John Tornlinson

The prayer book articles and homilies

Some forgotten facts in their history which may decide their interpretation

John Tornlinson

The prayer book articles and homilies
Some forgotten facts in their history which may decide their interpretation

ISBN/EAN: 9783337283490

Printed in Europe, USA, Canada, Australia, Japan

Cover: Foto ©Lupo / pixelio.de

More available books at **www.hansebooks.com**

BY

J. T. TOMLINSON.

LONDON:
ELLIOT STOCK, 62, PATERNOSTER ROW, E.C.
1897.

PREFACE.

THE fragmentary character of the following papers is due to the fact that several of them appeared originally in a periodical as replies to current fallacies. Additions and corrections have, however, been freely introduced, and it is believed that much of the information is either new, or not otherwise accessible to ordinary readers. Documents quoted from Strype, Cardwell and the Parker Correspondence have been carefully collated with the originals in the libraries of Lambeth, Corpus Christi, Cambridge, the Inner Temple, and the British Museum.

The photozincographs from the *Durham Book* are due to the courteous assistance of Canon Tristram and the Rev. H. E. Fox.

Every contribution, however humble, to a more intelligent understanding of the history and meaning of the Liturgy of the Church of England may hope for a share of that "favourable allowance" which the Preface to the Prayer Book itself bespeaks.

USEFUL MEMORANDA.

REGNAL YEARS OF EDWARD VI. (*New* Style.*)

1 Began January 28th, 1547	4 Began January 28th, 1550	6 Began January 28th, 1552
2 ,, ,, **1548**	5 ,, ,, 1551	**7** ,, ,, **1553**
3 ,, ,, 1549		"The latter year of Edward VI."
		(*Edward Died July 6th, 1553.*)

PARLIAMENTS OF EDWARD VI.

Parliament I.

Session I.	1 Edward VI.	1547, November 4th—December 24th, 1547
,, II.	2 & 3 Edward VI.	1548, November 24th—March 14th, 1549
,, III.	3 & 4 Edward VI.	1549, November 4th—February 1st, 1550
,, IV.	5 & 6 Edward VI.	1552, January 23rd—April 15th, 1552

Parliament II.

Session I.	7 Edward VI.	1553, March 1st—March 31st, 1553 (dissolved)

---

* Up to A.D. 1751 the year commenced on March 25th, so that (for example) any day in 1897 from January 1st to March 24th, both inclusive, would be reckoned as belonging to 1896 "Old Style."

Dates of Successive Prayer Books.

Year.	Title.	Enacted.	First Printed.	Use made compulsory.
1549	"First" Prayer Book of Edward	January 22nd	March 7th	June 9th
1552	"Second" Prayer Book, Edward VI. (Continued in use till December 20th, 1553)	April 14th	August	November 1st
1559	Elizabeth's version of *Second* Book of Edward VI.	May 8th	May 15th (?)	June 24th
1604	James's version of *Second* Book of Edward VI.	(Not enacted) Letters Patent February 9th	March	To come into use "Within such time as the Bishops shall think good to limit."
1662	Our present Book.	May 19th*	June ?	August 24th

* (*Subscribed by Convocation, December 20th, 1661.*)

CONTENTS.

		PAGE
I.	The Black-letter Holy Days	1
II.	The "Ministers and Mistakers" of the First Prayer Book	16
III.	The Injunctions of Elizabeth, 1559	34
IV.	The Advertisements of Elizabeth, 1566	61
V.	The Ornaments Rubric (Elizabeth, 1559-1661)	91
VI.	The Ornaments Rubric (Charles II., 1662)	137
VII.	The Ornaments Rubric (The Great Cosin Myth)	167
VIII.	"The Breaking of the Bread"	212
IX.	The First Book of Homilies	229
X.	The Second Book of Homilies	240
XI.	The Declaration on Kneeling	254
XII.	The Ordinal and Article XXXVI	269
XIII.	Article XXXI.	284
	Index	309

THE PRAYER BOOK ARTICLES AND HOMILIES

I

The Black=letter Holy Days

LONG before the Reformation in England, the interference with trade and agriculture which resulted from the frequent feast days of the Church had become a great social evil. Archbishop Langton, in 1222, and Archbishop Meopham, in 1328-33, had already sought to cut down the number of the non-working days;[1] and Archbishop Islip, who followed their example, explained the reason of the retrenchment to be—

"That disorderly meetings and negociations and other unlawful exercises are practised on such days, and what was intended for devotion is converted to lewdness, forasmuch as the tavern on these days is more frequented than the

---

[1] Goulburn's *Meditations on the Liturgical Gospels*, p. 15.

church . . not to omit that covenant servants . . do abstain from work on holidays (though of their own making) and on the vigils of saints, and yet take no less on that account for their weekly wages."[2]

Cardinal D'Ailly, in 1417, had advocated at the Council of Constance the reduction of the number of feast days,[3] and Erasmus proposed to abolish all festivals save the Lord's day and a few principal feasts. Mr. Denton, in his *England in the Fifteenth Century*, shews that these "Feasts" were a direct source of impoverishment and misery to the working classes. He says, "The wages of an agricultural labourer, man, woman, or child, were directed by Parliament to be paid daily, or perhaps all that is meant by the statute was that their wages should be paid after a daily, not weekly, reckoning. This, as the statute tells us, was to prevent labourers making any claim for payment for labour on festivals of the Church, or for more than half-a-day's wages on Saturdays and on the eves of their holy days."[4]

The words of this statute (4 Henry IV., cap. xiv.) throw light incidentally upon the meaning of the word "Noon"—"none other labourers shall take any hire for the holy days, nor for the evens of fasts, when they do not labour but till the hour of noon, but only for the *half day*, upon pain"—of a fine equivalent to £20 in our present money!

The State Paper which was presented to Henry VIII. as a petition from the Commons was drafted by Cromwell himself, and in it complaint is made to the

---

[2] Johnson's *Canons*, II.-427.
[3] Ffoulkes, *Christendom's Divisions*, p. 133.   [4] p. 221.
[5] Brewer's *State Papers of Henry VIII.*, V.-468.

King that—"A great number of holy days now at this present time, with very small devotion, be solemnized and kept throughout this your realm, upon the which many great, abominable, and execrable vices, idle and wanton sports, be used and exercised which holy days . . . might *be made fewer in number*."[6]

Accordingly (July 15th, 1536), Convocation acting under "the King's Highness's authority as supreme head in earth of the Church of England," declared that the number of holy days was—

"The occasion of much sloth and idleness, the very nourish of thieves, vagabonds, and divers other unthriftiness and inconveniences . . . and loss of man's food many times being clean destroyed through the superstitious observance of the said holy days, in not taking the opportunity of good and serene weather in time of harvest; but also pernicious to the souls of many men, which being enticed by the licentious vocation and liberty of those holidays, do upon the same *commonly* use and practice more excess, riot, and superfluity than upon any other days."[7]

That steps were taken by the executive to mitigate the evil is shewn by the fact that at Warwick the curate was imprisoned, September 9th, 1536, for tolling the bell on "St. Laurence's day."[8] Yet Cromwell himself interceded on behalf of the Cornish men that they might be allowed still to observe the "festum loci."

When the Reformation movement obtained freer course under King Edward, the *whole* of the blackletter saints were swept away completely. Some who profess to like the "First Prayer Book" of Edward VI. scarcely realize this fact, nor the peculiarity that the

---

[6] Froude's *History of England*, 1.-208.
[7] Stephens' *Ecclesiastical Statutes*, p. 333.
[8] Gairdner's *State Papers of Henry VIII.*, XI.-172.

title of "St." was then given to *none*, even, of the "red-letter" saints, except Peter. In the Second Prayer Book of Edward the names of St. George, St. Laurence, and St. Clement, were added, together with "Lammas," the "Dog Days," and "Term" days, obviously for reasons of secular convenience.

At the issuing of the earlier Prayer Book, Royal Injunctions accompanied it, directing "that none keep the *abrogate* holy days other than those that have their proper and peculiar service."[9]

In 1552 Dr. Morwen, President of Corpus Christi, Oxford, was committed to the Fleet "for using upon Corpus Christi day other service than was appointed by the book of service," which like our present Prayer Book was careful to ignore that "feast" altogether.[10]

The Act 5 and 6 Edward VI., cap. iii., which immediately followed upon the issue of the Second Prayer Book of Edward, ordered that "all the days hereafter mentioned shall be kept and commanded to be kept holy days, and *none other*." The list corresponds with our present "table," and shews by its omission of the names of George, Laurence, and Clement, and of Lammas, that these black-letter insertions, like "sol in aqua," &c., were intended merely for the convenience of the public, as in our modern "almanacs."

That statute was repealed by 1 Mary, Session 2, cap. ii., and Queen Mary issued on the purely "Erastian" authority of the Crown, in March, 1554, Articles commanding "that all such holy days and

---

[9] Cardwell's *Documentary Annals*, No. XV.
[10] Strype's *Ecclesiastical Memorials*, II.-ii.-52.

fasting days be observed and kept, as was observed and kept in the *latter* time of King Henry VIII." [11]

On the accession of Elizabeth, a bill was brought in to re-enact the 5 and 6 Edward VI., but the lofty notions of Royal prerogative which the Queen entertained, especially in matters relating to the Church, led to the adoption of a more irregular procedure. After being passed by the Commons and read twice in the Lords', the bill was dropped on April 30th, 1559 (D'Ewes, p. 27). Yet, as Mr. Perry, in his *Lawful Church Ornaments* (p. 140) observes, Edward's 19th Injunction was omitted from the Injunctions of 1559, of even date with the Prayer Book, "because the 5th and 6th Ed. VI., c. 3, A.D. 1552, had regulated the matter."

The Act of Uniformity (1 Elizabeth, cap. ii.) gave the sanction of *law* to the Calendar of Edward's Second Book: and we find accordingly that the earliest copies of Elizabeth's book had no black-letter days save those above mentioned.[12] But on January 22nd, 1561, Queen Elizabeth issued letters under her signet, directing the Royal Commissioners for Ecclesiastical Causes to draw up a new Calendar, which was ready on February 15th, and on February 27th an entry in the churchwardens' accounts at St. Michael's, Cornhill, runs:—" 1559, for paving where the high altar stood xd. Paid for the carriage of rubbish of the high

---

[11] Cardwell's *Documentary Annals*, No. XXX. The black-letter copy in C. C. C. Library (Vol. CCXXI., p. 521) is dated at foot "Excusum Londini in ædibus Johanni Cawodi typographi Reginæ Mariæ. Anno 1553. Mense Martio," shewing that it was printed before March 25th, 1554. Cardwell misprinted "late time" instead of "the *latter* time of King Henry VIII."

[12] See Clay's *Liturgies of Queen Elizabeth*, Parker Society, pp. xiii. and 47-52, where it will be seen that some astronomical notes had also been inserted.

altar xvi d. 1560 [*i.e.* 1561, New Style] Feb. 27 paid for the new orders of the service book and the X Commands v s. 1. d."[13]

This Calendar contained (all but three of) our present black-letter list. But it was preceded by a Table of Feasts, headed " these to be *observed* for holy days and *none other* "; and this list corresponds *verbatim* with that given in 5 and 6 Edward VI., cap. iii.[14] The mention in the Acts of the Privy Council of a payment of rent as " due at thinvention of the Cross," illustrates the purely secular character of these black-letter days. That entry is dated " June 24, 1552," when, by statute 5 and 6 Edward VI., cap. iii., any special religious observance of the day was entirely prohibited. Nevertheless as almanacs were unknown, the church kalendar was relied upon by the common people to furnish all such needful information ; and as matter of convenience (tending, moreover, to make people possess themselves

---

[13] *Parker Correspondence*, p. 136. Overall's *Accounts of St. Michael's, Cornhill*, pp. 150-5.

[14] Elizabeth was, however, acting *ultra vires*, as Mr. Droop (*Edwardian Vestments*, p. 20) remarks. Strictly speaking, the black-letter days of Edward's Second Prayer Book *alone* had any legal right to be printed in any Prayer Book until 1662. The " Notes " formerly attributed to " Bishop Cosin " state that these Elizabethan tables were " but the printer's work, no order of the Church," and he urged that the 5 and 6 Edward VI., cap. iii., had been repealed by Mary " and *not since revived*," a blunder which Mr. James Parker does not correct in his *History of the Revisions of the Prayer Book*, p. 125. Bishop Stubbs, in his *Draft Report*, similarly marks the 5 and 6 Edward VI. as " repealed " (*Report of Ecclesiastical Courts Commission*, p. 43). But that Act was revived in 1604 by 1 James I., cap. xxv. When Cosin grew older he grew wiser, and not merely adopted the very list which he had formerly denounced, but suggested various reforms, such as the omission of the names of St. Catharine, St. Faith, and Conception of Blessed Virgin Mary saying " better left out " (Nicholls' *Appendix*, p. 67). Mr. James Parker omits this pertinent fact, in his *History of the Revisions of the Prayer Book*, pp. 121-6.

of the new book), Elizabeth restored in her kalendar of 1561, a long list of such traditional memoranda. "Dog days," "Sol in tauro," &c., are among these black-letter days.

To prevent any misunderstanding, the Elizabethan Bishops in April, 1561, drew up some "Resolutions," among which was this one :—" That there be no other holy day observed besides the Sundays, but only such as be set out *in the Act of King Edward, An. 5 et 6 cap. 3.*" Cardwell notes [15] that those words in italic were inserted by Archbishop Parker's own hand, instead of the words crossed through in the original draft, viz. "in the Calendar of the Service Book, with two days following the Feasts of Easter and Pentecost." In 1564 it was further explained in the *Preces Privatae*,[16] published by authority, that the black-letter days were retained for secular reasons only—

"We have not done it because we hold them all for saints, *of whom we do not esteem some to be even among the good.* . . . but that they may be as notes and marks of some certain things, the stated times of which it is very important to know, and ignorance of which may be a disadvantage to our countrymen."

In March, 1566, the celebrated "Advertisements" of Queen Elizabeth appeared, directing "That there be none other holy days observed besides the Sundays, but only such as be set out for holy days, as in the statute 5 and 6 Edward VI., and in the new Calendar authorised by the Queen's Majesty."[17]

The Bishops who acted as "Commissioners under the Great Seal for causes ecclesiastical," like the other

---

[15] Cardwell's *Documentary Annals*, I.-206.
[16] Parker Society Edition, p. 428.
[17] Cardwell's *Documentary Annals*, No. LXV. Cf Cardwell's *Synodalia*, I.-124.

Elizabethan Ordinaries, enforced the Calendar on the principle that what was "not appointed" by the Prayer Book, was "abrogated" by it.

A few extracts from their Visitation Articles will shew this. In 1571 Archbishop Grindal asked throughout the Province of York—

"Whether any holy days or fasting days heretofore abrogated or *not appointed to be used* as holy days, or fasting days, by the new Kalendar of the book of Common Prayer, be either proclaimed and bidden by your parson, vicar or curate, or be superstitiously observed by any of your parish, and what be their names, that so do observe the same: and whether there be any ringing or tolling of bells to call the people together used in any of those days more or otherwise than is commonly used upon other days that be *kept as work days*?" [18]

Archbishop Parker asks, in 1575, "Whether any other holy days be kept than such as be *appointed in* the book of Common Prayer." [19]

Aylmer, Bishop of London, in 1577 repeats verbatim Grindal's inquiry, merely adding, "And whether any public feasts other than such as be appointed by law be by any private authority, without order from the Bishop, commanded or *used*." [20]

Middleton, Bishop of St. David's in 1583, in asking whether they are still "bidden to be observed by the minister in Churches," notifies that "old superstitious holidays be justly abrogated and put down." [21]

Indeed, the Jacobean and Laudian Bishops also speak of holy days "abrogated *by* the Book of Common Prayer" [22]; referring also to Canon 88, which forbids

---

[18] *Appendix to the Second Report of the Ritual Commission*, pp. 408-8 and 412-15.
[19] *Ibid.*, 417-41.   [20] *Ibid.*, 418-7.   [21] *Ibid.*, 427-6.
[22] *Ibid.*, 456-17, 515-13, 536-13, 574-17.

"Bells to be rung superstitiously upon the holy days or eves abrogated (*antiquatæ*), by the Book of Common Prayer." "The last part of this Canon," says Mr. Davis, in his edition of the Canons of 1604, "refers to the black-letter feasts and saints days, &c., which are excluded from the table in the Book of Common Prayer of ALL the feasts that are to be observed."

The passing of 1 James I., cap. xxv. (repealing 1 Mary, Session 2, cap. ii.), in May, 1604, followed close upon the issue (in March of the same year) of the Jacobean revision of the Prayer Book. In this way the 5 and 6 Edward VI., cap. iii., became thenceforth the legal standard.[23]

Lastly, at the final revision of the Prayer Book, the Bishops at the Savoy Conference declared "the other names are left in the Calendar, not that they should be so kept as holy days, but they are useful for the preservation of their memories, and for other reasons, as for leases, law days, &c."[24] Bishop Cosin in his *Regni Angliæ Religio Catholica*, written to give foreign churches a just idea of our Prayer Book, *takes no notice whatever* of the black-letter people, but heads the red letter days with the words "sacrati Deo apud nos sunt."[25]

Sir Robert J. Phillimore in *Elphinstone v. Purchas*, condemned as unlawful the practice of giving notice for the observance of "the feasts of St. Leonard, St. Martin, and St. Britius," under the rubric which bids the announcement of *all* days that "are in the week following to be observed."

---

[23] Coke's *Institutes*, II.-686.   [24] Cardwell's *Conferences*, p. 341.
[25] Cosin's *Works*, IV.-364.

All the older commentators on the Prayer Book, like Wheatly and Nicholls, explained the retention of the "Romish saints' days" on the ground that "those days were either quarter-days for payment of rent, or were days remarkable in the course of the law, or adapted to some secular account, so that some inconvenience would ensue if they were totally omitted from the Calendar." This, of course, was obvious when almanacs were not to be had, and when men habitually dated by the name of the day, not as now by the day of the month. But even in the nineteenth century we should feel the inconvenience of having no Calendar at hand when bequests, fairs, guild-anniversaries, wakes or antiquarian allusions escaped our recognition under some old-world designation. Hence it was, doubtless, that the Ritual Commissioners in their "Fourth Report,"[26] decided in 1870 to retain the black-letter days, but with this "Note—That although some other days are marked in the Calendar, yet the above mentioned [*i.e.* the red-letter days] are the *only* fasts, and feasts appointed to be observed throughout the year."

⁎

The defence set up by Romanisers for the intermingling of "joyful stories" of obscure or apocryphal "saints" with their Sunday sermons (as suggested by the *Kalendar of the English Church*) is, that a certain sentimental beauty, or pious feeling clings to the legendary "story." But the Act of Convocation in 1536, above referred to, said plainly—"the number of Holy Days is so excessively grown, and yet daily more and more by men's *devotion*, yea rather superstition,

---

[26] p. 8.

was like further to increase." And the preface to the Prayer Book tells us " some [ceremonies] entered into the Church by undiscreet *devotion*, and such a *zeal* as was without knowledge ; and for because they were winked at in the beginning, they grew daily to more and more abuses."

All the errors and superstitions of the dark ages were introduced by pious and well-meaning persons. And religion has ever suffered most " in the house of its friends." " Will ye talk deceitfully for God ? " said Job. Dean Hook admits that[27]—

"Their first great object was to encourage in the masses the sentiment of religion; and, although, as we shall presently see, the duty of upholding the truth was not in theory ignored, yet in dealing with the masses it was forgotten. Thus sanctification was the one object, but they forgot that man is to be sanctified through the truth . . . . this habitual postponement of the true to the useful, to the emotional, and even to the beautiful was applied to the ordinances of the Church, and even to articles of faith. It is not too much to say, that the almost exclusive regard to religious sentiment led to the gradual introduction of those superstitious observances, and those errors in doctrine, which, being authoritatively established at the Council of Trent, are the distinguishing characteristics of modern Romanism.

" The question asked, as they were gradually introduced, was not whether they were in accordance with the truth, but whether they tended to excite devotional fervour, sanctify the imagination, and

---

[27] *Sermon before Church Congress at Manchester*, 1863, pp. 2, 3.

conduce to the purposes of civilising the savage mind. Afterwards when they had been so far established as to have become part and parcel of the entire ecclesiastical system, the attempt to defend them by argument, against the assaults of the Reformers, became a necessity—but the origination of the evil is to be found rather in the separation of the truth of religion from its emotions."

But the nemesis of all falsehood followed, slowly indeed, but surely. As Dr. Johnson objected to a chattering deist who admitted that "one half of the Bible was inspired,"—"Yes, but *which* half?" For, is it to be believed that the mystery of the Incarnation, or of the Resurrection, is merely a "joyful story" of the same kind as the pious fables of hagiologists? Superstition was ever the parent of infidelity, and lying legends, and old wives' fables have largely alienated the intellect of Europe from the most sacred truths of the Gospel; since all alike, according to their "Catholic" teachers, are made to rest upon the *same* "authority." That lesson ought not to be lost upon us. A methodist friend used to say, when he heard a goody story, or a missionary platform-anecdote, "Is that a *fact*, or an anecdote?" The first and only question in laying foundations should be "Is this true? Is it written? What saith the Scripture?"

"Those who tell us that the Church now sanctions any religious observances of the days of St. Brice, St. Blaise, St. Valentine, &c., insult our understanding; and if they attempt to enforce such observance on the people, they aggrieve the conscience of the well-informed among them. They inflict on them, though in a less degree, the same annoyance and distress which the myths of the Roman breviary inflict on the learned and conscientious priests of France."²⁸

In the Abyssinian Church, Pontius Pilate, together with his wife Procla, is commemorated on June 25th. Even the Greeks reckon the wife among the Saints.

The "conception B. V. M." was a festival "introduced by private and unauthorised zeal in the eleventh century, [which] spread rapidly in spite of reason and the indignant remonstrances of St. Bernard, but, was not authorised by Rome until 1483. Fostered by this observance, an irrational heresy, which was utterly unknown when it commenced, gradually obtained and secured a footing, until at length in our own time, this day has been solemnly canonised as the feast of the Immaculate Conception."²⁹

These "joyful stories" have been scouted even by educated Romanists.

Tillemont in his *Histoire Ecclésiastique*, Vols. IV. and V., throws many of them over-board. Thus he says of St. Valentine "nothing certain" was known about him; of St. Blaise " we have many histories, but not one of which we dare make use ; " and of St. Katharine, that it would be hard to find any Saint more generally reverenced, and of whom so little is known. Even Mr. Blunt's *Annotated Prayer Book*, admits that the history of St. Prisca is "uncertain"; that of St. Fabian, a "*materialising allegory* "; that of St. George, "so obscure that some have doubted his existence." In fact, St. George is in exactly the same category as

---

[28] See *Lettres Parisiennes of the Abbé Laborde*, Paris, 1855, cited by Scudamore, *Exposure of the English Church Union Reply*, p. 6.
[29] Scudamore's *Remarks on English Church Union Petition*, p 5.

his dragon. Mr. Scudamore says, "It may be thought certain that there was a martyr of this name; but his age, country, and history are alike unknown. His early fame rested on a lying legend, that was condemned as apocryphal by a Council held at Rome in 494. All subsequent accounts of him are pure fictions" (p. 5). Whereupon, Dr. Littledale directs this rubbish to be sung (" To the praise and glory of God "?)—

> " O noble martyr, thee we sing,
> O soldier worthy of thy king:
> St. George our patron saint," &c. (*Hymn* 246.)

The *Invention of the Cross*, however, it seems " has not been disproved," (*sic*)—a faint praise, which might be applied to many other doubtful " inventions." Bishop Cosin,[30] however, notes that "this feast the Greeks lack"; that Dunstan "after his death was Sainted, but, God knows why!" and that " All Souls'" Day, " in ours and other reformed Churches was deservedly abrogated by us all."

Yet in obedience to the so-called *Kalendar of the English Church*, published by the "Church Printing Company," the adulteration of Christianity with "profane fables" goes on apace. The *People's Hymnal* gives *four* "suitable hymns" for "All Souls' Day," to commemorate the "joyful story" that certain monks heard at the mouth of the crater of Mount Etna, the lamentation of the fiends at the loss of " souls taken out of their hands by the prayers of Cluniac monks" (Wheatly). The *Hymnal*, therefore, deprecates purgatorial torment in these " suitable " words:—

---

[30] In Nicholls' *Appendix*, 11-14.

"Let not *penal fire* burn them,
Let not binding fetters chain,
Nor the worm which never dieth
Torture them with endless pain," &c., &c.
(*Hymn for All Souls*, 299.)

In a sermon on "the feast of St. Katharine," addressed to the inmates of St. Katharine's Home, Woodford, by the Rev. N. J. Devereux, "the preacher illustrated his remarks about the saint by directing attention to St. Katharine, as depicted in the banner lately presented to the chapel." To childish minds an object lesson like this, is very telling. "Seeing is believing," says the vulgar proverb; so the banner was irresistible. Yet Cardinal "Baronius actually brands the *Acta Sanctæ Catherinæ* of the Roman martyrology as a mixture of mendacity and truth (*mendacium veris admixtum*)."

The following is the "joyful story" of the banner, as told by Mr. Baring Gould :—

"A wheel set with razors was constructed for the execution of St. Catherine, but when she was placed on it the wheel broke and the razors flew about, hacking and cutting the throats of the bystanders. Then Catherine prayed that she might suffer death, and asked only two things—that after her death her body might be preserved from being touched by profane fingers, and that the world might be converted. Then her head was struck off with a sword, and angels came and carried off her body to Mount Sinai. Maxentius was defeated by Constantine, and the world became Christian."

Why not? With the sword of Constantine on the one side and "joyful stories" on the other, "the world" could have no difficulty in making its choice. The only doubt is whether the world would be a pin the better for a "conversion" of this kind.

II

The "Ministers and Mistakers" of the First Prayer Book

THE First Prayer Book of Edward VI. proved a failure. The original commission had to be cut down to less than half before the book could be got through committee,[1] yet, even then, five of its "compilers" disliked it; and Bishops Day, Skip, and Thirlby were among the eight Bishops who spoke and voted against it in the Lords'. It was rejected alike by Bonner on the one hand[2] and by Hooper on the other,[3] and "religious" rebellions in Devon, Buckinghamshire, and Oxfordshire attest its continued unpopularity. When it is remembered that the book only came into use on June 9th, 1549, and that no copy was printed after that year, it will be seen that the demand for it could never have been very great. As Mr. Walton (himself an ardent Ritualist) says:—

"The First Prayer Book, in fact, under the circumstances,

---

[1] Cardwell's *Two Liturgies of Edward VI. compared*. Preface, p. xi.
[2] Collier's *Ecclesiastical History*, V.-357.
[3] *Original Letters*, Parker Society, p. 79. See Pocock's *Troubles connected with the Prayer Book of* 1549, p. 26, and *Original Letters*, pp. 391, 467.

and at the time of its actual publication, was an expedient, or *temporary compromise, which can have really satisfied no one;* nor is it now easy (if we except the deprived Bishop Day) to point to any individuals or any party whose opinions or convictions it any longer expressed. It is surely as mistaken as it is ungenerous, in the present day, to quote the qualified approval of the First Prayer Book which was extorted, under the pressure of an iniquitous persecution, from Bishop Gardiner. An assent to its principles, under his circumstances, must be admitted as worth very little indeed."[4]

Mr. Walton had not seen the *Great Parliamentary Debate* which has only been brought to light since his death, or he could never have imagined that Bishop Day's "convictions" were expressed by this book.

As Prebendary Humphry truly said in his *Student's Commentary on the Book of Common Prayer*,[5] "The First Prayer Book of Edward appears to have been received with irreverence, and disregarded by a great portion of the clergy, with the connivance of the Bishops."

Within a twelvemonth it was already under revision, for the people of England evidently would not have it.

This is clear from the official statements both of the Privy Council and of the very same Parliament which had so recently enacted that book.

The second Parliament of Edward VI. did not meet till March 1st, 1553; so that the *same* parliament which had enacted the First Prayer Book was compelled (on April 14th, 1552) to rescind it, and to substitute for it the Second Prayer Book of Edward VI., which in all substantial respects is identical with our own.

Nothing but dire necessity, we may be sure, could

---

[4] *Letter to Canon Carter*, second edition, p 51   [5] p. 16.

have induced Parliament to consent to such a step. "It is ill swapping horses while you are crossing streams." And the danger of such a flank movement in face of a wary foe was obvious. It became necessary therefore to minimise as far as possible the nature and importance of the changes actually made. Hence the language of the Second Act of Uniformity (5 and 6 Edward VI., cap. i.) was almost apologetic. After admitting (what could not be denied) that "a great number of people in divers parts of this realm . . do wilfully . . refuse to come to their parish churches," the third section went on to say,—

"And because there hath arisen in the use and exercise of the aforesaid common service in the Church heretofore set forth, divers doubts for the fashion and manner of ministration of the same, rather by the CURIOSITY OF THE MINISTER AND MISTAKERS, than of any other worthy cause; therefore, as well for the more plain and manifest explanation hereof, as for the *more perfection* of the said order of common service, in some places where it is *necessary* to make the same prayers and fashion of service *more earnest and fit* to stir Christian people to the true honouring of Almighty God; the King's most excellent majesty . . hath caused the aforesaid order of common service, entitled 'The Book of Common Prayer,' to be *faithfully and godly* perused, explained, and *made fully perfect*."

According to this account, the Second Book was the First Book "godly perused" and made "fully perfect," especially in places where it needed to be "explained," or it was "necessary to make the same more earnest and fit." Moreover the First Book was repealed, and its future use was made illegal under penalties,[6] so that the preference of the Second Book, *by the very framers of the First Book*, was marked and decided.

---

[6] *Ibid.*, Sec. 6.

I have shewn elsewhere[7] that before the First Prayer Book was adopted, the Reforming Bishops who were its advocates publicly denied any "objective presence," or any reception by the wicked, or any "oblation" of the body of Christ. The sworn testimony of Bishop Day given on Gardiner's trial, in 1551, was that "My Lord of Canterbury hath made a book against the verity of Christ's body and blood *in* the sacrament: and that the Bishop now of London [Ridley] did openly impugn the verity of Christ's body and blood in the sacrament, in the parliament at Westminster."[8] I have shewn also that the First Prayer Book was regarded *at the time* as merely provisional until the English Reformers could give full effect to their own predilections.[9] On June 20th, 1549, *i.e.* within a fortnight of its coming into use, Ridley presided at a public disputation at Cambridge, which Alban Langdale, one of the disputants on the "Catholic" side, afterwards described in these terms. "Nor did they profess the heresy of the Lutherans (as they had put forth in their first axiom), but publicly before the world and pertinaciously adopted that of the Swiss."[10]

It has been contended, however, by the admirers of the semi-reformed book that the Act just quoted admits the First Book to have been "agreeable to the word of God and the primitive Church." That, however, is a mistake. Those words referred only

---

[7] *Great Parliamentary Debate in* 1548 (J F. Shaw), pp. 15-18.
[8] Foxe's *Acts and Monuments*, VI.-240.   [9] *Great Debate*, p. 19.
[10] Neque enim Lutheranorum (uti axiomate primo prae se tulerunt) sed Helvetiorum haeresim pertinaciter palam mundo profitebantur." *Catholica Confutatio*, p. 8. Compare Foxe's report of "Rochester's" (*i.e.* Ridley's) interpellations during this Disputation.—*Acts and Monuments*, VI.-311-318.

to Divine Service, being "*used in the Mother tongue within the Church of England*"—a practice rejected by the Papal party, yet in the main highly popular and therefore reaffirmed, and credit taken for it, in this unmistakable fashion by Edward's lay Parliament.

Anyone who compares the language of our Twenty-fourth Article as to "the word of God and the custom of the primitive church," with the very first proposition publicly debated in Westminster Abbey on March 31st, 1559, viz. "It is against the Word of God and the custom of the Primitive Church to use a tongue unknown to the people in Common Prayers and administration of the sacraments,"[11] will recognise the special allusion in Edward's second Act of Uniformity. The words "a very godly order set forth by authority of Parliament, *to be used in the mother tongue* within this Church of England, *agreeable to the Word of God and the Primitive Church*," were but the usual and accepted formula in vindication of the principle of a vernacular service book.

As Mr. Milton justly observes:[12]

"The words of praise contained in this act must be taken as applying to the book as a whole, of which the parts to be altered constituted in extent, a very small portion, not one-fiftieth of the whole volume. They must be regarded as dictated by policy. It was policy to say what they could for the book, but it was necessary to get rid of it; and they did get rid of it most effectually. The act made it an offence not only to read the service in that book, but even to be present and to hear it read."

It is true that the "Ministers and mistakers" of the First Prayer Book were censured by this later Act for

---

[11] Cardwell's *Conferences*, p. 24.   [12] *Church Perplexities*, p. 79.

having necessitated the revision of the book. But it is "unhistorical" to fancy, as Cosin and Wheatly have done, that foreigners like Bucer, Martyr, or Alasco were the persons intended. Yet it has been imagined that a concession to the scruples of these people caused the changes of 1552, and that the English Parliament in reluctantly making such changes, desired to brand their "curiosity" by using the words above quoted.

We can show, however, that this was not the case. Bucer, and the rest never were "Ministers" (*i.e.* officiants) under the Prayer Book of 1549. Up to the day of his death (February 28th, 1551) Bucer, like Martyr, could not even read the Prayer Book except by means of a Latin version, and had to rely upon an "interpreter," probably Fagius' son.[13]

Alasco never held office of any kind as a "Minister" of the Church of England. The "Ministre" of the service was clearly the ordinary Incumbent: the "Mystakers" were those who mistook, or wilfully misunderstood and wrested the meaning of the First Prayer Book. And there is really no difficulty in identifying these persons. Even in the earlier stages of reform, when the Cup so long monopolised by the clergy was being restored to the church, we find a letter from the Privy Council to the Bishops complaining that "a great number of the Curates of the realm, either for lack of knowledge cannot, or *for want of good mind will not* be so ready to set forth the same as we would wish." Similarly under Elizabeth a Royal proclamation was issued on March 22nd, 1559,

---

[13] See Clay's *Preface to Elizabethan Liturgies,* p. xxv. note. Compare *Original Letters,* pp. 332, 535.

bidding the parishioners who at the ensuing Easter might be (illegally) refused the cup by their own Minister, to "resort to some *other* honest, discreet, and learned priest and Minister."[14]

That illustrates what was meant by the "curiosity" (*i.e.* crotchetty scrupulosity) of the Incumbents. Unluckily, it was not confined to them. The Bishop of London, about a fortnight after the First Prayer Book began to be "ministered" at St. Paul's, was censured by the King's Council for allowing "Apostles' Communion" and "Our Lady's Communion" to be celebrated at side-altars, which they regarded as "a scorn to the reverence of the Communion of the Lord's body and blood." In any case, they said, it must be done "as it is appointed in the book of the public service without *cautele* or digression from the common order."[15] These *cautels*, which occupy nine pages in Maskell,[16] were the minute and punctilious directions given in the missal, and they were in every sense of the word highly "curious." The "Curiosity of the Minister," then, was the regard paid to such "abolished" cautels. Not only Bonner, but many of the other Bishops, were conniving at "curiosity" of this kind. Strype tells us[17] that he took from Bishop Thirlby's Register the letter which Cardwell[18] prints as directed also to Bonner on July 23rd, 1549, and concludes that "it was a common letter to them all." In this "common letter" to the Bishops, the Council

---

[14] Dyson's *Proclamations of Queen Elizabeth*. Compare *Documentary Annals*, No. XIV.
[15] Cardwell's *Documentary Annals*, No. XVI.
[16] *Ancient Liturgy of the Church of England*, pp. 168-176.
[17] *Ecclesiastical Memorials*, II.-i.-331. [18] *Documentary Annals*, No. XVII.

complain that the First Prayer Book "remaineth in many places of this our realm either *not known at all, or not used*, or at the least, if it be used, very seldom, and that in such light and irreverent sort, as the people in many places *have heard nothing*, or if they hear, they neither understand nor have that spiritual delectation in the same, that to good Christians appertaineth : the fault thereof like as we must of reason impute to you, and other of your vocation called by God through our appointment."

A hint is given to the Romanising Bishops that the King might through their neglect "consequently be occasioned thereby to see *otherwise* to the redress of these things, whereof we would be sorry."

Bonner took no heed, however, and on September 13th, he was duly articled before the Ecclesiastical Commissioners on the information of Latimer and Hooper, for nonconformity. Two of these articles ran

"Item, that ye know, or have heard say, that certain persons within your diocese, sith the time that the said Injunctions were given unto you, have heard, been at, or celebrate mass, or evensong in the Latin tongue, and after the old rite and manner, other than according to the King's majesty's book."

"Item, that the rites of the common service of the Church, now set forth, be in some parts of your diocese *diversely* used ; and you, knowing or hearing of the same, have not called any *ministers of the service* before you for the redress of such diversity, nor corrected the misusers thereof." [19]

The proceedings were protracted, but on October 1st, 1549, sentence of deprivation was pronounced, because, among other things, Bonner "had utterly neglected to search out those who followed the foreign

---

[19] Foxe's *Acts and Monuments*, V.-763.

and rejected (*non probatos*) rites whereof his diocese of London was specially complained of."[20]

The fall of the Duke of Somerset (October 12th, 1549) gave new hopes to the Romanists.[21] Hooper wrote anxiously,[22] "We hope that no alteration will be made." He complained of the negligence of the Bishops in enforcing the Prayer Book, saying "it is only the fear for their property that prevents them from reforming their churches according to the rule of God's word." Yet, oddly enough, this very letter which complains of, and describes the nonconformity of the Romish Incumbents and the negligence of the Romish prelates has been adduced as evidence of the authorised practice as prescribed by the Prayer Book!

Two days, however, before Hooper wrote this letter it had become necessary to call in and destroy the old service books "and all other bokes of service, the keeping whereof shold be a let to the usage of the said boke of commene prayers," so that the Commissaries of the Archbishop were everywhere to destroy them "that they never after may serve eyther to *anie soche use as they were provided for*, or be at anytime a let to that godly and *uniforme* Order."[23]

This Royal Order was soon afterwards enforced by the added "authority of Parliament," viz. The Act 3 and 4 Edward VI., cap. 10. Ridley's Visitation Articles of May, 1550 (followed verbatim in Hooper's of the following year) and based upon the Royal Visita-

---

[20] Foxe, V.-795. "Externos et non probatos ecclesiæ ritus." Some "abolished" and some "retained."
[21] *Documentary Annals*, No. XX.   [22] *Original Letters*, p. 71.
[23] *Documentary Annals*, No. XX.

tion Articles of 1549,[24] may be read in Miller's *Guide to Ecclesiastical Law*. They shew that all such practices were denounced *at the time* as being a violation of the First Prayer Book by one of the leading framers of that Book. Yet the Romish party then, as now, proved too strong for the law. Though Bonner had been deposed, "popery" still reigned at St. Paul's. Strype tells us that "even under Ridley, who was now Bishop, the communion was celebrated with such superstitions, as though it were a mass." The Privy Council then sent competent experts to vouch for the actual practice complained of. On October 11th, 1550, it was ordered "that Thomas Astely join with two

---

[24] The Injunctions of 1547 had lost their Parliamentary authority (if they ever had any) by the passing of 1 Edward VI. cap. 12, which took place on December 24th, 1547, in the *first* year of King Edward. Consequently they had no "authority *of Parliament* in the *second* year." Their Royal authority was, however, unaffected, and they were required to be read once a quarter by every incumbent. These Injunctions of 1547 were adapted to the altered ritual of the First Prayer Book by simply directing the clergy in 1549 to "*Omit* in the reading of the Injunctions all such as make mention of the Popish Mass." Such "omissions" in publishing official documents were the customary way of rescinding the older directions. Thus Archbishop Peckham when required by the King to withdraw certain excommunications, directed that "deleatur, et *pro non pronunciata habeatur* illa clausula." (Makower. *Constitutional History of the Church of England*, p. 32.) The Articles of 1549 are shewn to be later than the Prayer Book by their mentioning it, and its "catechism"; yet, prior to the second book, by their referring to "going to the sick with the sacrament." They must have been prior to Ridley's, which verbally correspond, inasmuch as no authority less than that of the Crown could have authorised an "omission" to read Royal Injunctions. Doubtless, Collier is right in saying they were Articles for the Royal Visitation set on foot in 1549 and intended to enforce the new Prayer Book. (Collier, V.-324.) Cardwell holds the same view (*Documentary Annals*, p. 75, second edition). "For an uniformity" they direct to "use no other ceremonies than are appointed in the King's book of common prayers." All the "omitted" ceremonies are described as "counterfeiting the Popish Mass": and thus the proof is complete that the "ministers" who were then violating "uniformity," were the crypto-papal incumbents.

or three more honest gentlemen in London for the observation of the usage of the communion in Paul's: whereof information was given, that it was used as the very mass." "Such a secret goodwill did many of the priests and churchmen belonging to the Cathedral still bear to the old former usages." [25] This was the more marked an instance of non-conformity, because in the previous April, Bishop Ridley "Commanded the lytt of the aulter to be put owte or he came into the qwere" [26] at St. Paul's, and in his diocesan Visitation in May, he had forbidden any setting of lights upon the Lord's board, &c., as being contrary to the Prayer Book of 1549.

Perhaps the best account of the situation is to be found in Bucer's letters, written as they were at the time, and without any thought of publication. On Whit-Sunday, 1550, he wrote to Calvin—

"Many of the parochial clergy so recite and administer the service, that the people have no more understanding of the mysteries of Christ, than if the Latin instead of the vulgar tongue were still in use. And when complaints respecting these shocking abuses of the church are laid by godly men before the rulers of the kingdom, they say it is the business of the bishops to remedy the evil: when they are laid before the bishops, those, namely, who have long since made a profession of the gospel, their reply is, that they cannot rectify them without an act of parliament." [27]

In November of the same year he writes to his friend the martyr-bishop Hooper—

---

[25] Strype's *Ecclesiastical Memorials*, II.-i.-372.
[26] *Greyfriar's Chronicle*, p. 67. The marginal heading was "Puttynge ovte the lyttes' (plural) 'at the [a]ulter in Powlles." Howlett's *Monumenta Franciscana*, II.-227. [27] *Original Letters*, p. 547.

"All the Divine offices are recited by many pseudo Parish-priests or vicars, so frigidly, slovenly, and mumblingly, that they are understood by the common people just as well as if they had been read in an African or Indian dialect. . . In many places the Lord's Supper so takes the place of Mass, that the people do not know in what respect it differs from it, except that it is celebrated in the vulgar tongue."[24]

During the same year Bucer wrote his *De Regno Christi* for presentation to King Edward on New Year's Day, 1551, in which he said—

"Some turn the prescribed form of service into a mere papistical abuse. Although it is now in the vulgar tongue, the 'sacrificers' recite it of set purpose so indistinctly that it cannot be understood, whilst the people altogether refuse to understand or to listen. Not a few of the priests show forth the sacred communion of Christ as the papistical mass and the people are present with no other intention than to assist at the mass itself. Hardly anyone takes the sacrament from the table of the Lord, except the sacrificer alone, or a churchwarden, and even he does so unwillingly—(*sacrificulum unum, vel aedituum cumque invitum*").

Fox, who was ordained a deacon at St. Paul's by Ridley on June 24th, 1550, describes as an eye-witness this "curiosity of the ministers." He says—

"Through the perverse obstinacy and dissembling frowardness of many of the inferior priests and ministers of the Cathedrals and other churches of this realm, there did arise a marvellous schism and variety of fashions in celebrating the common service and administration of the sacraments and other rites and ceremonies of the Church. For some, zealously allowing the king's proceedings, did gladly follow the order thereof: and others, though not so willingly admitting them yet dissemblingly and patchingly use some part of them; but many, carelessly contemning all, would still exercise their old wonted popery."
—*Acts and Monuments*, V.-720.

[24] Gorham's *Reformation Gleanings*, p. 201.

We have no difficulty then in identifying the "Ministers"; but who, it may be asked, were the "Mistakers" mentioned in the Act?

Bishop Cosin tells us in his "Second Series of Notes,"[29] that—

"In the first edition of the Liturgy, indeed, under King Edward VI. even the name of 'Mass' (as it was commonly then called) had been retained; but when men leavened with the doctrine of the Papists were twisting it to a bad sense, it seemed good to the bishops that in the second publication of that Liturgy, it should be altogether omitted."

That mention of "homines papistarum doctrinâ fermentati" who "*ad pravum sensum detorquebant*" exactly hits off the "mistakers" of the statute. Of these Gardiner was the chief. Gardiner's own attitude toward the Prayer Book was very characteristic. He had no part whatever in the "consultations" which resulted in its being adopted, and he must have taken some pains to avoid seeing it, since even so late as June, 1550, he still refused even to look at it.

"Whereupon it was agreed, that the said book should be brought unto him by the lieutenant of the Tower: who within a day or two, by order of the whole Council, brought the said bishop not only that book of common prayer, but also the book for making of bishops, priests, and deacons."[30]

The new Ordinal came out in March, 1550,[31] and this mention of two separate books (which is noticed also in the testimony of several of the witnesses) shews that the *First* Prayer Book was the one under discussion;

---

[29] *Works*, V.-301.
[30] Foxe, VI.-172. He had, however, been careful to read the Act of Uniformity itself. *Ibid.*, p. 72.
[31] *Original Letters*, p. 81.

for, in the Second Prayer Book, the Ordinal was incorporated into the same volume. On the occasion above referred to, Gardiner—

"Said, that albeit at the beginning, he would not give his assent to the making the said book in such form as it is made, yet the same book being now set forth as it is, he would both observe the same himself, and cause all others to do the like in all his diocese."

But he refused, all the same, to subscribe a declaration to this effect when tendered to him for signature. "And touching the Book of Ordering of Priests, &c., he saith, he misliked the same." [32]

Lawyer-like, though disliking the new Liturgy, Gardiner for polemical and strategic reasons sought to put on the new book a Roman gloss. And it is very instructive to observe that *in every instance* in which this was done *the Prayer Book was altered* to avoid what Cranmer insisted was, if not a wilful "mistaking," yet a real perversion of its true meaning. When, therefore, we find that Gardiner's "mistakings" were obviated by a series of alterations which eliminated all possibility of such "mistakings" in the future, we can hardly refuse to recognise in "wily Winchester" the type and leader of the "mistakers" denounced in the second Act of Uniformity.[33]

Among such alterations were the following.

1. Gardiner deduced an argument in favour of masses for the dead from the fact that prayer for the departed was incorporated into the "Prayer of Consecration" of 1549.[34] All such prayers were accordingly removed, and the prayer itself transposed.

---

[32] Foxe, VI., p. 172.   [33] 5 and 6 Edward VI., cap. i.
[34] See *Cranmer on the Lord's Supper*, p. 84

2. Again, take the alteration made in the Prayer of Consecration itself—

1549.	1552.
Hear us, O merciful Father, we beseech thee, and with thy Holy Spirit and word vouchsafe to bl+ess and sanc+tify these thy gifts and creatures of bread and wine that they may be unto us the body and blood of thy most dearly-beloved Son Jesus Christ, who, in the same night that he was betrayed,	Hear us, O merciful Father, we beseech thee, and grant that we receiving these thy creatures of bread and wine according to thy Son our Saviour Jesus Christ's holy institution, in remembrance of his death and passion, may be partakers of his most blessed body and blood, &c.

Bishop Gardiner, in 1550, argued in favour of transubstantiation from the

"Prayer which is ordered to be made in the Book of Common Prayer now set forth. Wherein we require of God, the creatures of bread and wine to be sanctified, and to be to us the body and blood of Christ, which they cannot be, unless God worketh it, and maketh them so to be."

To which Cranmer replied—

"The bread and wine be made unto us the body and blood of Christ (as it is in the Book of Common Prayer) but not by changing the substance of bread and wine into the substance of Christ's natural body and blood, but that in the godly *using* of them they be *unto the receivers* Christ's body and blood. . . . And therefore, in the book of the Holy Communion, we do not pray *absolutely* that the bread and wine may be made the body and blood of Christ, but that *unto us* in that holy mystery they may be so: that is to say, that we may so worthily receive the same, that we may be partakers of Christ's body and blood."[35]

Who that reads these concluding words, and remembers the share taken by Cranmer in the

---

[35] *On the Lord's Supper*, p. 79.

liturgical reforms of Edward VI. can fail to identify the "mistakers" to whom the alteration was attributed by the Act.

3. Another instance is the Rubric of 1549 bidding the wafers to be

"*divided in two pieces at the least, or more, by discretion of the minister, and so distributed. And men must not think less to be received in part than in the whole, but in each of them the whole body of our Saviour Jesus Christ.*"

This rubric had been designed no doubt to forestall the superstitious prejudice of those who had been wont to have an unbroken wafer placed within their mouths by the celebrant. It is worth notice that in Ireland so late as 1867 a Maynooth professor recommends priests to divide the wafer, if necessary, but "it is recommended that, if possible, the parts thus broken be given to the better instructed, for some ignorant persons might suppose that there is an important difference between one of these and the whole particle."[36] Gardiner adroitly availed himself of the seeming admission of a local residence within "each" fragment. "And where in the Book of Common Prayer it is truly said, in each part of the bread consecrate broken to be Christ's whole body," &c. Cranmer could only reply that—

"As for the Book of Common Prayer, although it say, that in each part of the bread broken is *received* the whole body of Christ, yet it saith not so of the parts *unbroken*, nor yet of the parts or whole *reserved*, as the Papists teach."[37]

The objection still remained which Bucer pointed out,[38] viz. that it was "as though in these words it

---

[36] O'Kane's *Notes on the Roman Rubrics*, sec. 691.
[37] *On the Lord's Supper*, p. 64.   [38] *Censura*, p. 459.

were affirmed that the body of Christ is offered as locally shut up in the particles of the bread."

The rubric was struck out in the Second Prayer Book, and the Romish "ministers" who still clung to their benefices had no longer any chance of "mistaking" this ambiguous sentence.

4. Gardiner had claimed "the prayer of humble access" as being an act of adoration paid directly to the Flesh of Christ then lying upon the altar, because in the First Prayer Book this prayer stood *after* the consecration and before the distribution. Gardiner wrote—

"As touching the adoration of Christ's flesh *in* the sacrament . . (it) is well set forth in the Book of Common Prayer, where the priest is ordered to kneel and make a prayer in his own, and the name of all that should communicate, confessing therein that is prepared there." [39]

Cranmer replies that such adoration is "idolatry": nevertheless the prayer itself was transposed so as to be used thenceforth only while the elements remained *un*consecrated.

5. The words of "distribution" were alleged (incorrectly) by Gardiner as teaching his doctrine of "the presence." [40] Cranmer disputed the accuracy of the citation, but for all that the words themselves were changed.

6. Gardiner insisted before the Privy Council "that although the elevation was taken away, yet the alteration, in one special place, was indeed reserved: and showed it to them, adding it must needs be so." [41]

---

[39] *On the Lord's Supper*, p. 229.   [40] *Ibid.*, pp. 51-53.
[41] Foxe's *Acts and Monuments*, VI.-114. No. LXIV.

The allusion was to the Rubric of 1549: —

"*As touching kneeling, crossing*, holding up of hands, *knocking upon the breast and other gestures: they may be used or left as every man's devotion serveth without blame.*"

Gardiner was ordered (July 14th, 1550) to subscribe a declaration that "it is ordered in the said book and Order that the sacrament should not be lifted up, and shewed to the people to be adored." [12] Gardiner refused to subscribe: the rubric, however, was not merely struck out, but the manual acts, which under pretence of "taking" the bread were often used as a pretext for elevating the host, were also abolished.[13]

In each of the above instances, Cranmer denied that his opponent was giving the true meaning of the First Prayer Book, and as the drafting of the Second Act of Uniformity was exclusively in the hands of his own friends, it is clear that the "Mistakers," blamed in it for having rendered changes necessary, were the "sesqui-conforming" clergy who to-day are known as the "Romanisers."

[12] Dasent's *Acts of the Privy Council*, III.-75: or Foxe, VI.-83.
[13] See Hooper's *Early Writings*, p. 534; and Bishop Middleton's *Injunctions of* 1583, quoted below at p. 218.

III

The Injunctions of Elizabeth

THE right of the Crown to issue Injunctions binding on the clergy has long been recognised in English law. "Prerogative" and "custom" were reinforced at the Reformation by statutory declarations professing to be declaratory of constitutional law, but certainly claiming very wide if not arbitrary powers for the Civil ruler.[1] Under Elizabeth, the title of the Sovereign was changed from that of "Supreme Head" to that of "Supreme Governor;" but the authority vested in the "Governor" by the statute 1 Elizabeth, cap. i., was not a whit less than that claimed by Henry and Edward; indeed, it explicitly *added* "schisms" to the subjects which were to be thenceforward liable to Regal correction. And the 18th section of that Act gave the Queen authority to delegate her jurisdiction to "visit" ecclesiastical offences to "Commissioners under the great seal for causes ecclesiastical." These Royal Commissioners constituted a court of first instance, whose decisions were without appeal. Their powers were wide, and extended even to deprivation; and the process of their Court was

---

[1] Makower's *Constitutional History of the Church of England*, p. 258.

THE INJUNCTIONS OF ELIZABETH 35

comparatively swift and summary. It followed that the "Royal Supremacy" was then a thing in everyday evidence before the whole nation.

The 17th section of the Act, which is still unrepealed, is—

"Such jurisdictions, privileges, superiorities and pre-eminences, spiritual and ecclesiastical, as by *any* spiritual or ecclesiastical power or authority hath heretofore been, *or* may lawfully be exercised and used for the visitation of the ecclesiastical state and persons, and for reformation, order and correction of the same, and of all manner of errors, heresies, schisms, abuses, offences, contempts and enormities, shall for ever, by authority of this present parliament, be united and annexed to the imperial crown of this realm."[2]

The Government decided to hold a Royal Visitation of the whole country simultaneously with the issue of the Prayer Book, so as to make clear what were the requirements of the altered Liturgy.

The *second* Prayer Book of Edward was to come into use again on June 24th, 1559, and preparations had been made to ensure its prompt enforcement. On May 28th, 1559, a letter was written by a clergyman in Kent to John Abel at Strasburg, which stated that fourteen persons named were to be Visitors, "*and also* the Queen's Commissioners for all ecclesiastical matters."[3] On June 13th, Cecil, the Prime Minister, writes to Throckmorton, the Ambassador, that Injunctions and Articles were "*already* framed for general Visitation."[4] Dr. Lewis thinks these were prepared "probably in April."[5] At any rate, printed copies were

---

[2] Section 17. [3] Churton's *Life of Nowell*, Appendix, 394.
[4] *State Papers, Foreign*, Elizabeth, p. 313.
[5] *Reformation Settlement*, p. 198.

"annexed"[6] to the Commission dated June 24th (i.e., *of even date with the Prayer Book itself*), and copies were also to be delivered by the Royal Commissioners to every incumbent. In North's *Chronicle of St. Martin's, Leicester*,[7] the entry "paid for the service book" comes just after the fee paid to the Visitors.

The clergy were required to subscribe a declaration "acknowledging" the two Acts of Supremacy and Uniformity (1 Elizabeth, cap. i. and ii.), "and the orders and rules contained in the Injunctions given by the Queen's Majesty and exhibited in this present Visitation, to be according to the true Word of God," &c.[8]

Dr. Stephens, in the Introduction to his *Notes Legal and Historical on the Book of Common Prayer*,[9] following Burnet,[10] says the Royal Visitors of 1559 constituted the "first High Commission."

Richard Cosin, Dean of the Arches and Vicar-General under Archbishop Whitgift, says the Injunctions were "under the great seal of England";[11] and in a later work published in 1591, *An Apology of and for sundrie proceedings by Jurisdiction Ecclesiastical*,[12] he described them as "Injunctions which were set out by the Queen's majesty in the first year of her reign, and are under the great seal of England for better record of the matter, her Highness being thereunto authorised by act of parliament."

Two Commissioners were added to the Visitors for

---

[6] "Injunctiones presentibus annexas." *Annals*, No. XLV.
[8] Strype's *Annals*, I.-i.-255.
[10] *History of the Reformation*, II.-i.-800.
[11] *Answer to an Abstract*, p. 63, A.D. 1584.
[12] p. 22; or p. 45 of the edition of 1593.
  Cardwell's *Documentary*
[7] p. 140.
[9] p. ciii.

the North on August 14th,[13] and that Commission was opened at Nottingham on August 22nd, 1559.[14] Meantime, at St. Paul's Cathedral, a like Commission sat on August 11th, 1559,[15] the reserved wafer having been removed from St. Paul's as early as June 11th,[16] and from the Royal Chapel on May 9th, *i.e.* the very next day after the Royal Assent had been given to the Act of Uniformity.[17] The like was done throughout England, and the list of Commissioners included the names of the revisers of the Prayer Book, the Secretaries of State, and the newly-nominated Bishops, Privy Councillors, &c.

"This thing was not done in a corner," nor by persons either ignorant or uninterested as to the requirements of the restored Prayer Book. We naturally turn, therefore, to their Articles and Injunctions to see how "ritualism" was then[18] dealt with. Among the Articles were these:—

"Whether they minister the Holy Communion any otherwise, than only after such form and manner, as it is set forth by the common authority of the Queen's Majesty and the Parliament."

"Item, whether you know any man in your parish secretly, or in unlawful conventicles say or hear Mass, or any other *service prohibited by the law.*"[19]

Mr. James Parker says that the Injunctions were

---

[13] *State Papers, Domestic,* Elizabeth, p. 136.
[14] *Zurich Letters,* I.-73.   [15] Strype's *Grindal,* p. 36.
[16] Hall's *Letters from Simancas,* p. 62.   [17] Froude, VI.-209.
[18] The Visitors under Edward VI. had their Commission "passed under the Great Seal." Dasent's *Acts of the Privy Council,* IV.-219, under date February 16th, 1552.
[19] Cardwell's *Documentary Annals,* I.-213, 216.

"almost entirely a repetition of those of Edward VI."[20] But this is not so. Ten of Edward's were altogether omitted, while twenty-four of Elizabeth's were entirely new; and among these new ones was the Thirtieth, which ran as follows:—

THIRTIETH INJUNCTION, 1559.

"Item, Her Majesty being desirous to have the prelacy and clergy of this realm to be had as well in outward reverence, as otherwise regarded for the worthiness of their ministries, and thinking it necessary to have them known to the people in all places and assemblies, BOTH IN THE CHURCH and without, and thereby to receive the honour and estimation due to the SPECIAL MESSENGERS AND MINISTERS OF ALMIGHTY GOD; willeth and commandeth, that all Archbishops and Bishops, and all other that be called or admitted to preaching or ministry of the Sacraments, or that be admitted into vocation ecclesiastical, or into any society of learning in either of the Universities, or elsewhere, shall use and wear such seemly habits, garments, and such square caps, as were most commonly and orderly received in the LATTER YEAR of the reign of King Edward the Sixth; not thereby meaning to attribute any holiness or special worthiness to the said garments, but as St. Paul writeth: 'Omnia decenter et secundum ordinem fiant,' 1 Cor. 14 cap."

Now, the *out-door* garb of the clergy underwent no change whatever from the earlier to the later years of Edward VI. The reason for so emphatically fixing "the latter year" is to be found in the fact that in that year *alone* during the whole reign of Edward was the surplice "only" prescribed as the exclusive dress of ministration. It will be observed that the regnal year—"the year of the reign"—is mentioned: and regnal years are always computed from the monarch's

---

[20] *History of the Revisions of the Prayer Book*, p. 46.

accession to the throne. The sixth regnal year of Edward ended on January 27th, 1553, so that the SEVENTH year of his reign, commencing from that date, was the period fixed on. And we have quite a considerable number of assignments by the Edwardian Royal Commissioners dated " in the *seventh* year" of his reign. The *Surrey Inventories*, published by Mr. Tyssen, shew how the copes were converted into table cloths or " carpets," and the albs into surplices by direction of the Royal Visitors.[21]

The Commissions for the *last* Royal Visitation under Edward are commonly dated after the enactment of the Second Prayer Book: and even when the Commission itself is of an earlier date, the Commissioners' return is dated "in the viith yearre of the raingne of our Sovereign Lord Edward the Sixth."[22]

The Act of Uniformity itself (1 Elizabeth, cap. ii.). in its opening words, refers directly to the order of common service which " *remained* at the DEATH of our late sovereign lord King Edward VIth." On March 17th, 1559, a still earlier Bill had been read twice in the Commons, " that no persons shall be punished for using the religion used in King Edward's *last* year."[23] So Jewel, writing in 1559, soon after the passing of the Act of Uniformity, told Peter Martyr that religion was to be " restored to the same state as it was during your *latest* residence among us, under Edward."[24]

---

[21] See *Inventories of the Goods and Ornaments of Surrey*, published by Wyman and Sons ; and Second Report of Ritual Commission, p. 57

[22] Cussans' *Hertfordshire Inventories*, p. 22. Peacock's *English Church Furniture*, pp. 221, 225-7.

[23] D'Ewes' *Journal*, p. 52.   [24] *Zurich Letters*, 1.-23

It will be seen by-and-by that the Thirtieth Injunction, above quoted, was understood by everybody in authority at the time of its issue to relate to the ministerial dress, and to require the "surplice only," which was exclusively the legal standard of the "*latter year of the reign of King Edward VIth.*" This fact is felt to be so inconvenient that Ritualistic writers can hardly ever bring themselves to divulge the actual wording of this Thirtieth Injunction. Their method of citing it is peculiar. First, they habitually quote the Injunction *omitting* the words printed above in capitals, for which words they are careful to substitute a row of dots. Mr. James Parker does this at pages 21 and 156 of his *Letter to Lord Selborne*, and also at page 44 of his *Ornaments Rubric*. At page 73 of his *Letter*, he says the Thirtieth Injunction "relates wholly to the 'apparel,'" and he marks with inverted commas the word "apparel," as though it were taken from the Injunction, in which, however, no such word occurs. Next, he quietly assumes[25] that the "sixth year" (*i.e.* the penultimate year), was "the latter year of the reign." The motive is obvious. The "sixth" year of Edward began January 28th, 1552, whereas Edward's "second" Prayer Book did not come into use till November, so that for nine months of that "sixth year" the Mass ornaments were in legal use. Hence, Mr. James Parker on his own authority substitutes the "sixth" year, *i.e.* the *last year but one* for "the latter year of Edward VI."

The Rev. T. W. Perry, in his *Notes on the Purchas Judgment*,[26] quotes the Injunction in this fashion, "Her

---

[25] *Letter to Lord Selborne*, p. 21.   [26] p. 30.

Majesty . . . willeth and commandeth," &c.; thus omitting altogether the first half of the Injunction: and in his *Lawful Church Ornaments*,[27] he summarises the Injunction thus:—" 30. Orders a particular dress for the members of the universities and for the clergy *when not officiating*" (!). Canon MacColl is, however, *facile princeps*, for he actually quotes a statement from the *Zurich Letters*,[28] viz. that "*in the Injunctions, however, published by the Queen, after the Parliament*, there are prescribed to the clergy some ornaments such as the Mass-priests had and still retain" to prove that Eucharistic vestments, properly so called, were *enjoined!*[29] And by suppressing the words given above in italics he makes it appear as though the Act of Uniformity were the document referred to in 1560 by Lever.

From the pains systematically taken to suppress the witness of this Thirtieth Injunction, it is evident that it is felt to be a formidable foe to the contention of the Ritualists.

***

A more difficult question, however, arises, viz. whether the Injunctions of 1559 derived their authority from the Supremacy Act, 1 Elizabeth, cap. i., or from the Act of Uniformity, 1 Elizabeth, cap. ii. If from the former, the Injunctions must be regarded as executive and administrative acts of the "Supreme Ordinary" enforcing the rubric of the *second* Prayer Book of Edward, which had just been re-enacted under penalties by the second, third, and fourth sections of the Act of Uniformity.

---

[27] p. 141.   [28] *Zurich Letters*, I.-84.
[29] MacColl's *Lawlessness*, pp. 70, 71, third edition.

That view would be consistent with all that was done at the time, except so far as a local and partial connivance at the wearing of copes here and there in the "great churches" must be admitted to conflict with it. But then this wearing of copes by Epistoler and Gospeller was an irregularity equally inexplicable on any *other* hypothesis: it was a relaxation of the law, and not a sample of law-abiding, whatever explanation we may choose to adopt.

But, if we prefer to suppose that the Injunctions were issued under the final provisoes of the Act of Uniformity (1 Elizabeth, cap. ii.), we may regard them, with Mr. Kennion, as being "other order taken" under the 25th section of that Act.

That section ran—

"Provided always, and be it enacted, that such ornaments of the church and of the ministers thereof, shall be retained and be in use, as was in this church of England by authority of Parliament, in the second year of King Edward the Sixth, until *other order* shall be therein taken by the authority of the Queen's majesty, with the advice of her commissioners appointed and authorised under the great seal of England for causes ecclesiastical, or of the metropolitan of this realm."

The "advice" of the Metropolitan could not then be had, for Archbishop Parker was not "confirmed" till December 9th, 1559, his first act of "jurisdiction" being dated December 11th, *i.e.* six days *before* his consecration.[30]

But it is by no means so certain that "Commissioners under the Great Seal for causes ecclesiastical" did not exist at the date of the issue of the Injunctions. The Fifty-first Injunction expressly refers to "such

[31] Haddan's *Apostolical Succession*, p. 323

Her Majesty's Commissioners, or three of them, as be appointed in the City of London to hear and determine divers causes ecclesiastical tending to the execution of certain statutes made the last Parliament for Uniformity of order in religion." The Commission to the Royal Visitors in the north, dated June 24th, authorises them to appoint persons to present the disobedient to " Our Commissioners sitting at London, and Delegates for reformation of ecclesiastical affairs.[31]

And the Royal Visitors were themselves also "Commissioners under the Great Seal" appointed by Letters Patent not merely to "visit ecclesiastical persons," but the laity also, and "to examine, hear, and finally determine causes of every kind," to sequestrate or deprive incumbents, who "obstinately and peremptorily refused to subscribe to the religion received," to inflict censures, and suitable penalties on those who disobeyed the Injunctions, to examine letters of orders, give licenses to preach, and to restore those who had been deprived under Mary.[32]

These Visitors might legitimately be described as "Commissioners appointed under the Great Seal of England for causes ecclesiastical," and, if so, their official acts in the Visitation of 1559 would be the "taking further" or "other order" contemplated by the statute. But, before the Injunctions issued, there were also, in addition, other "Commissioners" qualified to give the statutory "advice" needed. Lord Coke says that the Marian Bishops were deprived by

---

[31] *Documentary Annals*, I.-221.
[32] Cardwell's *Documentary Annals*, No. XLV., "Statum tam ecclesiasticum quam laicum visitare . . . clerumque et populum." Compare the subsequent Commission of 1562, price one penny, published as *Tract CVII.*, by the Church Association, 14, Buckingham Street, Strand, W.C.

Royal Commissioners under a Commission "said to be lost, and enrolled it is not as it ought to have been, and it is affirmed by some that *have seen it* that it passed not above twenty sheets of paper copywise." [33]

Moreover, on May 5th, 1559, an Act was passed, " That the Queen's Majesty *by Commission* may examine the deprivation of spiritual persons, and restore them again." [34] On May 6th, Bishop Bonner's last collation was given,[35] on May 29th he was deprived,[36] and the spiritualties of his see were in the hands of the Dean and Chapter of Canterbury on June 2nd.[37] On June 22nd, the *congé d'élire* to elect his successor recited the vacancy of the see " by the privation and deposition of Edmund Bonner." [38] On June 21st the Bishops of Lichfield (Baynes), Worcester (Pates), Carlisle (Oglethorpe), Chester (Scot), and Llandaff (Kitchen) were deprived.[39] On June 25th the Bishop of St. Asaph was deprived, the spiritualties being seized July 15th;[40] and on June 26th the Bishops of Winchester and Lincoln were deprived." On the 18th of July the *congé d'élire* for Ely mentions " the lawful removal of Thomas [Thirlby] the last bishop," [42]

---

[33] Coke's *Fourth Institute*, Ed. 1681, pp. 322-326.
[34] D'Ewes' *Journal*, p. 31-I.
[35] Burnet, *History of the Reformation*, II.-791.
[36] Machyn's *Diary*, Camden Society, p. 200.
[37] Collier, VI.-252.   [38] Rymer, *Fœdera*, XV.-532.
[39] Machyn, p. 200. Strype, *Annals*, I.-i.-210. Bramhall's *Works*, A-C.L. III., p. 232. On July 12th the Spanish ambassador reported that " it is feared he [Kitchen] may take the oath, as he is wearing a bishop's garb again." On July 18th Kitchen gave a written promise to enforce the oath of supremacy upon his clergy, the Queen consenting to " defer " his own taking of it : and on that same day the Queen issued her licence to elect Parker. Hume's *Spanish State Papers*, I.-86. Lamb's *History of the Thirty-nine Articles*, p. 11.
[40] Bramhall, p. 232.
[41] Machyn, p. 201. Strype, p. 210, says June 25th.
[42] Rymer, XV.-537.

who was deprived along with Archbishop Heath on July 5th.⁴³ On July 13th, the Spanish Ambassador reported to Philip that "they have deprived the Bishops of St. David's [Morgan] and Exeter [Tuberville] this week." ⁴⁴

The subsequent Act, 39 Elizabeth, cap. viii., refers to the "*sentence* and *sentences* of deprivation" which had been pronounced. This Act was passed in 1597, when Coke was Attorney-General, and when the Parliament also must have known all the facts.

Strype says, " the venerable Commissaries went to the Chapter House of the said Cathedral, and there sat *judicially*. The Queen's Letters Commissional signed by her own hand and seal, were read by Peter Lylly, Principal Register of the Queen in that behalf."⁴⁵ So Lord Coke said, " sentence is given by Commissioners Delegates by the Prince, as by the late Visitors, Ann. I., Elizabeth, &c.⁴⁶

Hence we may feel certain that " Commissioners under the Great Seal for causes ecclesiastical " must have been in existence at the time when the Injunctions issued : and seeing that the actual Visitation did not commence till August, there was ample time for the Injunctions to have received the formal sanction of the " High Commission."

***

Archbishop Parker wrote to Cecil, the prime minister, on January 8th, 1571, that "the Injunction hath authority by proviso of the statute," and " by virtue of which law

---

⁴³ Machyn, 203. Strype, 211.
⁴⁴ Hume's *Spanish State Papers*, Vol. I.-80.
⁴⁵ *Annals*, I., Part I., p. 249.   ⁴⁶ *Fourth Institute*, p. 340.

she published *further order* in her Injunctions." He adds that Queen Elizabeth herself told him that she had insisted on the addition of this proviso to the Act of Uniformity expressly with a view to such "orders" as the Injunctions contained [48]; and that this was also the recognised view taken of the Injunctions by the nation at large is shewn by the language of the Order respecting "the tables in the church" which was appended to the Injunctions. It says that "in some other places, the altars be not yet removed, upon opinion conceived of some *other order therein to be taken* by her Majesty's Visitors." Archbishop Parker, writing to Cecil, expressly mentions this order "for the placing of the tables *within the quire*" as being a "further order" under the Act of Uniformity. Mr. Maskell recognises that "Elizabeth, in her Injunctions which were supplemental to her Act of Uniformity, and were grounded upon an especial clause in that Act," took order as to singing.[49] And even Mr. T. W. Perry admits that Archbishop Parker's letter "shews that the Injunctions were an exercise of the powers given in the 25th section relative to ornaments, no less than to (*sic*) the 26th section."[50]

Whether, however, the Injunctions were issued under the Act of Uniformity, or under the Supremacy Act, is matter rather of antiquarian, legal, and literary interest. What Churchmen are more concerned to know is that their legal authority was undoubted,[51] and that from

---

[48] *Archbishop Parker's Correspondence*, Parker Society Edition, p. 375.
[49] *Ancient Liturgies*, Preface, XIV.
[50] *Notes on Purchas Judgment*, p. 14.
[51] See Article XXXVII. of the Thirty-nine Articles.

the first they were held to require the surplice to the exclusion of all "massing gear."

The evidence of this may be conveniently thrown into the form of a

Chronological Catena.

1559, October 20th.—Queen Elizabeth to her Commissioners respecting " certain Ecclesiastical persons who refuse to observe the Rites, Ceremonies, and Divine Service ordained and provided by our laws, statutes, and *Injunctions.*" [52] Recusants were to be certified to the Queen in Chancery, *i.e.* to the Delegates.

1560, April 1st.—Sandys, then Bishop of Worcester, one of the Royal Commissioners for the North, reports, after his visitation, that " all images of every kind were at our recent visitation not only taken down, but also burnt, and that too by public authority. . . . There remain only in our church (Ecclesiâ), those Popish vestments *I mean copes* (copas intellige); which we hope will not continue long." [53] In October of the same year he writes to Archbishop Parker:—" I visited with your consent; I proceeded orderly, according to laws and Injunctions; I innovated nothing; I was altogether led by laws." [54]

1561, September.—Archbishop Parker visiting the cathedral and collegiate churches within his Province inquires, " Whether your Divine Service be used and the *Sacraments ministered* in manner and form prescribed by the Queen's Majestie's Injunctions, and none other way." [55]

1562.—Alley, Bishop of Exeter, said, " I know one preacher, not of the basest sort nor estimation, which did glory

---

[52] Rymer, *Fœdera*, XV.-547.
[53] *Zurich Letters*, I., Appendix 43. Canon Raine observes "our church " would mean Worcester Cathedral.
[54] *Parker Correspondence*, p. 126. [55] Strype's *Parker*, I.-146.

and boast that he made eight sermons in London
against surplices, rochets, tippets, and caps, . . . matters
indifferent; which are made politic by the prescribed
Order of the Prince." [56]

1563, August 16.—Humphrey writes to Bullinger to ask,
"Whether at the command of the Sovereign (the
jurisdiction of the Pope having been abolished) and
for the sake of order and not of ornament (*cultus*),
habits of this kind may be worn in church (*vestes
ecclesiæ*). . . . I am speaking of that round cap and
Popish surplice, which are now enjoined us, not by
the unlawful tyranny of the Pope, but by the just and
legitimate authority of the Queen." [57]

1563.—Archbishop Parker issued his own injunctions asking,
"Whether your . . . prestes, curates or ministers do
use in the time of the celebration of Divine Service to
wear a *surplice prescribed by the Queen's Majesty's
Injunctions*, and the Book of Common Prayer." [58]

1564, January.—Archdeacon Mullins, sitting by commission
from Grindal, Bishop of London, at St. Sepulchre's
Church, "Signified to them the Queen's pleasure,
which was that all orders should wear the square cap,
surplice and gown. They were therefore prayed in
a gentle manner to take on them the cap, with the
tippet to wear about their necks, and the gown; . .
and *to wear in the ministry of the Church the surplice*
ONLY." [59] This was *not* subsequent to Archbishop
Parker's letter of January 30th, 1564-5, as Dr. Lewis
(p. 237) supposed, for the plague had ceased in
London on January 23rd, 1564—see Gairdner's
Three Fifteenth Century Chronicles, pp. 125, 128.
"And it is certain from Strype's remark that the
plague was then 'slacking,' that the London clergy
were summoned in January, 1564, and not 1564-5."

---

[56] Strype, *Annals*, I.-i.-520.   [57] *Zurich Letters*, I.-134.
[58] Parker's *Letter to Lord Selborne*, p. 195.
[59] Strype's *Grindal*, p. 144.

Grindal's "Form of thanksgiving to God for ceasing the contagious sickness of the plague" is dated January 22nd, and was published January 26th, 1563-4.[60]

1564.—"On the 24th of March following." Archbishop Parker, with Grindal and other Commissioners, sat at Lambeth when the chancellor is reported by Strype to have said,[61] "My masters and the ministers of London, the Council's pleasure is that strictly ye keep the unity of apparel like to this man. . . . that is, a square cap, a scholar's gown (priest-like), a tippet, and in the church a linen surplice: and inviolably observe the rubric of the Book of Common Prayer and the Queen's Majesty's Injunctions."

1565.—Bishop Horn, who had returned to England early in 1559 and took part in the public dispute "in Westminster Quire" on March 31st, 1559, was not a member of the House of Lords until after the passing of the Act of Uniformity, having been made Bishop of Winchester on February 16th, 1560. On July 17th, 1565, *i.e.* prior to the issue of the "Advertisements," he wrote to Gaulter respecting "The Act of Parliament, which passed before our reinstatement, (*restitutionem*,)[62] by which, though the rest of the dregs were taken away (*sublatâ reliquâ fæce*), the use of square caps and surplices remained to the clergy, though without superstitious conceit *which was expressly guarded against in the very terms of the Act* (*decreti*). It was enjoined us (*Injunctum*) who then had not any authority to sanction or repeal, either to wear the caps and surplices, or to give place to

---

[60] See Grindal's *Remains*, pp. 115, 267, and Clay's *Liturgies set forth in the Reign of Queen Elizabeth*, p. 518. Stow's *Memoranda*, Camden Society, p. 128.

[61] *Life of Grindal*, p. 144.

[62] The Deanery of Durham which he had held under Edward, was restored to him in 1559. *Le Neve's Fasti*, III.-299.

others."[63] The mention of "caps" and "the express words" relating to "superstitious conceit" are not found in the Act, but in the concluding sentence of the Thirtieth Injunction, which is regarded by Bishop Horn (who was himself one of the Visitors in 1559) as practically identified with the Act and as of the same purport and authority.

1565, May.—Humphrey writes to the Bishops against the apparel now ordered to be adopted. See above under 1563.[64]

1565, August.—Gualter writing to Humphrey:—"Yt troblyth me not a lytle that the Quenes Mai. Ordynaunce for ye weryng of the surplisse and prests cappe, whereas ther had bene greater nede of the reformacyon and amendment of other thinges at this tyme then to sett up agayne such Ordnances."[65]

1565, November 3rd.—Bullinger writes to Bishop Horn, "It is expressly provided, as you write, in that decree that square caps with surplices are to be retained (*retineri*) without any superstition."[66]

1565, November 26th.—"Beaumont, Kelke, Matthew Hutton, Longworth, respectively Masters of Trinity, Magdalene, Pembroke, St. John's, and Whitgift, Lady Margaret Professor, addressed Cecil their Chancellor, that they had heard that all the students were to be placed under a necessity of obeying an old injunction (*præscriptum vetus*) in regard to vestments."[67]

1565, December 18th.—Richard Longworth, Master of St. John's, Cambridge, speaks of the "Queen's Injunctions for wearing surplices."[68]

---

[63] *Zurich Letters,* I. Appendix, 84.
[64] *State Papers, Domestic,* Elizabeth, No. 64, p. 253.
[65] *Lansdowne MSS.,* IX., Article I.
[66] Burnet's *History of the Reformation,* III.,ii.,426.
[67] Swainson's *Historical Inquiry,* p. 52. Strype's *Parker,* Appendix, No. XXXIX.
[68] *State Papers, Domestic,* Elizabeth, p. 263.

1565.—Bishop of Lincoln (Bullingham, a Commissioner under the Great Seal and one of the framers of the Advertisements) visited King's College, Cambridge, and gave injunctions to the Romish Provost, Dr. Philip Baker, "to destroy a great deal of Popish stuff, as mass books, legends, couchers, and grails, copes, vestments, candlesticks, crosses, pixes, paxes, and the brazen rood; which the Provost did not perform, but preserved them in a secret corner. . . . He used one Mr. Woolward very extremely (who was afterwards Fellow of Eton) because he would not execute the service at the Communion with his face towards the east and his back towards the congregation[69] according to the manner of the Mass; for the denial of which he was like to be expelled, and had been, had not one of the Queen's Injunctions been his warrant."[70] This Ritualistic Provost was deprived by the Royal Commissioners and bolted to Louvain.

1565, December 22nd.—Bishop Jewel declined to institute Humphrey "in respect of this vain contention about apparel."[71] (See above under "1563.")

1565.—Bishop Geste " in the month of December, this year " (i.e. 1564-5), drew up for the Prime Minister, a paper to shew "that the apparel of priests may be worn."[72] In it, he says the Puritans "have been borne withal herein *almost these six years*."[73] He twice expresses the wish that "it were in print declared" that the priest's dress was worn "not for religion, but for order and obedience." This (coupled with the "6 years") fixes the date, because the Advertisements

---

[69] This word "congregation" in the *Lansdowne MSS.*, VIII., No. 53, has been carelessly altered by Strype into "table."
[70] Strype's *Grindal*, p. 210. Grindal's *Remains*, p. 308.
[71] Jewel's *Works*, IV.-1265.   [72] Strype's *Life of Parker*, I.-339
[73] Dugdale's *Life of Geste*, p. 204.

4 *

of 1566 contained this very declaration "in print."[74] Geste urges "It is most plainly known, that [it] is the Queen's Majesty's Injunction and commandment, that we ministers should wear priests' apparel."[75] That this related to the dress of "ministration" is shewn by the "third reason" attributed by Geste to Puritans in which they cite Romish writers on ritual to prove "that priests' apparel hath many superstitious significations: and hath been and should be sanctified' [which the outdoor dress never was]: 'and judgeth it so necessary, that ministers cannot serve God well in *the church* without it."[76] In reply Bishop Geste takes each of the items of dress complained of and parallels it with an existing secular usage of the same vesture by laymen. He says :—

"The lawyer weareth a *tippet and a gown*, like a papistical priest: yet no man judgeth him to sin, or to be a papist therefore. The mourner weareth a *cap* like a priest: yet no man reproveth him, or thinketh him to be a papist for it. The porter, the horsekeeper, sometime wear a linen garment, like a *surplice*, yet no man judgeth them to do amiss, or to be papists for it. Therefore, it is not the fashion of priests' garments that hath the appearance of evil."[77]

1566, January 20th.—The Vice-Chancellor to Cecil: "Mr. Beaumont wished to know if he can deprive a man for not wearing a surplice."[78]

1566, February 8th.—Bishop Jewel writes: "The contention respecting that linen church dress (de Ecclesiastica veste lineâ) is not yet at rest . . . but the Queen can

---

[74] Cardwell's *Documentary Annals*, I.-289. Strype's *Parker*, III.-85.
[75] Dugdale, p. 205. [76] *Ibid.*, p. 206.
[77] *Ibid.*, p. 208. Crowley, the Puritan Vicar of St. Giles', Cripplegate, called the choristers' surplices "porters' coats." *Parker Correspondence*, p. 276. Gairdner's *Three Fifteenth-Century Chronicles*, p. 136.
[78] *State Papers, Domestic*, Elizabeth, p. 267.

bear no change in religion at this time."[79] He had spoken of it as "ista λαιοστολία" on February 7th, 1562.[80]

1566, March 20th.—Archbishop Parker and Grindal write to Cecil, stating that "we intende particulerly to examine every of them, whether they will promyse conformytie in there mynistrations and outwarde apparell, stablished by lawe and Injunction."[81]

1566.—"The xxvj day of Marche, in anno 1566, beyng Twesday, ye parsons and mynystars of ye churches in and abought London were (by commaundyment) at Lambethe, before ye Archebyshoppe of Caunterbury and othar of ye cownsell, wher charge was gyven to them to sarve theyr churchis and were theyr aparayll *accordyng to ye quens Injunctions*, or ells to do no sarvyce. And that same weke or ye begynyng of ye next came forthe a boke in print subscribyd by ye Archebyshope of Cauntorbury, ye Byshopps of London, Wynchester, Elii, and dyvers othar," viz. the "Advertisements (see below, p. 62) of Queen Elizabeth."

*_**

All the instances above cited, it will be observed, were prior to the publication of the Advertisements, when the Rubric and the Thirtieth Injunction were the only "laws" regulating the dress of the clergy at "all times of their ministration." Mr. Kennion is of opinion that the Thirtieth Injunction of 1559 was that "other Order" by the Queen contemplated in the proviso of her Act of Uniformity. If so, a statutory authority supplanted from the very first the provisional adoption of the vestments of the First Prayer Book— supposing, that is, that the popular theory is correct

---

[79] *Zurich Letters*, I., Appendix p. 89.   [80] *Ibid.*, p. 59.
[81] *Lansdowne MSS.*, VIII., No. 86.

which assumes that such ornaments were authorised either by the proviso itself, or by the illegitimate fraud-rubric which in Elizabeth's *printed* Prayer Books had been, without authority, substituted for the statutory Rubric of 1552, then freshly enacted by the third section 1 Elizabeth, cap. ii.

For myself, I prefer the alternative theory, viz. that the Rubric of 1552 was designed by the Elizabethan Act of Uniformity to stand in full legal force from the first, and that the proviso in the Act merely related to the retention and utilisation of the *discarded and illegal* ornaments of 1549 by the legal custodians of the parish goods, until "order" could be "taken" by the Royal Visitors to ensure their disposal without waste or loss. That theory, however, will require separate treatment in another paper. See p. 91. But if, for the moment, we may assume that theory to be true, the Injunctions of 1559 will be seen to fall into line as administrative enforcements by the executive of the Statutory Rubric of 1552 which, until 1661, remained in law (and, very nearly, in fact) the sole standard of ministerial dress.

But the proof that the Thirtieth Injunction related to the dress of the Officiants in Divine Service, and coincided with the standard of the Advertisements of Elizabeth (instead of conflicting with it, as has been popularly supposed), would be incomplete without further evidence of the action of the authorities during the reign of Elizabeth, subsequent to 1566. We therefore continue our chain of witnesses. At the very moment of issuing the Advertisements, Archbishop Parker (in his official letter to the Dean of Bocking, enclosing a copy of the new book), wrote on

1566, March 28th.—"Divers parsons . . . have not conformed themselves to the Queen's Majesty's laws and Injunctions in the administration of public prayers and sacraments and in outward apparel."[82] And an undated letter of George Withers to the Elector Palatine about the same time said: "In what way the Sacraments are disfigured by human inventions, will easily appear from the public form of prayer, the royal Injunctions, and the admonitions, or (as they call them) the Advertisements of the Bishops."[83]

1566, May 1st.—Bullinger replying to two letters of February 9th and 16th says: "Surely I like it not in anywyse that (if ye were commanded) ye should say service at an altar, rather burthened than beautified with the image of a crucifix, in massing apparel, that is in an alb and in a Vestment, which hath the picture of Christ hanging on the back." This is quoted from the official translation put forth by Archbishop Parker[84] and his brother Bishops, and printed by Jugge *cum privilegio* in 1566, of which there is a copy in the British Museum "877.6.3." In the margin opposite the word "vestment" is printed "*casula.*" In the *Lansdowne MSS.*, IX.-44, is a copy which reads "in veste missatica, hoc est in alba et casula." Strype also correctly gives the word "casula."[85] Bishop Burnet, however, carelessly misprinted the word as "*copa,*" and was followed by the Parker Society's translator.[86] But Mr. Pocock in his edition of *Burnet* (VI.-489) has ascertained that the original letter at Zurich reads "casula." Burnet's blunder, however, misled the counsel employed on both sides in the *Case and Opinion* published by

---

[82] Archbishop Parker's *Register*, I.-257.   [83] *Zurich Letters*, II.-163.
[84] Strype's *Annals*, I.-ii.-175. Both Grindal and Horn claim to have "printed" Bullinger's letter (*Zurich Letters*, I.-168, 175), and this is explained by Abel's letter of June 6th, 1566, in which he says it was done "by order of the Commissioners" (*Zurich Letters*, II.-120).
[85] *Annals*, I.-ii., Appendix, No. 24.   [86] *Zurich Letters*, I.-345.

"several Archbishops and Bishops," and by the English Church Union, respectively, in 1866. The true reading is important, because the cope never was a "mass garment," and the meaning of the rubrical word "Vestment" (which Dr. Lewis had questioned) is conclusively shown to be the Chasuble. Bullinger enclosed a copy of his letter in another (dated May 3rd, 1566) to Bishops Horn, Grindal, and Parkhurst, by whom it was published, greatly to the disgust of the Puritans.[87] Bullinger goes on to say that he learns from his English correspondents that there "is now no dispute concerning habits of this kind, but the question is, whether it be lawful for ministers of the Gospel to wear a round or square cap, and a white garment, which they call a surplice."

1566, July.—In their reply to Bullinger, the Puritan leaders do not pretend that the alb or chasuble were in question, but they complain "the surplice and cope are being brought back" (*revocantur*) by the Advertisements.[88]

1566.—The Vicar of Southbemfleet was presented, "because he doth not observe the Injunctions, and will not minister in a surples." Other like instances will be found in Hale's *Precedents in Criminal Cases*, pp. 126, 149, 177, 196, 210, 226, 243.

1567.—Archbishop Parker inquired from each of the Cathedral and Collegiate churches of his Province—I. "Whether they use seemly or priestly garments, according as they are commanded by the Queen's Majesty's Injunctions to do?"—"III. Whether your Divine Service be used, and your sacraments ministered in manner and form prescribed by the Queen's Majesty's Injunctions, and none other way?"[89]

1569.—Archbishop Parker's articles for his diocese—"III. Whether your priests, curates, or ministers do use in

---

[87] *Zurich Letters*, II.-124.   [88] *Ibid.*, I., Appendix, p. 94.
[89] Cardwell's *Documentary Annals*, I.-304.

the time of celebration of Divine Service to wear a surplice prescribed by the Queen's Majesty's Injunctions and the Book of Common Prayer ? "[90]

1569.—Parkhurst's Visitation Articles, "Imprimis, whether your Divine Service be said or sung in due time and reverently, and the sacraments duly and reverently ministered in such decent apparel as is appointed by the laws, the Queen's Majesty's Injunctions, and other Orders set forth by public authority in that behalf."[91]

1570, September 25th.—Queen Elizabeth wrote to Bishop Parkhurst to take proceedings against any that had " in any of the rites of the Church, as in the ministration of the sacraments or other ceremonies, used any innovation, by making alterations from the orders prescribed and established by the statutes and ordinances of the realm, or explained by the Queen's Injunctions."[92]

1571, August 20th.— Queen Elizabeth writes to Archbishop Parker, *directly referring the Advertisements to her letter of January 25th, 1565* (see below, p. 77)

"Where we required you, as the Metropolitan of our realm, and as the principal person in our Commission for causes ecclesiastical, to have good regard that such uniform order in the Divine Service and rules of the Church might be duly kept, as by the laws in that behalf is provided, and by our Injunctions also declared and explained," charging him "by all means lawful to proceed herein as you have begun," and insisting on " the observation of our laws, Injunctions, and commandments."[93]

---

[90] Cardwell's *Documentary Annals*, I.-321.
[91] *Ritual Commission, Second Report*, Appendix, p. 405.
[92] Strype's *Parker*, II.-36.
[93] *Parker Correspondence*, p. 386. Cardwell has misprinted "require" instead of *required*, and thus obscures the Queen's reference to her *former* letter of January, 1565.

1571.—Bishop Cox, Visitation Articles for Ely, "Every parson, vicar, and curate shall use in the time of the celebration of Divine Service to wear *a surplice, prescribed by the Queen's Majesty's Injunctions* and the Book of Common Prayer, and shall keep and observe all other rites and orders prescribed in the same Book of Common Prayer and Injunctions, as well about the celebration of the sacraments, as also in their comely and priestlyke apparel, to be worn according to the precept set forth in the book called Advertisements." [94]

1573, November 7th.—The Privy Council write to urge the Bishops "to the keeping of the orders allowed by the said Parliament and by Her Majesty's Injunctions." [95]

1573, November 24th.—Archbishop Parker directs Sandys, Bishop of London (as Dean of the Province of Canterbury), to require each of his suffragans to see "that one uniform order in the celebration of Divine Service and ministration of the Sacraments should be used and observed in all places of this Her Highness' realm and dominions, according to the Book of Common Prayer set forth by public authority and Her Majesty's Injunctions." [96]

1573.—Archbishop Parker's Visitation Articles for the Diocese of Canterbury are in the British Museum ($\frac{775}{9}$). Questions 1 and 4 speak of the "Advertisements lately set forth by public authority"; and Question 3 asks for the surplice "prescribed by the Injunctions and the book of common prayer."

1574.—Cartwright, speaking of the surplice, says: "They pretend, I confess, the Queen's Majesty's Injunctions, and obedience to them." [97]

1575.—Archbishop Parker in Visitation of Winchester asks, "XVI. Whether they . . . minister the Sacraments reverently in such sort as is set forth by the laws of

---

[94] *Second Report of the Ritual Commission,* Appendix, 406.
[95] Cardwell's *Documentary Annals,* I.-352.
[96] *Parker Correspondence,* p. 451.   [97] Whitgift's *Works,* II.-7.

this realm, the Queen's Majesty's Injunctions, and the Advertisements."⁹⁸

1576.—Archbishop Grindal, Visitation Articles, "Whether your Divine Service be used, and the Sacraments ministered in manner and form prescribed in the Queen's Majesty's Injunctions, and none otherwaies." ⁹⁹

1578, July 1st.—Williams, a Fellow of Manchester Collegiate Church, was bidden to "Wear the surplice . . . according to the Queen's Injunctions." ¹⁰⁰

1584.—Archbishop Whitgift Visitation Articles, "Whether doth your minister in public prayer-time wear a surplesse and go abroad apparelled, as by Her Majesty's Injunctions and Advertisements prescribed." ¹⁰¹

1585.—Archbishop Whitgift, in Articles for Chichester, repeats verbatim the last inquiry.¹⁰²

1588.—Archbishop Whitgift, Articles for Salisbury, "Whether have you in your church all things necessary for the common prayer, and due administration of the Sacraments according to Her Majesty's laws and Injunctions?" ¹⁰³

1589.—Archbishop Whitgift repeats verbatim the above in his Visitations of Canterbury and Rochester.¹⁰⁴

1598.—Chaderton, Bishop of Lincoln, asks in his Visitation "Whether your parson . . administer the sacraments, wearing a surplice according to the Queen's Injunctions." ¹⁰⁵

At that date the printing of the Injunctions had probably ceased, their place having been taken by the Advertisements, as afterwards by the Canons of 1604.

---

⁹⁸ *Second Report of the Ritual Commission,* Appendix, p. 416.
⁹⁹ Cardwell's *Documentary Annals,* I.-364.
¹⁰⁰ Raine's *Chetham Miscellanies,* Vol. V., p 6.
¹⁰¹ Droop's *Edwardian Vestments,* p. 17.
¹⁰² Cardwell's *Documentary Annals,* II.-35. Edition 1844.
¹⁰³ *Documentary Annals,* II.-14.
¹⁰⁴ Strype's *Whitgift,* I.-594.
¹⁰⁵ Article 15, British Museum, "5155 a. 20."

They continued to be cited, however, in the Visitation Articles down to (and long after) the latest of those reprinted by the Ritual Commission. Strype in 1709 spoke of "the apparel prescribed to ministers by the Queen's Injunctions, viz. . . . in their ministration the surplice."[106]

Archdeacon Sharp in 1735 said, "Her Injunctions have the sanction of that Parliament which granted her the said power, and the sanction too of the Act of Uniformity after the restoration, which by this Rubric now under consideration refers, according to the explanation now given to it, to her Injunctions."[107] And Mr. Droop in his *latest* edition says,[108] "The most probable view seems to me to be, that when the Injunctions were issued in July, 1559, Elizabeth and her advisers intended their Thirtieth Injunction to apply 'both in the Church and without,' and to prescribe only the surplice in church." It will be noticed that in the extracts dated after 1566 the *identity* of the requirements of the Injunctions and Advertisements and the undoubted application of both to the dress of ministration, is always assumed.

---

[106] *Annals*, I.-ii.-125, Edition 1824. [107] *On the Rubric*, p. 66.
[108] *Edwardian Vestments*, p. 80.

IV
The Advertisements of Queen Elizabeth

DR. Littledale wrote in the *Times* of January 26th, 1886, as follows :—
"It is certain, and the Court had the fact laid before it, that these Advertisements were not issued by Queen Elizabeth at all, since Archbishop Parker declares, in a letter to the Prime Minister, Sir William Cecil, on March 28th, 1566, that he had not been able to get the Queen's authority for the Advertisements, which he thought had nothing in them against the law of the realm, and that he had been obliged to assay his own authority in issuing them; while Strype tells us that Cecil's own copy was endorsed with the words 'These not authorised nor published.' Here then is indisputable evidence from the chief personages in Church and State at the time, entirely overthrowing the inferential guesswork with which the Privy Council sought to establish the royal character of these Advertisements."

The statement bristles with mistakes. "Cecil's own copy," of what Strype called "Articles or Ordinances," was in MS. only, bearing the above "endorsement" made in "1564" (Old Style), and was *not* "The" Advertisements, but was a document differing from the printed book sent by Archbishop Parker for Cecil's perusal on March 28th, 1566 (New Style). It was the former, and not the latter which Parker said had failed to gain the Queen's approval; for which very reason it had been in the interval extensively altered. Archbishop Parker does not say a word about "assaying with his own authority to *issue*" the book, but to *execute* and *administer* the laws which were in force prior to that "issue." And at least five separate Elizabethan editions still remain out of the many "published" during Cecil's lifetime, which he himself personally assisted in enforcing.

Since the Ridsdale Judgment was delivered, the Camden Society have published a contemporary chronicle by John Stowe, which enables us to fix the date of the Advertisements with tolerable certainty. In Gairdner's *Three Fifteenth-Century Chronicles*, p. 135, we have the following entry in Stowe's diary :—

"The xxvj day of Marche, in anno 1566, beyng Twesday, ye parsons and mynystars of ye churches in and aboughte London were (by commaundyment) at Lambethe, before ye Archebyshoppe of Caunterbury and othar of ye cownsell, wher charge was gyven to them to sarve theyr churchis and were theyr aparayll accordyng to ye quens injunctions, or ells to do no sarvyce. And *that same weke or ye begynyng of ye next* came forthe a boke in print subscribyd by ye Archebyshope of Cauntorbury, ye Byshopps of London, Wynchester, Elii, and dyvers othar, whiche apoynted ye sayd mynistars to were theyre gownes and clokes with standynge colars and corneryd capse, and at theyr servyce to were syrplysys, or els not to mynstar, &ct.'

This corresponds with the date fixed in Archbishop

Parker's letter to Cecil of November 15th, 1573, in which he says "Order hath been taken publicly *this seven years* by Commissioners, according to the statute, that fonts should not be removed."[1]

"Seven years" from 1573 brings us back to 1566: and the allusion was to the direction of the Advertisements, "that the fonte be not removed, nor that the curate do baptize in parish churches in any basons," &c.[2] Mr. James Parker tries to evade this by suggesting that the Order of 1561 may be the one referred to, or that it is a "reference to nothing more than the Rubric"![3] But the Rubric (which says nothing about "removing" fonts) was not an "Order by Commissioners"; and 1561 was not "seven years" before 1573: so that we may reasonably prefer to the ingenuity of Mr. James Parker the candour of the Rev. T. W. Perry, who admits that "the 'Order' here referred to is, no doubt, the direction of the Advertisements."[4]

We know also from the very letter referred to by Dr. Littledale as having been sent by Archbishop Parker to Cecil on March 28th, 1566, that the "new printed" book and the draft letter issuing it had both been submitted to Cecil and were "yet stayed" for Cecil's approval. It had been previously sent to him in the rough, on March 12th, 1566.[5] Alterations had been made by Cecil, as, for instance, the penalty of "sequestration, not deprivation," which on March 12th

---

[1] *Parker Correspondence*, p. 450.   [2] *Documentary Annals*, I.-292.
[3] *Letter to Selborne*, pp. 164, 208.
[4] *On Purchas Judgment*, p. 70.   See *Zurich Letters*, II.-149.
[5] *Parker Correspondence*, p. 263.

had stood as part of the MS. draft,⁶ was struck out before the book was "new printed," and finally submitted to Cecil on March 28th. No penalty whatever was retained in the Advertisements as "issued."

In the form ultimately agreed upon between Cecil and the Metropolitan, the "new printed book" (having been found to agree with the draft previously settled between them) was "issued" by the Archbishop (in a formal series of letters to Grindal, Bishop of London, to the Dean of the Arches, and to three Ordinaries of Peculiars) immediately on his getting back the "printed book" from the Queen's Secretary. These letters are all entered in *Archbishop Parker's Register* at Lambeth, Vol. I., p. 257, *et seq.* On April 4th, Archbishop Parker writes to Cecil that "my lord of London and I dismissed them all' [the London nonconforming Ministers] 'with our Advertisements."⁷ Before this, on March 26th, Parker had told Cecil that he and Bishop Cox were of opinion that "if London were reformed, all the realm would soon follow."⁸

Having therefore thus dealt, by way of example, with the "London ministers," Grindal (as Dean of the Province) sent out on May 21st to the other Bishops of the Province of Canterbury, and to the Dean and Chapter of St. Paul's, for their own "deanery," the printed book. The covering letter to the Dean of St. Paul's is printed in the *State Papers, Domestic,* Elizabeth, Vol. XXXIX., No. 76.

"After my hartie cõmendacyons these are to require

---

⁶ *Parker Correspondence*, p. 264. Strype's *Parker*, III.-92.
⁷ *Parker Correspondence*, p. 277. ⁸ *Ibid.*, p. 270.

and to give yo" in especyall charge that wch all
convenyent speed yo" call before yo" all & singuler the
mynisters and Ecc̅liasticall psons wth^{in} yor deanry of
Poules and office, and to ps̅cribe & enjoyne everie of
them upon payne of deprivac̅on to prepare forthw^{th} and
to weare such habit and apparell as is ordeyned by the
Queenes majesties authoritie expressed in the treaty
intituled the advertisemen^{ts}, &c. which I send heerein
enclosed unto yo" and in like to injoyne everie of them
under the said payne of deprivac̅on as well to observe
the order of mynistrac̅on in the Church with surples,
and in such forme as is sett forth in the saide treatie,
as alsoe to require the subscription of every of them
to the said Advertisem^{ts}. And yf yo" shall pceive any of
them to be disobedient wch shall refuse to conforme
themselves heerein, that then w^{th}out any delay yo"
certifie me the names of all such before Trynitie
Sundaie next ensuinge to the intent I maie pceed to
the reformac̅on and deprivac̅on of everie of them as
appertayneth in this case with a Certificate allsoe of
the names of such as pmiseth conformytie. And thus
I bidd yo" farwell from my howse in London, this
xxith of Maie, 1566."

Yo^r in Christ,

Indorssed   EDM. LONDON.
To the right-worshippfull the DEANE & CHAPTER
OF POWLES, Yeve theise.

This fixes the date of the "issue" as between
March 28th and April 3rd, 1566, for London (compare
Stowe as above cited), and May 21st for the rest of the
Province of Canterbury. In the interval (just before
April 28th) "the Queen's Majesty willed my lord of

York to declare her pleasure determinately to have the Order go forward,"[10] and thus the Northern Province also came under the same rule.

The following chronological table may enable the reader to take a bird's-eye view of the changes which preceded the "issue" of the Advertisements:—

TABLE.

A.D. 1561 [11] (March?).—"Interpretations" (in MS.) of the Injunctions partially drafted by Bishop Cox (according to Strype; the C. C. C. Cambridge copy being also annotated by Archbishop Parker), but never finished, nor authorised. These *may* possibly be the "Articles partly *of old* agreed upon amongst us," mentioned in Archbishop Parker's letter of March 3rd, 1565. Portions have been published by Strype and Cardwell, but the whole of them have never yet been printed.

A.D. 1562, July 20th.—Letters Patent appointing as Royal Commissioners the first four signatories of the Advertisements.[12]

A.D. 1565, January 25th.—Queen's Letter to Archbishop Parker, saying, "We do by these our present letters require . . . you being the Metropolitan . . . (as the like we will order for the province of York) to confer with your brethren, namely, such as be *in commission for causes ecclesiastical* . . so to proceed by Order, injunction, or censure, according to the order and appointment of such laws and ordinances as are *provided by Act of Parliament* . . .

---

[10] *Parker Correspondence*, p. 280. The High Commissioners enforced "the Advertisements" by name in the diocese of Durham in 1577. Balme's *Church and the Ornaments Rubric*, p. 78.

[11] That this, and not 1559, is the true date. See *Perry on Purchas Judgment*, p. 450. Parker's *Letter to Selborne*, p. 98.

[12] Prothero's *Select Statutes*, p. 232.

so as uniformity of order may be kept in every church, and *without variety* and contention."[13]

A.D. 1565, February 28th.—Certificates sent in from every church as to "varieties in the Service." Archbishop Parker had written for these on January 30th.[14]

A.D. 1565, March 3rd.—Rough draft of "Ordinances" as devised by the Commissioners under the Great Seal for Causes Ecclesiastical, sent by Parker to Cecil.[15]

A.D. 1565, March 8th.—Fair copy of revised MS. "Ordinances" endorsed by Cecil as "not authorised nor published."[16] Da Silva said "the order has been dropped by Leicester's help."[17]

[An interval of twelve months remains without record.]

A.D. 1566, March 10th.—Archbishop Parker's "first" interview with Queen Elizabeth respecting enforcement of discipline. (*Parker Correspondence*, p. 278.)

A.D. 1566, March 12.—Archbishop Parker sends rough draft of the Advertisements to Cecil. (*Parker Correspondence*, p. 263.)

A.D. 1566, March 17 *circa*.—Archbishop Parker's special interview (Grindal being also sent for) with Queen Elizabeth. (*Parker Correspondence*, p. 273.)

A.D. 1566, March 28th.—Parker sends the printed Advertisements to Cecil, and writes to Grindal an official letter reciting how "The Queen's Highness hath expressly charged both you and me, of late being *therefore* called to her presence, to see her laws executed, *and* good Orders DECREED." He charges

---

[13] *Parker Correspondence*, p. 223.
[14] *Parker Correspondence*, p. 227. Lamb's *Letters* from C. C. C. Library, p. 314.
[15] *Parker Correspondence*, p. 233.
[16] This endorsement is not on the Petyt MS., but someone has added at the beginning the date "14 Marcii, 1564" (*i.e.* 1564-5). Strype says his copy was dated "Mar. 1564." The outside wrapper may have been lost. Strype's *Parker*, 1-314.
[17] Hume's *State Papers, Spanish*, I.-401. Compare *State Papers, Foreign*, Elizabeth, under date June 4th.

him as he will answer "To Her Majesty, to see Her Majesty's laws and injunctions duly observed within your diocese, and also these our convenient Orders described in these books," &c. (*Parker Correspondence*, pp. 271, 273.) This letter also fixes the date of the Advertisements by speaking of the Queen's letter of January 25th, 1565, as "addressed to them now, a year past and more."

A.D. 1566, April 4th.—The Advertisements publicly enforced in London. (*Parker Correspondence*, p. 276.)

A.D. 1566, April 28th.—The Order to go forward in Province of York. (*Parker Correspondence*, p. 280.) Archbishop Parker and (May 4th) Grindal write to Cecil to get members of the Privy Council to sit with the Commissioners. (*Parker Correspondence*, p. 280, and Grindal's *Remains*, p. 289.)

A.D. 1566, May 21st.—Advertisements issued by Grindal to Bishops of Canterbury Province, "according as hath been heretofore used." (*Parker Correspondence*, p. 273.)

A.D. 1566, May 27th.—Privy Council enforced the Advertisements for "Crossed Caps." (*State Papers, Domestic*, Elizabeth, Vol. XXXIX., No. 82.)

A.D. 1566, June 6th.—Ditto for Surplice, &c. (2 *Zurich Letters*, pp. 119, 143. *Parker Correspondence*, p. 285.)

A.D. 1565, June 6th.— Before this date Parker and the Commissioners published Bullinger's "Resolutions." See p. 55. (*Zurich Letters*, II.-120, 124.)

Looking back over the above table, it will be readily perceived that Dr. Littledale has transferred Cecil's "endorsement" upon the rejected MS. "Ordinances" of March 8th, 1565. to the printed Advertisements which alone were "authorised and published," and which were issued for London between March 28th and April 4th, 1566. The title, preamble, form, penalties, provision for doctrinal subscriptions, and very many other details had been changed in the "printed book" which was signed by Geste, Bishop of Rochester, and "others": whereas the MS. "Ordinances" of 1565 were devised "only" by the Bishops of London, Winchester, Ely, Lincoln, and Parker himself.[18]

Let us next examine Dr. Littledale's statement that "evidence from the chief personages in Church and State at the time" overthrows "the Royal character of the Advertisements."

Who were these "chief personages"? Clearly *not* the anonymous Puritan pamphleteers who published without either printer's or author's names, and without even a date. These unscrupulous and obscure controversialists would have readily appealed to the Court of Queen's Bench for protection against any unlawful attempts to "deprive" them of their freeholds, if there had been the smallest substance in their fanciful contention. In Sampson's case præmunire was, in fact, threatened.[19]

We know that under Elizabeth, prohibitions habitually and frequently took causes not only "out of the Archbishops' and Bishops' Courts, but even out of the hands of the Queen's Ecclesiastical Commissioners and her Court of Delegates."[20] But in no single instance did a Nonconformist venture to challenge before the courts of law the "Royal authority of the Advertisements." Like Dr. Littledale, they preferred to make their appeal from the decisions of the Queen's Courts to the ill-informed "religious" public. But, unlike Dr. Littledale, they abused "the chief personages in

---

[18] *Parker Correspondence*, p. 233. Geste's name (alone) is added at foot of the Petyt MS., p. 521, after those of "the devisers."
[19] Strype's *Cranmer*, Ecclesiastical History Society Edition. II.-129 note.   [20] Strype's *Whitgift*, II.-427.

Church and State" for procuring a "*Royal* edict" as they habitually call the Advertisements. True, they sometimes affect to doubt the Royal authority; but the insincerity of this inconsistent conduct is laid bare by Withers (one of their leaders), who warned the Prince Elector Palatine "you must take especial care to *transfer all the blame* from the Queen unto the Bishops, who do not act the part of her advisers with the freedom that becomes them, and which it is right they should exercise. For as to their asserting both at home and to foreigners that they do not themselves approve these measures, but that they execute them at the instigation of the Queen, they both themselves command them in books publicly set forth for that very purpose, and STATE *that it is done by the Queen* after a good and pious counsel."[21] The "chief personages both in Church and State" were quite alive to this Puritan device. Archbishop Parker wrote to Cecil: "As for the Queen's Majesty's part, in my expostulation with many of them I signify their disobedience, wherein, *because they see the danger*, they cease to impute it to Her Majesty."[22]

Bishop Cox, in 1572, makes this very charge against them.[23] Barrow and Greenwood practised the same course, carefully exempting the Queen in order to fasten blame upon the Bishops.[24]

No respectable writer on the Puritan side who published anything *with his own name* to his book ever adopted this shabby artifice. Cartwright, and the "Admonition to Parliament" ignore it. On the other

---

[21] *Zurich Letters*, II.-164.
[23] *Zurich Letters*, I.-235.
[22] *Parker Correspondence*, p. 237.
[24] Strype's *Whitgift*, II.-187.

hand, let us see what the responsible Ordinaries who had to administer the law (at their own risk if they exceeded their powers) *publicly* stated in Elizabeth's own lifetime as to the "Royal character of the Advertisements."

That the risk was keenly felt is shown by a memorandum (in Cecil's handwriting) of a Privy Council meeting on June 4th, 1565—" The Bishops complain that they dare not execute the ecclesiastical laws to the furtherance of religion for fear of the præmunire wherewith the judges and lawyers of the realm being not well affected in religion, threaten them, some authority might be given them from the Queen to continue during her pleasure."[25] Leicester's influence steadily declined from this time.[26]

1566, May 21st.—In the letter before referred to as sent by Grindal with the copies distributed to the Bishops of the Province of Canterbury, he said : Every minister "upon pain of deprivation to prepare forthwith and to wear such habit and apparel as is *ordained by the Queen's Majesty's authority* expressed in the Treaty intituled the Advertisements, &c., which I send herein enclosed to you."

Now, to obviate the force of these words, Mr. James Parker has first of all, at p. 56, interpolated a comma after the word "authority" and before the word "expressed," and then further interpolated the word "as" before "expressed" (*ibid.*), for which he finally

---

[25] Stevenson's *State Papers, Foreign*, Elizabeth, June 4th, 1565.
[26] See Lewis' *Reformation Settlement*, p. 255. This same fear of præmunire was felt in 1562, and even in 1571 on the part of subscribers to the Thirty-nine Articles. See Bennet's *Essay*, pp. 208, 270.

substitutes the word "and". So that at p. 207 of his "letter to Lord Selborne" he prints in parallel columns the Ridsdale Judgment and his own counter-statement as follows:—

Mr. Jas. Parker's "Synopsis," p. 207.

Immediately after their issue on May 21st, Bishop Grindal wrote to the Dean of St Paul's, *stating* they were issued by the Queen's authority. *Ridsdale*, p. 9.	Grindal does *not* state this. He says: "Such habit as is ordeyned by authority and expressed in the Advertisements." *Letter* 56, 57.

This method of quotation is adopted in order to show how the "chief personages" repudiated "Royal" authority!

1566, May 25th.—Guzman da Silva, the Spanish ambassador, reports to his master: "Although by order of the Queen, and after much exhortation, measures have been taken to make clergymen wear their ancient garb as I wrote some time ago, not only have many refused to obey, but have written against it, and even against the Queen, who, they say, had no right to make such an order." He mentions too that "the Queen believed, or was informed that the Bishop of London [Grindal] would not execute the order very zealously, and she rated him soundly, and threatened to punish him for an anabaptist, with other expressions of the same sort."[27] It is interesting to compare this with the *Parker Correspondence*, p. 278.

1566, June 6th.—Abel writes of "the Queen's command respecting the cap and surplice."[28]

---

[27] Hume's *Spanish State Papers*, I.-553.   [28] *Zurich Letters*, II.-119.

1566, June 29th.—The Privy Council put forth an order that no one "should print any book against . . . any injunction, letters patent, or *ordinances* passed or *set forth*, or to be passed or set forth *by the Queen's grant, commission*, or authority." And a Royal pardon spoke of divers, who " for refusing to wear such distinct and decent apparel as by public Order is commanded, by due order of law already are *deprived*."[28b]

This explains why the criticism of the Advertisements was anonymous, why no printer dared to put his name to these " books," and also the view taken of them by the "chief personages in Church and State at the time."

1566, October (27th?).—In a minute of the Privy Council, Mr. Crowley was said to have been committed "in summer last," " for disobeying such Orders as were thought requisite by the Queen's Majesty."[29] Now Crowley's committal took place on that 4th of April, 1566, when " my Lord of London and I dismissed them all with our Advertisements."[30] Crowley immediately published " A Declaration of the doings of those ministers of God's Word and Sacraments in the city of London, which have refused to wear the upper apparell and ministering garments of the Pope's Church." As a side-heading is the title "The Bishop's Advertisements." Thus what the Puritans (for strategic reasons) called " the Bishop's Advertisements " were recognised by the Privy Council as " Orders " emanating from the Queen.

[28b] Strype's *Parker*, I.-442, III.-154. Dasent's *Acts of the Privy Council*, VII.-315.

[29] Shaw's *Argument in Ridsdale Case*, p. 529. The *Lansdowne MS*, 982, folio 104, gives the date as October 28th.

[30] *Parker Correspondence*, p. 277.

1567.—Archbishop Parker's articles for the visitation of Norwich are in the British Museum. T $\frac{1013}{10}$. They are preceded by "instructions to the Commissioners," the first of which is "to reduce the clergy unto one uniform order in their ministration and preaching; and that without any partial respect you will put in due execution the Queen's Majesty's ecclesiastical laws, statutes, injunctions, and her Highness's *other commandments* given and published in that behalf." The fifth was the articles "together bound with the Advertisements, fourpence." Cardwell, who correctly says[31] that these same articles were designed for *all* the Cathedrals in the Province of Canterbury, unfortunately omitted these preceding directions.

In answer to the "Third Article" the return from Canterbury Cathedral made by George Gardyner, Prebendary, was—"The communion is administered in a chalice contrary, as he saith, to the Advertisements of the Queen."[32]

1569.—Archbishop Parker[33] and Bishop Parkhurst[34] both refer to the Advertisements as "set forth by public authority"; Parkhurst specifying for use at perambulations in the Rogation Days "homilies as be appointed by the Queen's Majesty's authority."[35] Now, "the use of homilies at perambulations was prescribed, not by the Injunctions of 1559, but by the Advertisements." In these same Articles of 1569, No. xxv., Archbishop Parker spoke of "the Queen's

---

[31] *Documentary Annals*, I.-303.
[32] Strype's *Parker*, Appendix No. LIV. As to the unlawfulness of the chalice, see below, p. 95.   [33] *Documentary Annals*, I.-320.
[34] *Second Report of the Ritual Commission*, Appendix, p. 405-1.
[35] *Ibid.*, p. 404-4.

Majesty's ecclesiastical laws, statutes, injunctions, and all *Her Highness' other* commandments." " Public authority " is a phrase constantly used for the highest authority common to the whole community.[36] A good example of this is seen in Canon lxv.

1571.—The authority of the Advertisements was repeatedly recognised by Convocation,[37] as also by Canon xxiv. of 1604, which adopts the direction of the Advertisements for the dress of epistoler and gospeller just where the Advertisements *contradict and contravene* the requirements of the Rubric of 1549 (First Book of Edward). See p. 120.

1571, August 20th.—Queen Elizabeth to Archbishop Parker refers to her former letter of January 25th, 1565, and to Bishops Horn and Cox, as Commissioners for the "observation of Our laws, Injunctions *and* commandments."[38]

1573, November 15th.—Archbishop Parker's language as to the Order relating to fonts has already been cited, p. 63. His Diocesan Visitation Articles of this year are in the British Museum,[39] in which he twice refers (Queries 1 and 4) to "the Advertisements lately set forth by public authority."

During the same year, Queen Elizabeth herself stated that she had " caused at several times since the beginning of her reign certain Injunctions and *other* Orders to be published by the advice of her clergy."[40]

In 1574 (Archbishop) Whitgift, then Vice-Chancellor

---

[36] See Mr. Benjamin Shaw's *Argument*, p. 536. Compare Bishop Cox in *Zurich Letters*, I.-236. Strype's *Parker*, III.-154.
[37] Cardwell's *Synodalia*, I.-119, 124, 126, 127.
[38] *Parker Correspondence*, p. 387. [39] British Museum, ???.
[40] Strype's *Parker*, II.-352.

of Cambridge, wrote in reply to the "Second Admonition" of the Puritans as follows:—

"They note certain contrarieties in this church as betwixt .... the Communion Book and Advertisements concerning church vestures. .... But in these same matters they are much deceived; for, as I suppose, in matters of *Ornaments of the Church and of the Ministers thereof*, the Queen's Majesty, together with the Archbishop or the Commissioners in causes ecclesiastical, have authority *by Act of Parliament* to alter and appoint such rites and ceremonies as shall from time to time be thought to them most convenient."[41]

In 1573, the year before the above was published, Dr. Thomas Sparke was ordained, who acted as one of the Puritan representatives at the Hampton Court Conference in 1604. In 1607 he published *A Brotherly Perswasion to Unitie*, dedicated by permission to King James, and "commanded by publicke authoritie to be printed." In chapter v. of this work he says—

"It can never soundly be proved that a surplice, as it is prescribed to us, *with long and large sleeves*, hath been at all any of their idolatrous Mass garments. .... Her Majesty, by virtue of the said statute, with the consent of the Archbishop and High Commissioners, in the seventh year of her reign (as it appears by the book of Advertisements then *by authority* published), belike of purpose to remove the scandal taken by the Popish alb, appointed the surplice in this form and manner that we wear it, to be used instead thereof."[42]

1575.—Archbishop Parker's Articles for Winchester[43] speak of "the Queen's Majesty's Injunctions, and other Her Highness' commandments, orders, decrees, and Advertisements."

---

[41] Whitgift's *Works*, III.-510.   [42] p. 20.
[43] *Second Report of the Ritual Commission*, Appendix, p. 418-50.

1576.—Grindal, as quoted by Strype,[41] speaks of not opposing "the Queen's Injunctions, nor the Ordinations, nor Articles made by some of the Queen's Commissioners, . . . January the 25th, in the seventh year of the Queen's reign."[45]

This is very interesting as showing the sense in which the *undated* Advertisements of 1566 came to be spoken of as "made" the seventh year. It was "by virtue of the Queen's Majesty's letters commanding the same," her letter being dated "January 25, 1564" (*i.e.* 1565, New Style). Grindal, who was himself a "Commissioner under the Great Seal for Causes Ecclesiastical," and as such was one of the signatories of the Advertisements of 1566, refers their "making" to the Queen's Letter of the *preceding* year, which, he said, empowered the Commissioners to "*decree* good Orders." Thus the Bishops' Advertisements and the Commissioners' Advertisements were also the Queen's Advertisements, as being "made" by her Commission.

This also explains what had misled Strype, Cardwell, &c., and puzzles so many people, viz. why Archbishop Parker placed on the forefront of the Advertisements at the time of their being "newly printed," in March,

---

[41] *Life of Parker*, I.-319.
[45] "Item volumus et injungimus ut Decanus, Prebendarii, et minores Canonici ubique (nisi valetudo impedierit) eo vestitu, habitu, et piliis utantur quibus ecclesiasticas personas uti decet. Neque vel Injunctiones Regiæ Majestatis vel Ordinationibus aut Articulis per nonnullos *Regiae Majestatis Commissarios videlicet* Matthæum Cantuariensem Archiepiscopum, Edmundum Londiniensem episcopum, Ricardum Eliensem, Edmundum Roffensem, Robertum Wintoniensem, Nicholaum Lincolniensem respective episcopos subscriptis et vicesimo quinto die mensis Januarii anno serenissimæ dominæ nostræ reginæ Elizabethæ, &c., septimo *datis et publice editis* in hac parte sub pœna in dictis injunctionibus contraveniant."—Grindal's *Register*, fol. 110.

1566, the words "by virtue of the Queen's letters commanding the same, the 25th day of January, in the seventh year of the reign of our Sovereign Lady Eliz." Cardwell puts in a second comma after "letters." Mr. James Parker, who in his *Letter to Lord Selborne*, p. 145, introduces a full-stop after "same," says he is "not called upon to justify, *or even explain*, the expression 'Advertisements *by virtue of*': it is perhaps vague"![46] Vague? Not a bit! The Royal Orders of October 10th, 1561, were similarly entitled "Orders . . . *by virtue of* Her Majesty's Letters addressed to Her Highness' Commissioners for Causes Ecclesiastical."[47]

1582.—The Privy Council sent to the commissaries of Archbishop Grindal "a special letter to urge the Book of Advertisements" which "were commonly at Visitations printed and dispersed."[48]

1583.—Draft of Articles endorsed by Cecil as presented *to Queen Elizabeth* herself by Archbishop Whitgift and Bishop Piers, signed by them and four other bishops, in which they speak of "the Advertisements set out by Her Majesty's authority."[49]

Before November 6th, 1583, was published *An Abstract of certain Acts of Parliament*, which at p. 210 calls them "Advertisements published in the 7th year of her Grace's reign, and subscribed with the hands of one Abp. and 5 Bishops, her Highness' Eccl. Commissioners."

---

[46] *Letter*, p. 146.
[47] Miller's *Guide to Ecclesiastical Law*, Sec. 83. An original is in British Museum, "5155. aa. 7." [48] Strype's *Whitgift*, I.-200.
[49] Lord Selborne's *Notes*, p. 77. *State Papers, Domestic*, Elizabeth, Vol. CLXIII., No. 31.

In 1584 appeared *An Answer to an Abstract of certaine Acts of Parliament*, by Richard Cosin, Dean of the Arches, and "published by authority" in which he rebuts the contention of the Puritan writer, who had said that "though Her Majesty's excellent name be used by the publishers of the said Advertisements for confirmation of them, and that *they affirm Her Majesty to have commanded them thereunto* by Her Highness' letters," yet they lacked credit because "not printed by Her Majesty's printer," and "without Her Majesty's privilege." [50]

The Dean of the Arches, who, at p. 67, speaks of "Her Majesty's Injunctions and Advertisements," thus replied (p. 74, chapter cxxx.): "And is any man to surmise that those reverend and wise Fathers, who subscribed unto the said Book of Advertisements, would or durst publish them in Her Majesty's name, and as by Her Highness' *authority and letters, dated such a certain day*, if it were not so: or that they would enterprise to forbid or restrain that which the law had so exactly charged and commanded?"

On this the Rev. T. W. Perry, of the English Church Union, says: "It is certain that Cosin could not have been defending their authority as being the 'other order' of Elizabeth's Act of Uniformity, because he considered that that order had never been taken." In proof of this, he refers to *John* Cosin's notes of 1640 as his voucher for what *Richard* Cosin in 1584 must have "considered." [51] Admirable critic!

---

[50] Such a test was, of course, worthless. But the words "cum privilegio" *are* on the title-page, and Wolfe is called "Nostrum Typographum" in Queen Elizabeth's letters patent, 1560. Clay's *Elizabethan Liturgies*, p. 301. See also Droop's *Edwardian Vestments*, p. 95.   [51] *Perry on Purchas Judgment*, p. 155.

1585.—Archbishop Whitgift, in the fifth of his Articles for Chichester, speaks of "Her Majesty's Injunctions and Advertisements."[52]

In the same year Rishton (who went to Brasenose College, Oxford, in 1568), wrote: "The Queen issued Her orders on the apparel and dress of Ecclesiastics," evidently referring to the Advertisements.[53]

1587.—Hooker, in a letter to Archbishop Whitgift, intended to be laid before the Privy Council (of which Whitgift had been sworn a member in February, 1586), described the Advertisements as "a decree agreed upon by the bishops, and confirmed by Her Majesty's authority."[54]

1629.—Bishop Andrewes in his notes on the Common Prayer says, "for cathedral churches it was ordained by the Advertisements, in Queen Elizabeth's time (that authority being *reserved, notwithstanding this book, by an act of parliament*), that there should be an epistler and a gospeller, besides the priest."[55]

1640.—In Canon VII. the Laudian Convocation of this year appealed to "the Injunctions and *Advertisements of Queen Elizabeth* of blessed memory."[56] The Visitation Articles drawn up by Heylyn and authorised by Convocation in their Ninth Canon, also refer to the "Injunctions and Advertisements of Queen Elizabeth."[57]

1641.—The Sub-Committee of Divines appointed by the House of Lords had before them a list of the

---

[52] Cardwell's *Documentary Annals*, II.-6.
[53] Sanders' *Anglican Schism*, Edition 1877, p. 281.
[54] Keble's *Hooker*, III.-587.
[55] *Nicholls on Common Prayer*, Appendix, p. 39.
[56] Cardwell's *Synodalia*, I.-404.
[57] *Second Report of the Ritual Commission*, Appendix p 591.

"innovations in discipline" complained of by the Puritans, among which were "by pretending for their innovations, the Injunctions and *Advertisements of Queen Elizabeth*, which are not in force, but by way of commentary and imposition."[58] The Committee apparently thought that the Canons of 1604 had superseded these Orders, but they made no question of their "Royal" authority.

1641.—Bishop Wren, in his defence written for presentation to Parliament, says—"Now these Injunctions [of 1559] are allowed and confirmed by the Queen's Advertisements, cap. I. art. 3, and those Advertisements *are authorized by law*, 1 *Eliz., c.* 2, *sec. penult.*"[59]

1655.—Anthony Sparrow, in his *Rationale of the Book of Common Prayer*, says:—"The minister at the time of his ministration shall use such ornaments as were in use in the second of Edward VI., viz., a surplice in the ordinary ministration, and a cope in time of ministration of the Holy Communion in cathedral and collegiate churches.—Queen Elizabeth's Articles set forth in the seventh year of her reign." Sparrow, who had been a Savoy Commissioner, and took part in Convocation at the last Revision of the Prayer Book, re-published this statement in 1664, 1672 (as Bishop of Exeter), and 1684 (as Bishop of Norwich), the year before his death.

1659.—L'Estrange, in his *Alliance of Divine Offices* (reprinted in 1690 and 1699), says:—"*The minister shall use such ornaments, &c.* In the latter end of the Act of Uniformity there was reserved to the Queen a power to make some further order, with the advice of her

---

[58] Cardwell's *Conferences*, 273. [59] *Parentalia*, p. 75.

commissioners, &c., concerning ornaments for ministers; but I do not find that she made any use of that authority, or put her power into exercise further than is *expressed in her Advertisements* of the seventh year of her reign, by which it is ordered that 'in cathedrals the chief minister officiating at the Communion shall wear a decent cope, with gospeller and epistoler agreeable.'" Edition 1846, p. 104.

1661.—Peter Heylyn, chaplain to Charles the First, published his *History of the Reformation*, in which he said :—

"The Queen thought fit to make a further signification of her royal pleasure,—not grounded only on the sovereign power and prerogative royal, by which she published her Injunctions in the first year of her reign, but legally declared by her Commissioners for Causes Ecclesiastical, according to the Acts and Statutes made in that behalf; for then it was to be presumed, that such as had denied obedience to her sole commands, would at least give it to the laws. . . . which being accordingly performed, presented to the Queen, and by her approved, the said rules and orders were set forth and published in a certain book, entituled 'Advertisements,' &c. . . . . . . And that they might be known to have the stamp of royal authority, a preface was prefixed before them, in which it was expressed, 'That the Queen . . . . . . had required the Metropolitan, by her special letters, that, upon conference had with such other Bishops as were authorized by her Commission for Causes Ecclesiastical, some order might be took, whereby all diversities and varieties in the premises might be taken away;' and finally, that, in obedience unto her commands, the said Metropolitan and the rest there named had agreed upon 'the rules and orders ensuing, which were by her thought meet to be used and followed.'" [Robertson's edition, Vol. II., pp. 408-10.]

1661.—Anthony Sparrow presented to Convocation his collection of Articles, containing the Advertisements, "to vindicate the Church of England, and to *promote uniformity* and peace in the same."

In the same year Prynne published his *Sober and Pacific Examination*, at p. 61 of which he mentions "Q. Eliz. Advertisements in the 7th year of her reign, by her High Commissioners' advice."

1662.—Archdeacon Pory's Visitation Articles refer to the "Injunctions and Advertisements of Queen Elizabeth."[60] Pory is the reputed author of the *Prayer for the High Court of Parliament*, and had been on many important committees during the revision of the Prayer Book in 1661.[61]

1708.—Dr. Thomas Bennet in his *Paraphrase and Annotations on the Common Prayer*, after quoting the proviso from 1 Elizabeth, cap. ii, continues,—" This clause explains Queen Elizabeth's Rubric, and, consequently, the present one, which is in reality the same. So that those ornaments of the church and its ministry, which were required in the second year of King Edward, were to be retained till the Queen (and, consequently, any of her successors), with the advice before specified, should take Order. Now such Order was accordingly taken by the Queen in the year 1564, which was the seventh of her reign. For she did then, with the advice of her Ecclesiastical Commissioners, particularly the then Metropolitan, Dr. Matthew Parker, publish certain Advertisements, wherein are the following directions. 'Item, in the ministration, &c. . . . .' From hence it is plain that the parish priests (and I take no notice of the case of others) are

---

[60] *Second Report of the Ritual Commission*, Appendix, pp. 627-3.
[61] Parker's *History of the Revisions of the Prayer Book*, p. 83.

obliged to no other ornaments but surplices and hoods. For these are authentic limitations of the Rubric."[62]

Thus, during 144 years, up to the date of the publication of this work of Dr. Bennet, not a single writer among the professedly loyal members of the Church of England had ever expressed the smallest doubt as to the Royal authority belonging to the Advertisements of Elizabeth. As Lord Selborne truly said, "No writer of reputation, in any work published before the Eighteenth Century, seems to have suggested a doubt that the Advertisements were, as matter of *fact*, authorized by Queen Elizabeth."

***

We come now to a very curious illustration of the growth of a "tradition." In 1661, as before mentioned, Anthony Sparrow published an edition of the Advertisements (which had by that time become exceedingly scarce), but, unfortunately, his reprints were not very accurate. His alterations in the Thirty-nine Articles of 1571 from the text of John Day (which he professed to follow) have been noted by Dr. Lamb. Similarly, the title-page of the Advertisements was altered by the omission of four words from the title, and by the addition of the false date, "A.D. 1564," at the foot of the title-page. In some editions "Anno 7. Eliz. R." is also added.

Strype, who published in 1711 his *Life of Archbishop Parker*, tells us that "these Articles were *printed* with a preface in 1564, by Reginald Wolf, *according to Bp. Sparrow's collections.*" This, however, was an entire mistake. The Articles were *not* printed at all till

---

[62] Cited in *Archdeacon Harrison on the Rubric*, p. 131.

1566; and the source of the mistake is shewn to be this inaccurate reprint of Bishop Sparrow, who mistook the date of the Queen's letter for that of the Advertisements themselves. The result was that Strype, who had seen the MS. Ordinances of March 8th, 1565 (*i.e.* 1564, Old Style, see p. 67 *supra*), and knew that they "were not authorized or published," confused them with the printed Advertisements, to which Bishop Sparrow had given the wrong date, "1564."

By an odd coincidence, Nicholls also published, in 1709-10, his *Comment on the Book of Common Prayer*, which (unluckily for the Church of England) contained in the Appendix some posthumous notes (made long before he became a Bishop) by the Rev. John Cosin, who died some forty years before their publication. In many of these Notes, Cosin expressed the opinion that the pre-Reformation Canons, the usages of 1548, and the Rubric of 1549 (which abolished and superseded those usages), were all alike legalized by the so-called Ornaments Rubric of Elizabeth! Yet he adopted Bishop Andrewes' Note mentioned above, viz. that the authority of Queen Elizabeth's Advertisements was "reserved, *notwithstanding this book*, by Act of Parliament."[63]

These crude and inconsistent notions had been derived in part from reading an anonymous Puritan pamphlet called *A Survey of the Book of Common Prayer*, published in 1606, to which the *Notes* make frequent reference. But the point of importance to notice is that Strype's blunder, *plus* Cosin's *Notes*, produced a complete revolution in the "Tradition of the elders." Collier (1714) and Neal (1732) were but the first of a long line of undiscriminating copyists, who "took over"

[63] Cosin's *Works*, V.-90.

without examination the Strype-Cosin theory. What
makes this more ludicrous is that Cosin, after he
became Bishop, and indeed in all his official acts, and
Strype himself in his *later* chapters both of the *Annals*
and *Life of Parker*, supported the older view. Bishop
Cosin's *Notes* will be subjected to a detailed analysis in
another paper. See p. 171. As to Strype, as Lord
Selborne points out,[64] "After having spoken of the
rejection of the first draft of the Advertisements . . .
he added that those difficulties were finally overcome
. . . ascribing all that was done, as distinctly as
possible, to the will and commandment of the Queen."

There is one other writer, Archdeacon Sharp, who, as
the son of Archbishop Sharp (who had been chaplain to
Charles II., and was himself made Archdeacon of Berks
in 1672) is a competent witness to the received belief of
the Restoration Churchmen. Writing in 1753 he says:
—"Now putting these things together, that the Rubric
hath an immediate reference to the Act; and that the
Act is made with express reservation to the Queen's
future appointments; and that the Queen, pursuant to
this power given her, did in the year 1564, publish her
Advertisements (as they are called) concerning the
habit of ministers to be worn by them in time of divine
service; it will appear that her injunctions thus set
forth are authentic limitations of this Rubric."[65] This
though quoted with approbation by Bishop Mant, is
one of the last witnesses to the older belief. The later
writers, such as Gibson[66] (1713), Burn (1763), and

---

[64] *Notes on Liturgical History*, p. 15.   [65] *On the Rubric*, p. 66.

[66] Yet even Bishop Gibson speaks of the Advertisements as "Articles
published by the Queen in the 7th year of her reign" (*Codex*, p. 245),
and marks the Ornaments Rubric of 1549 as "obsolete," p. 390.

Cardwell (1839), copy the *ipsissima verba* of Cosin's *Notes* without so much as a pretence of original research.

***

The directions of the Advertisements which bore upon " the ornaments of the ministers " were as follows—

Item, In the ministration of the holy communion in cathedrall and collegiate churches, the principall minister shall use a cope with gospeller and epistoler agreeably ; and at all other prayers to be said at that communion table, to use no copes but surplesses.

Item, That the deane and prebendaries weare a surplease with a silk hoode in the quyer; and when they preach in the cathedrall or collegiate church to weare their hoode.

Item, That every minister sayinge any publique prayers or ministringe the sacramentes, or other rites of the churche, shall weare a comely surples with sleeves, to be provided at the charges of the parishe ; and that the parishe provide a decente table standinge on a frame for the communion table.

The original draft (in 1565) proposed to direct that—

" In the ministration of the communion in cathedral and collegiate churches, the executor, with Pisteler and Gospeller, minister the same in copes ; and at all other praiers to be said at the communion table, to have no copes, but surplesses." [67]

That draft was rejected on other grounds, but this particular direction underwent merely verbal alterations.

It will be noticed that the Advertisement pointedly and flatly contradicted the Rubric of 1549. The First Prayer Book of Edward ordered the cope to be worn at the ante-communion precisely where the Advertisements forbad its being so worn. The First Prayer Book ordered the Epistoler and Gospeller to wear "albs with tunacles," thereby creating a *distinctive*

---

[67] *Petyt MS.*, 538-47, p. 516.

dress for the celebrant, as such, since he alone might wear a "vestment or cope." Thus it was no question of "maximum and minimum," as is sometimes represented, but of direct conflict, and express contradiction. If the Advertisements (or the Canons of 1604) are to be obeyed, the Prayer Book of 1549 *cannot* be complied with, and *vice versâ*.

"Agreeably" here, and in the 24th Canon, meant "*congrue*," "*convenienter*," "to match." So Spenser wrote in his *Faerie Queen*, VI.-vii.-3.

> "At last he met two knightes to him unknowne
> The which were armed both *agreably*."

Or to take a pastoral parallel (VI.-ii.-36)

> "Both clad in shepherd's weeds agreeably."

In the Latin translation of the Advertisements sent to Zurich the word is rendered "apposite."[68] The Puritan author of the *Survey of the Common Prayer*, 1606, gives a reference to this Advertisement in the margin of his commentary—"seeing in cathedral churches special men (forsooth) in copes, must read at the high altar, or communion table, one the epistle and is therefore called the Epistler, the other the gospel and is therefore called the Gospeller."[69]

Hence, when referred to in official documents of the period, copes are always mentioned in the plural. Thus, in the paper of "Varieties in the Service," handed in to Cecil the Prime Minister, by Archbishop Parker, to shew the actual condition of things before the issue of the Advertisements, under the head of

---

[68] *Staatsarchiv. Zurich*, Gest VI.-164, fol. 148, m. et seq.
[69] *Ibid.*, p. 36. See below, p. 120.

"Administration of the Communion" we read, "Some with surpless and copes."[70] The 24th Canon itself has the heading "Coenam administrantibus capparum usus injunctus": and Bancroft, who drafted that canon and presided in the Convocation which enacted it, gave at St. Paul's, in 1608, the direction that the Epistle and Gospel be read "in copes."[71] Thus the meaning of the canon was fixed at the time and on the highest authority. One of Smart's charges against Cosin was "the wearing a cope to read the Epistle and Gospel."[72] "Without the rich copes the Epistle and Gospel naked,"[73] grumbled the Puritans in 1640. And this triple cope-wearing was in strict accordance with Elizabethan usage. "The sub-dean and Epistler in rich coaps assistant to the said bishop" is the direction given in the *Cheque Book of the Chapel Royal*, published by the Camden Society. At the consecration of Archbishop Parker, the Epistoler and Gospeller (though not Bishops) wore copes; so, too, at St. Paul's on September 9th, 1559, at Durham House in 1626, and on various other occasions (some of which are detailed in *Hierurgia Anglicana*, pp. 149, 156, 298) the rule was observed which is prescribed by the statutes of Hereford Cathedral "in copis induantur tam qui celebrat, quam qui Epistolam et Evangelium recitant."

The 24th Canon of 1604 was designed to do honour to the "principal Feast days," *i.e.* to those days which

---

[70] *Lansdowne MSS.*, Vol. VIII., Article VII., folio 16. Stryre in copying this carelessly dropped the *s*.
[71] Wilkin's *Concilia*, IV.-436.
[72] Lewis' *Reformation Settlement*, p. 397. Mr. Dickenson in his Preface to the Sarum Missal, p. xiv, admits this usage.
[73] *Hierurgia Anglicana*, p. 382.

have "proper Prefaces" appointed in honour of our Lord, or of the Blessed Trinity. For this purpose (the "*Minister ibidem maximè eminens*" as the Latin version expresses it, *i.e.*) the highest dignitary on the staff who could be procured was required to celebrate in a "Cathedral or Collegiate Church" (for the cope continued to be illegal in parish churches, and was suppressed therein by Ordinaries like Bancroft and Laud), both he and his assistants wearing copes on such occasions to mark the eminence of the festival. Any superstition as to a "distinctive dress" for the "sacrificer" as the worker of an invisible miracle, was obviated by attiring the other "ministers of the word and sacraments" equally and alike in similar garments, since the Epistoler and Gospeller no less than the "principal minister" are the administrators and distributors of the sacred feast which through them is "given unto us" as the Catechism teaches. It follows that the action of Bishop Creighton and others in officiating sometimes with a cope, sometimes without, but never with "Gospeller and Epistler agreably" is unhistorical as being contrary to any known law of this Church and Realm at any period of its history, and therefore a violation of the Thirty-fourth Article of Religion.

V

The Ornaments Rubric. No. I

(ELIZABETH, 1559-61)

IN 1857 it was ruled by the Supreme Court of Appeal, in *Liddell* v. *Westerton*, that "the authority of Parliament" mentioned in the rubric means the first Act of Uniformity (2 and 3 Edward VI., cap. i.), and that the word Ornaments "applies, and in this rubric is confined, to those Articles the use of which in the services and ministrations of the Church, is prescribed by the [First] Prayer Book of Edward VI."[1] The Judges in that case were careful to say they "had nothing to do with the 'ornaments of the minister' or anything appertaining thereto."[2] In the subsequent cases of *Hebbert* v. *Purchas*, and *Ridsdale* v. *Clifton*, the same doctrine was extended (though with certain modifications) to the dress of the officiating clergy.

Nevertheless, the Folkestone Judgment laid down also as a principle, that no Judgment, even of the Supreme Court, can bind after any "new Light" has been discovered which destroys the (supposed)

---

[1] Brooke's *Six Privy Council Judgments*, p. 51.
[2] Moore's *Separate Report*, p. 31.

"historic" basis on which that Judgment had been made to rest. This principle was again affirmed by the Supreme Court in the Bishop of Lincoln's case; and though it has doubtless been abused to bolster up findings that were politically convenient, the principle is in itself sound and equitable. For it cannot be denied that the ritual litigation of the last forty years has brought to light much buried antiquarian learning, and has cleared up many obscure passages in Church history.

The net result of the several suits has been to declare that ever since the introduction of the "Ornaments Rubric" in 1559, all ornaments of the First Prayer Book became binding by law until 1566, when the statutory "Advertisements of Queen Elizabeth" altered that law by reducing the dress of ministration to the "surplice" for ministers "at all times of their ministration" with a hood according to their several degrees, except in cathedral churches, for which the novel arrangement of three copes to be worn simultaneously was prescribed for use on certain occasions.[3]

This rule being *statutory* could not be repealed by any mere Canons, so that if enacted (directly or indirectly) "by the authority of Parliament" in 1559, it must have remained binding (at least) until the passing of the last Act of Uniformity in 1662.

Such is the theory of "Law" as formulated by the Courts, and it is now proposed to shew that if judged by contemporary history it cannot be sustained. For the moment we apply to it the test of history, that theory breaks down.

---

[3] See pp. 59, 120.

Even as regards the "Ornaments of the Church" the same Judgment which affirmed the standard of the First Prayer Book admitted that the "altar" of that book had been universally discarded by the executive authorities in both Church and State. The Judgment therefore ordered the removal of the "altar," and the substitution for it of an "honest table," movable, and of wood.

It might be replied that the "altar" itself never was an "ornament." Indeed this had been judicially decided beforehand by Sir H. J. Fust in *Falkner* v. *Litchfield*.[4] And the Judicial Committee of the Privy Council has further ruled in *Parker* v. *Leach*[5] that no conclusion of law can possibly be drawn from the pre-Reformation "altar" to the Lord's "table." But the latter *is*, though the former was not, an "ornament." Its being now a lawful "ornament of the Church" depends, however, not at all upon the language of the "Ornaments Rubric," or of the First Prayer Book, but upon other rubrics of later Prayer Books, all of which required a "Table." Leaving the "altar" question on one side, the following list, taken from the First Prayer Book, will shew how inapplicable it became as a standard after the repeal of the First Prayer Book in 1552.

"*Ornaments of the Church*" *in 1549.*

1. A Bible, viz. the "Great Bible of Henry VIII.," which followed the Septuagint, and from which our Prayer Book version of the Psalms is taken.

---

[4] 1 Robertson's *Reports*, p. 254.
[5] 2 Moore, *P. C.*, N.S. 199.

2. A Prayer Book, viz. the First Book of Edward VI.

3. The Poor Men's Box, placed near the High Altar, into which each communicant dropped his separate offering.[6] This was quite distinct from the Parish Chest kept in the Vestry. (Canon lxxxiv.)

4. A Corporas, *i.e.* the linen cloth, about a foot square ("frequently inserted in the middle of a large piece of coloured silk," velvet,[7] &c.), *upon* which the bread was consecrated.[8] This was quite different from the "fair linen cloth" which is now used to *cover* the consecrated wine.[9]

5. A vessel for oil used at Baptisms.

6. Vessels for oil to anoint the sick (viz. a cruet and cup).[10]

7. Vessels in which both the consecrated elements were in 1549 conveyed from the altar to sick men's houses. (Article XXVIII.)

8. Chalice.

9. Paten.

10. Bell.

11. Font.

12. Pulpit.

Of these Nos. 2 to 7 were illegal during the first six years of Elizabeth's reign. Perhaps the water cruet might be added, for even the eccentric "Lambeth Judgment" admitted the illegality of any *ritual* mixing during the service: and it forms part of the very definition of an "ornament" that it is for use *in the service* by the officiants.

Even the "chalice" was illegal until it was again

---

[6] Injunction 29 of 1547. Archdeacon Harrison's *Historical Inquiry*, pp. 279-308.

[7] Cussan's *Church Goods in Hertfordshire*, pp. 108, 128.

[8] "Laying the bread upon the corporas, *or* ELSE in the paten." Rubric of Edward's First Book. See Jewel's *Works*, II.-705. Hooper's *Later Writings*, p. 146.

[9] Walker's *Ritual Reason Why*, Q. 241 note.

[10] Cussan's, pp. 11, 128.

restored at the revision of 1661. Hence we find the two great Elizabethan Archbishops of Canterbury and York repeatedly forbade the use of "old massing chalices," or "chalices heretofore used at Mass," and required their clergy to use "no chalice . . . but a Communion Cup of silver."[11] Nor was it until 1662 that a change in the law again legitimated any use of the "chalice."[12]

So then, as regards the "ornaments of the Church" we are entitled to say that the standard of 1549 was at variance with the requirements of *all* the later Liturgies.

We come next to the

"*Ornaments of the Minister*," *of the First Prayer Book*.

The following is a list of these dresses, &c.

1. A Surplice, to be worn (as an alternative to No. 3) along with Nos. 7 and 8 in "any public ministration" by the Bishop, who also wore No. 5 or No. 4. Also with No. 5, by the "Minister" in the ante-Communion, *on days when there was no Communion*. Also with No. 2, in Cathedrals and Colleges. Also, without any other ornament, in Parish Churches by the "Minister" at Matins, Evensong, Public Baptisms, and Burials.

2. University Hoods, permitted (but not ordered) to graduates *on the foundation*, in their own Cathedrals and Colleges; and in Parish Churches to the Preacher, if a Graduate.

3. An Alb ("white" and "plain"), to be worn instead of a

---

[11] *Second Report of Ritual Commission*, Appendix, pp. 408-7, 411-4, 416-17. Cardwell's *Documentary Annals*, I.-321, and British Museum, ¹⁄₅' Qv. 5. North's *Chronicles of St. Martin's, Leicester*, p. 169.

[12] See Gardyner's return in 1567 above, p. 74.

surplice with Nos. 4 or 5 by the Celebrant, and with No. 6 by the Assistant Clergy at the Administration of Holy Communion. Also by Bishops (who might have them of coloured silk and embroidered), in lieu of No. 1.

4. The "Vestment," *i.e.* Chasuble, worn by the Celebrant only at the actual Administration of Holy Communion. A Bishop *might* wear it at other times; but neither Protestant nor Papist would then have thought it seemly to do so.

5. A Cope, to be worn with No. 1 by a Bishop at any time, and by a Priest in the Ante-Communion *if there was no Communion.* Also with No. 3 by the Celebrant, in lieu of No. 4.

6. A Tunacle, worn (with No. 3) by the Assistant Clergy at Holy Communion.

7. A Rochette, worn by Bishops with No. 1 or No. 3, and with No. 4 or No. 5, and with

8. A Pastoral Staff.

It is true that the Advertisements of Queen Elizabeth *afterwards* authorised the use of the surplice by the celebrant at the Lord's Supper, and that these Advertisements had *statutory* authority under the Act of Uniformity, 1 Elizabeth, cap. ii. But this does not and cannot explain why nobody ever paid the slightest heed to the standard of 1549 during the six years, 1559-66, which elapsed *before* the issue of the Advertisements. Not a single Bishop then wore alb, or chasuble, not a single priest wore alb or tunacle, still less a "vestment," during all those six years when, on the received theory, those "ornaments" were not merely permissible but compulsory. That difficulty has never yet been fairly faced. Although Elizabeth herself, the Bench, the Bar, and a majority probably of the House of Lords with a large section of the people, especially of the landed gentry, are supposed to have been in favour of a high ritual, and although very many of the Marian clergy retained their livings—yet we do not find *one clear instance* of the ritual of 1549 being followed in any one church during the crucial years 1559-66 when, on the received hypothesis, *all* the ornaments of 1549 were required by law.

That would certainly be "strange if true." But is the hypothesis true?

Then again, the received theory would require us to believe that Elizabeth's Act of Uniformity was so absurdly framed that it first enacted *under a penalty* the Ornaments Rubric of 1552 ("and none other or otherwise"), and then, as an addendum and afterthought, went on to provide that a totally different set of ornaments should be worn and used "until other order be taken by the Queen"; yet forgetting to provide any penalty whatever for a disregard of this subsequent and inconsistent "proviso." That would have been an exceedingly fatuous thing to do, and very unlike the style of Elizabethan draftsmanship. But, the previous question arises—" Is it true?"

It is not true: and fortunately, the Queen's printers having begun to restore the old Act of Elizabeth which forms in law *part of the present Prayer Book*, every reader can now test this for himself.

The mistake arose from a misunderstanding of the 25th and 26th sections of the Act of 1559. These ran as follows—

Section XXV.—Provided always, and be it enacted, That such Ornaments of the Church and of the Ministers thereof, shall be retained and be in use, as was in this Church of *England* by Authority of Parliament, in the Second Year of the Reign of King *Edward* the Sixth, until other Order shall be therein taken by the Authority of the Queen's Majesty, with the Advice of her Commissioners appointed and authorised under the Great

Seal of England for causes Ecclesiastical, or of the Metropolitan of this Realm.

Section XXVI.—And also, That if there shall happen any contempt or irreverence to be used in the Ceremonies or Rites of the Church, by the misusing of the Orders appointed in this Book, the Queen's Majesty may, by the like Advice of the said Commissioners or Metropolitan, ordain and publish such further Ceremonies or Rites, as may be most for the Advancement of God's Glory, the Edifying of his Church, and the due Reverence of Christ's Holy Mysteries and Sacraments.

The "ordaining and publishing" mentioned in the 26th section was a totally different thing from the "taking order" of the 25th. "Taking order," according to the usage of that day, merely meant the giving some practical directions (such as were deemed applicable in each case), and were executive and administrative rather than legislative acts. A good illustration of the difference between "ordaining" and "taking order" is seen in Archbishop Parker's letter to the Warden of All Souls, in which (after reminding him that "vestments and tunicles serve not to use at these days") he says the Royal Commissioners were to "*take* such *order* and direction therein as shall appertain . . . to the fulfilling of the Queen's laws and *orders*."[13] Thus "taking order" was the giving practical "directions," at the discretion of the Visitors, in fulfilment and application (and at times, as the result shewed, in exceptional modifications) of the Queen's Orders.

So, in 1549, the Royal Visitors at Cambridge reported to the Protector that they "had set a stay" at Clare Hall, "so that they cannot alter, alienate, or dispose

---

[13] *Parker Correspondence*, pp. 296, 297.

anything, . . . leaving them in expectation of a further *order to be taken* by us, before our departing."[14]

Archbishop Grindal in his Injunctions for the Laity (1571) directed the churchwardens to "*take* some *order* among the parishioners, that every one may pay such a reasonable sum towards" defraying the cost of the sacramental elements as was expedient.[15]

An excellent illustration is found in the wording of the official "assignments" by the Royal Visitors in 1553. They wrote, "delivered unto the hands of the said wardens unto the use of the said church there to be occupied according to the effect of the commission directed unto the commissioners appointed for the sale of the church goods and other *order* to be therein *taken* for the same as followeth."[16]

These examples, *in pari materiâ*, might be indefinitely multiplied; but it is clear that by customary usage the words "take order" suggested primarily a purely administrative discretion on the part of some executive officer, and did not suggest any act of a legislative character. Now it has been shewn elsewhere (p. 43) that the Royal Visitors in 1559 were "Commissioners under the Great Seal for causes ecclesiastical," having power judicially to decide a variety of "causes," and were *also* executive officers of the Crown charged with the "taking order" wherever needed to give effect to the requirements of the new Prayer Book and to

---

[14] Bradford's *Writings*, Parker Society, II.-370.
[15] Grindal's *Remains*, p. 134.
[16] Tyssen's *Surrey Inventories*, p. 184 *et seq.*

The Royal Commission itself specified "the honest and comely furniture of coverings for the Communion Table, and surplice or surplices for the minister or ministers." (Cussan's *Hertfordshire Inventories*, p. 5.)

secure its acceptance in the particular neighbourhoods which they respectively "visited." Under the 25th section of the Act of Uniformity they had to "take order" as to the (1) retention; (2) the having "in use" certain ornaments which by the third and fourth sections of the same Act (1 Elizabeth, cap. 2) had been expressly forbidden to be used *by the minister* in his *ministrations*. It has been assumed, too hastily, that these two sections of the Act neutralise and contradict one another, and, stranger still, that the one which had no penalties attached to it must override the one which had.

But the proviso itself says nothing whatever about "the minister," nor about the "times of ministration." It had in fact nothing to do with either. It had the much more prosaic object of reserving for the Queen the goods which, being no longer required by law, would have been wasted or embezzled, as former experience in the days of King Edward had amply demonstrated. The custody of the ornaments was in the hands of the churchwardens because the ornaments themselves were the property of the parish, and were in fact customarily sold and bought by the wardens under the orders of the Parish Vestry. Toulmin Smith, in his work on *The Parish*, gives numerous illustrations of the control of the Vestry over their church ornaments. In Peacock's *Lincolnshire Church Furniture*, sales "by consent of the parish" were always returned as being a sufficient quittance of the churchwardens from further responsibility. Similar returns were sent in from every diocese. But a typical illustration is furnished by Gardiner, who had held the office of Lord Chancellor, and might be supposed, therefore, to know the law of the Church. Writing to Ridley, he observes:

"Ever since I was born, a poor parishioner, a layman, durst he so bold at a shift (if he were also churchwarden), to *sell to the use of the church* at length, and his own in the meantime, the silver cross on Easter Monday that was creeped to on Good Friday."[17]

That "retaining" ornaments did not necessarily imply their use by the officiant is seen from the fact that things *confessedly illegal* are constantly described as "retained." Archbishop Grindal in 1576 inquired whether any persons "of late have *retained* or kept in their custody" any of the prohibited books published abroad by the recusants at Louvain.[18]

When King Edward's Visitors visited Northampton they were directed to make complete inventories and deliver one copy to the Privy Council and another "to them in whose hands the said goods, plate, jewels, bells and ornaments shall remain to be kept preserved"; or, as another version says, "the same goods, &c., should be safely kept and appointed to the charge of such persons as should keep the same safely and be ready to answer to the same at all times."

Another directs that "they and every of them do safely keep unspoiled and unembezzled and unsold all such bells . . . the same to conserve until Our pleasure be therein further known."[19]

King Edward had entered in his own diary how "a letter was written" to the Captain of the Isle of Jersey "that he take heed to the church plate that it be not stolen away, but kept safe till further *order* be *taken*."[20]

---

[17] Ridley's *Works*, p. 498. [18] Grindal's *Remains*, p. 169.
[19] Stephens' *Notes, Legal and Historical, on the Book of Common Prayer*, I.-355. *Seventh Report of Deputy Keeper of Public Records*, p. 312.
[20] Burnet's *History of the Reformation*, II.-ii.-86.

And the Guernsey Commissioners, under Elizabeth, recommended a sale of the church bells to be "employed on fortification of the castle which was done with Jersey in King Edward's time."[21]

The other phrase, " Be in use," is peculiar. It seems studiously vague, and it is remarkable that that precise collocation of words *does not occur anywhere else* in the contemporary literature. But the word "use" in this connection seems precisely equivalent to "*ad opus*" in the old wills when directing money or chattels to be employed or utilised. In many cases the particular "use" intended was specified; but in others, especially where changes consequent upon an alteration in worship came in, they were directed *either* to be "used to the intent that they were first given, *or to some other* necessary and convenient service of the Church."[22]

The College of Eton was allowed to "enjoy still their church goods, the bells only except, so as they *convert* the same from monuments of superstition to *necessary uses* of the said College."[23]

The old Canon Law had directed "let the chrysomes be made use of for the ornaments of the church only,"[24] which Johnson explains to mean "they might be used for the making or mending surplices, amits, albs; or the wrapping up the chalices," &c.[25] So in the first year of King Edward VI. the churchwardens

---

[21] *State Papers, Domestic,* Elizabeth, Addenda, Vol. XIII., No. 117, p. 45.
[22] Strype's *Cranmer*, Ecclesiastical History Society edition, II.-90.
[23] Dasent's *Acts of the Privy Council*, IV.-270.
[24] *Constitutions of Archbishop Edmund*, No. 13.
[25] Johnson's *Canons*, II.-136.

of Mortlake returned among their receipts "received
for 2 altar cloths *to the use of the Church* for making of
the pulpit and seats by the consent of the parish,
3li 10s."[26] This "use of the Church" was understood
in the widest sense; it included the covering the roof
with lead, glazing the windows, repairs of the church,
clerk's house and schoolhouse, the poor men's box,
and indeed any legitimate expense which the churchwardens were then entitled to incur. "Use" meant
simply employment, utilisation. Thus "sold to the use
of the Church," "sold to the King's use," were phrases
continually recurring. So Archbishop Grindal in 1571
orders the churchwardens to "shew what cost they
have bestowed in reparations and other things for the
use of the Church," and directs that the "rood lofts
be *sold* by the churchwardens *to the use of the Church*, so
as *no part thereof be kept* and observed."[27]

Bishop Horn, as Visitor of Trinity College, Oxford,
ordered in 1570 that the crosses, censers, &c., be
defaced, "and to convert the matter thereof to the
godly *use*, profit, and behoof of your house."[28]

Archbishop Piers in 1590, on learning from the
churchwardens of St. Denis', York, that "there be
certain copes and vestments defaced belonging to the
parish not converted to any good use," orders "that
they be converted to the use of the Church."[29] In
short the albs were made into surplices, table-covers,

---

[26] Tyssen's *Surrey Inventories*, p. 118; similar entries occur at pp 88,
124, 184, *et seq*. At Pendock, Worcester, "One cope of green silk,
with a vestment the which is *turned to the use* to serve upon the table"
(*Report of Worcester Architectural Society*, Vol. XI., p. 329).

[27] Grindal's *Remains*, pp. 133-4.

[28] Warton's *Life of Sir T. Pope*, Appendix XIX.

[29] Raine's *Vestments in the Northern Province*, p. 16

font-covers, &c., the chasubles into table-carpets and pulpit-cloths, while the tiny chalices were converted into communion cups.[30] Thus all the ornaments of 1549 might "be in use" by the churchwardens, who "retained" them, without any resulting violation of the Ornaments Rubric of 1552 by the clergy.

Now the best way to test whether this theory or the popularly received view is the truer interpretation is to see how the law was understood and acted upon at the time, and especially how it was enforced by those in authority when the Elizabethan Act was fresh from the mint. Unless we rigidly exclude the conjectures of Strype and other writers of the eighteenth century, whose guesses have too long been mistaken for "history," we shall never get at the truth.

Perhaps the best way is to arrange the evidence in chronological order. In 1558 we have, first of all, the report sent to Cecil by Geste of the recommendations made by those who were consulted by the Government as to suggested alterations in the Liturgy. That report dissuaded from the use of any distinctive dress, even the cope, at the Communion, on the ground that

"Because it is thought sufficient to use but a surplice in baptizing, reading, preaching, and praying, therefore it is enough for the celebrating of the Communion. For if we should use another garment herein, it should seem to teach us that higher and better things be given by it than be given by the other service, which we must not believe."[31]

The Protestant party was strong in the Commons, and as early as February 15th, 1559, "the bill for

---

[30] Tyssen, pp. 75, 133. [31] Dugdale's *Life of Geste*, p. 145.

order of service and ministers in the Church" was read a first time.[32] Unwilling to wait till this measure had passed, on March 17th, 1559, "The bill that no persons shall be punished for using the religion used in King Edward's LAST year, was read the first and second time, and ordered to be engrossed."[33] The "*last*" year of Edward's reign was its "Seventh year," commencing January 28th, 1553, when the Second Prayer Book was *exclusively* in use. "The *latter* year of K. Edward" was also the standard subsequently enforced by the Thirtieth Injunction of Elizabeth.[34] But the Romish party was known to be strong in the Lords, so that to aid in getting the Bill through it was decided to hold a public disputation, to be conducted as in 1548, by leading representatives of both sides, in order to debate the Scriptural authority for the sacrifice in the Mass, the right of National Churches to "take away and change ceremonies," and the use of the vernacular, both of which last the Romish disputants opposed. Probably as a result of the threatened opposition in the Lords, a fresh Bill was introduced into the Commons on April 18th, which on May 8th received the Royal Assent and became the Act 1 Elizabeth, cap. ii. Every Bishop then on the bench spoke and voted *against* the Prayer Book, and according to Lingard, the Bill passed the Lords by a majority of only three: two Bishops of the Romish party being detained in prison, and Abbot Feckenham, who spoke against the Bill, being also absent at the division.[35] It began by reciting that

---

[32] D'Ewes' *Journal*, p. 47.   [33] *Ibid.*, p. 52.
[34] See p. 38.   [35] Lingard's *History of England*, Vol VI.-16.

"Where at the DEATH of our late Sovereign lord King Edward VIth there *remained* one uniform order of common service . . which was *set forth in one book* . . which was repealed and taken away by act of parliament in the first year of the reign of our late Sovereign lady Q. Mary, to the great decay of the due honour of God, and discomfort to the professors of the truth of Christ's religion ":—

The Act went on to repeal Mary's statute "*only concerning the said book*, and the service administration of sacraments, rites, and ceremonies *contained and appointed by* the said book," and to re-enact that book, *eo nomine*, "with the alterations and additions *therein* added and appointed by this statute." So that no new MS. or other Liturgy was enacted: and any alterations, to be legal at all, must be those statutably made "*therein*," *i.e.* in the Prayer Book of 1552.

The third section enacted (with the significant omission of all mention of the "Lords Spiritual") that the service should be "in such order and form as is *mentioned* in the said book . . with one alteration or addition of certain lessons to be used on every Sunday in the year, and the form of the Litany altered and corrected, and two sentences only added in the delivery of the sacraments, AND NONE OTHER OR OTHERWISE."

Those last words indicate the jealousy of the Commons against any interference by the Government with the result of their labours; and their wise precaution had the effect in law of re-enacting the two following rubrics of the book of 1552.

The Morning and Evening Prayer shall be used in such place of the Church, Chapel, or Chancel, and the Minister shall so turn him, as the people may best hear. And if there be any controversy therein, the matter shall be referred to the ordinary, and he or his deputy shall appoint the place, and the chancels shall remain, as they have done in times past.

And here is to be noted, that the Minister *at the time of the Communion and at all other times* in his ministration *shall use neither Alb, Vestment, nor cope, but being Arch-Bishop, or Bishop he shall have and wear a Rochet, and being a Priest or Deacon, he shall have and wear a surplice* only.

The Crown had no authority to tamper with the book, and any "printed" variation from the text which had been sanctioned by the statute was irregular, illegal, and *ultra vires*. The fourth section of the Act accordingly prescribed penalties for using "any other rite, ceremony, order, form, or manner of celebrating of the Lord's Supper. . . . than is *mentioned* and *set forth in* the said book." Thenceforward, any celebration in "the sacrificial vestments" became penal. Hence we have a very simple test as to the true meaning of the Act, viz. what did the Ordinaries and the State authorities *do* in reference to this question? Did the Elizabethan Bishops wear their mitres, pastoral staves, and vestments or copes "at all times of their ministration"? Did the Elizabethan clergy wear albs with vestments or copes, and their assistants wear "albs with tunacles" during the six years before the Advertisements of Elizabeth were issued?

The answer is that not once, anywhere, was the ritual of the First Prayer Book, in respect of the use of ornaments, followed by any one Bishop, priest or deacon.

On the other hypothesis which I am vindicating, these persons would be required to wear the "surplice only," or (in the case of Bishops) the Rochet.

Let us therefore resume our chronological recital of the evidence of history.

The earliest commentary is found in a letter written from London, two days after the passing of the Act, by Sandys (afterwards Archbishop of York), to his friend Parker (afterwards Archbishop of Canterbury).

"The Parliament draweth towards an end. The *last* book of service is gone through with a proviso to retain the ornaments which were used in the first and second year of King Edward, until it please the Queen to take other order for them. Our gloss upon this text is that we' [clergy] 'shall not be forced to *use* them, but that others' [churchwardens &c.]' in the meantime shall not convey them away, but that they may remain for the Queen." [36]

Sandys was one of those who are reputed to have met as a "Committee" to revise the Prayer Book, and according to Camden he was one of the Protestant representatives at the public debate in Westminster Abbey.[37] On the very day that the new Prayer Book became compulsory, Sandys was appointed one of the Royal Commissioners under the Queen's "own hand and seal"[38] to visit the churches and to enforce the new Act. No higher "authority" could be produced as to its true meaning: and his "gloss," *i.e.* interpretation, "turned out to be true."

The Visitors included among their number the Prime Minister, the Secretaries of State, the noblemen and Members of Parliament who had voted in favour of the Reformation, and the future Bishops; in short, the list included every name of those most deeply engaged in securing the success of the new book.

London, the seat of the Court and of the legislature, was promptly visited by them and the result is recorded in Machyn's *Diary*, and in Grindal's *Register*. Every-

---

[36] *Parker Correspondence*, p. 65.
[37] Camden, edition 1688, p. 21. Foxe, VIII.-679. Oglethorpe, whom Foxe gives as Sandys' opponent, was fined £250 and compelled to attend at the Privy Council meetings along with the rest of the disputants. Dasent's *Acts of the Privy Council*, VII.-79 *et seq.*
[38] Strype's *Annals*, I.-i.-248.

where the roods, crosses, and altars were pulled down, and at St. Paul's, "they further enjoined and gave in command that none in the said cathedral church henceforth use any shaven crowns, amices, or clothes called copes." [39]

"So that from Bartholomew-tide and so forward, within a month's time, or less, were destroyed all the roods, church images, church goods, with copes, crosses, censers," &c. [40]

Strype reprints the Interrogatories issued by some Ordinary during this visitation which were "joined to" the Visitation Articles of the Visitors, and inquiring "whether any images, books of service, or *vestments, not allowed by law*, be reserved of any man?" [41] and he quotes in his *Life of Parker* (III.-145) from a paper by "Bishop Cox, or Bishop Jewel" a reply to Puritan attacks, of somewhat later date, in these words—" in that they are said to be monuments of idolatry, that cannot be. For if some of the attire wherewith the mumbling Mass hath been said be *put away and abolished*, why term they the like form, and that which never served the like use, to be monuments of idolatry?"

On August 12th, Grindal (Bishop Elect of London) and May (Dean Elect of St. Paul's) ordered the prebendaries and petty canons of St. Paul's "to use only a surplice in the service time." [42]

---

[39] Strype's *Annals*, I.-i.-252. Hume's *Spanish State Papers*, 1.-89.
[40] Strype's *Grindal*, p. 37. Machyn's *Diary*, p. 208.
[41] *Strype's Annals*, I.-i.-245. I.-ii.-497. Cardwell's *Documentary Annals*, I.-210. "The use of these Vestments," says Mr. Tyrrell Green, "was distinctly understood at the time to imply a recognition of the sacrificial character of the Sacrament." *On the Articles*, p. 261.
[42] Wriothesley's *Chronicle of England*. Camden Society, II.-146. Holinshed, III.-1184. b. edition 1586.

In 1560, Pilkington, one of the reputed "revisers," a Royal Visitor for the University of Cambridge (and, before the close of the year, Bishop of Durham), mentions "copes" among distinctively "popish gear."[43] On June 5th of the same year the Canons of Salisbury commuted the (previously) customary payment of a cope at the first election of a new member of the chapter, for a money payment.[44] In the same year, Sandys reports to Archbishop Cranmer's old colleague, Peter Martyr, that "images of every kind were at our last Visitation not only taken down, but also burnt, and that too by public authority"; but, he adds, "only the popish vestments remain in our church' (*i.e.* Worcester Cathedral). 'I mean copes (*Copas intelligc*), which we hope will not last very long."[45] We learn afterwards from the taunt of Robert Johnson, the Nonconformist, that Sandys himself "refused the cope." See p. 134 *infra*. But this Worcester case is one of several instances (to be discussed hereafter) illustrating the dispensing power in respect of the cope which under the pretext of "taking order" the executive assumed to itself as matter of public policy.

In 1561, Parkhurst, Bishop of Norwich, asks whether any " vestments *not allowed by law* be reserved of any man," language which could only apply to the Rubric of 1552.[46]

In 1561-2, Alley, Bishop of Exeter, complains (apparently to the Privy Council) that he knew

---

[43] *Works*, pp. 77, 129.
[44] *Statuta et Consuetudines*, p. 113, B.M. 5155, cc. 1.
[45] *Zurich Letters*, I.-74 and Appendix, p. 43.
[46] *Second Report of the Ritual Commission*, Appendix, pp. 402-3.

"one preacher, not of the basest sort or estimation, which did glory and boast that he made eight sermons in London against surplices, rochets, tippets and cappes, counting them not to be perfect that do wear them. And although it be one in effect to wear either round caps, square caps, or button caps, yet it is thought, &c."[47]

This is intelligible, *if* the rubric of 1552 were then in use, because the dresses mentioned represent accurately enough the outdoor and ministerial garb of 1553.

Bishop Cooper, in his *Admonition to the People of England*, referring to the earliest Puritan objectors, said, "*At the beginning*, some learned and godly preachers, for private respects in themselves, made strange to wear the surplice, cap or tippet."[48] And Hooker himself says, "Under the happy reign of her Majesty which now is, the *greatest matter* awhile contended for was the wearing of the cap and surplice, till there came *Admonitions* directed unto the high court of Parliament," viz. in 1571.[49] George Cranmer's letter to Hooker also describes the successive stages of the Puritan revolt. He says, "The *first* degree was only some small difference about cap and surplice."[50] Such complaints would certainly not have been regarded as the "greatest" on either side had the sacrificial vestments been either customary or legal. Bishop Jewel's account given on February 7th, 1562, to Peter Martyr, quite bears out the same conception of the situation. He says—

"Now that the full light of the gospel has shone forth, the very vestiges of error must as far as possible be removed, together

---

[47] *Petyt MSS.*, Vol. XLVII., p. 448.
[49] *Ibid.*, p. 141.
[48] Keble's *Hooker*, I.-142.
[50] *Ibid.*, II.-509.

with the rubbish and, as the saying is, with the very dust. And I wish we could effect this in respect to that linen surplice." [50]

In the original Latin, Jewel borrows from Plutarch the word λινοστολία "linen-dressiness" to express the grievance of the advanced Protestants.[51] Later on, Jewel again recurs to the controversy in writing to Bullinger—" the contest respecting the linen surplice (ecclesiasticâ veste lineâ) is not yet at rest." Jewel himself wished to abolish the surplice, " But the Queen at this time is unable to endure the least alteration." [52] The date of that letter is February 8th, 1566, which is of interest as bearing on the question whether the Advertisements of 1566 were designed to change the vestiarian law.

In 1563 the Second Book of Homilies was published sometime before August 1st. The Homily " On Peril of Idolatry " was edited by Elizabeth herself (see below, p. 250), and the "Third Part" "teacheth the sumptuousness amongst the Jews to be a figure to signify, *not an example to follow*," adding " Rabanus at large declareth that this costly and manifold furniture of vestments *of late used* in the church was fetched from the Jewish usage and agreeth with Aaron's apparelling almost altogether "—whereas it is urged " the vestures used in the church in old time were very plain and single and nothing costly."

In the same year the Archbishop of Canterbury asks [52a] " whether your altars be taken down," and " ministers do use in the time of the celebration of divine service to wear a surplice . . and do use all rites and orders

---

[50] *Zurich Letters*, I.-100. [51] *Ibid.*, Appendix, p. 59.
[52] *Ibid.*, I.-149. [52a] *Second Report, Ritual Commission*, p. 403.

prescribed in the book of Common prayer, &c., and none other."

Such language does not point to a law as then requiring Vestments, albs and tunicles. (See above, p. 96.)

On August 16th, 1563, Humphrey wrote to Bullinger "*de re vestiariâ*," asking " Whether at the command of the sovereign (the jurisdiction of the Pope having been abolished) and for the sake of order, and not of ornament [? *Cultûs*] habits of this kind may be worn in church by pious men, lawfully and with a safe conscience. I am speaking of that round [*sic*] cap and popish surplice, which are now enjoined us."[53]

In January, 1564, Archdeacon Mullins visited the London clergy by commission from Grindal, Bishop of London, and requested them to "wear in the ministry of the church the surplice *only*. And lastly they were to subscribe with their hands that they would observe it."[54]

"On the 24th of March following, this reformation in ministers' habits began, when the use of the scholar's gown and cap was enjoined from that day forward : the surplice to be worn at *all* divine administrations : and the observation of the Book of Common Prayer *as was appointed by statute, and the rubric* of the said book."

The Archbishop, the Bishop of London, and other Ecclesiastical Commissioners were present when the Bishop's Chancellor, pointing to the Rev. Robert Cole, "canonically habited," said—

---

[53] *Zurich Letters*, I.-134.
[54] Strype's *Grindal*, p. 144. The plague " slacked " before January 26th, 1564. See Gairdner's *Three Fifteenth Century-Chronicles*, Camden Society, pp. 125, 128, which fixes the date to 1564, *not* 1564-5. Grindal's *Remains*, p. 115.

"My Masters and the Ministers of London, the Council's pleasure is that ye strictly keep the unity of apparel like to this man as you see him, that is, a square cap, a scholar's gown priest-like, a tippet, and in the church a linen surplice: and inviolably observe the rubric of the Book of Common Prayer, and the Queen's majesty's Injunctions."

Refusal was followed by deprivation;[55] so that had these requirements been contrary to law, the Nonconformists would at once have had a legal remedy by applying for prohibition.

Thus *before* the Advertisements of Elizabeth were issued, we have the High Commission declaring the "pleasure" of the Privy Council (*i.e.* of the Government of the day) as to the "unity of apparel," and as to the meaning of the Rubric and Injunctions.

In the following year (July 17th, 1565) a letter was written by Bishop Horn to Gualter which is only second in importance to the testimony of Sandys before quoted. Horn had returned to England in 1559 and took part in the public dispute in Westminster Abbey, held on March 31st, but he was not in Parliament till after the Act passed, having been made Bishop of Winchester on February 16th, 1560. Horn had been deprived by Mary of the Deanery of Durham, which had not been restored to him on April 28th, when the Act passed. Hence he describes it as passed "before our restitution" (*restitutionem*). The Parker Society unfortunately mistranslated this "before our *return*," which contradicts the previous statements on pp. 6, 11 and 15, in the same volume. Horn tells his correspondent that by this Act—

---

[55] *Parker Correspondence*, p. 270.

"though the other habits were taken away (*sublata reliqua faece*) the wearing of square caps and surplices was continued to the clergy, though without any superstitious conceit, which was expressly guarded against by the terms of the Act. . . . It was enjoined us (who had not then any authority either to make laws or repeal them) either to wear the caps and surplices, or to give place to others."[56]

Is it credible that Horn could have spoken of the "rest of the dregs being taken away" if they were still notoriously required by law?

It deserves notice, too, that Horn regards the language of the Injunctions of 1559, enforcing the new regime, as identified with the Act itself: for the "express terms" are not found in the Act, but in the Thirtieth Injunction. (See p. 38.)

1565.—Bullingham, bishop of Lincoln, as Visitor of King's College, Cambridge, ordered the Provost "to destroy a great deal of Popish stuff, as mass books . . copes, vestments, candlesticks, crosses, pixes, paxes, and the brazen rood."[57]

In the same year, the Commissioners for removing superstitious ornaments told Downham, Bishop of Chester, that they had taken away "vestments, albe, altar cloth, corporas, and other idolatrous gear."[58]

In the same year, Harding the Jesuit published his *Confutation*, in which he taunts his opponent, "If peculiar vestments for deacons, priests, bishops, be taken away . . judge ye whether ye have duly kept the old ceremonies?" To which Jewel replied, "Ye

---

[56] *Zurich Letters*, I.-142, and Appendix, p. 84.
[57] Strype's *Grindal*, p. 210.
[58] Gastrell's *Notitia Cestrensis*, II.-41, quoted in Bailey's *Lancashire Inventories*, II.-31.

come in with .. tunicles and chesibles .. as if all these things had descended directly from the apostles .. but you have so misused them, or rather so defiled and bewrayed them with your superstitions .. that we can no longer continue them without great conscience." [59]

The *Visitation of Lincolnshire Churches*, published by Mr. Peacock, shews the general destruction of vestments, albs, &c., and their conversion into cushions, carpets, antependiums, &c., and the alteration of albs to make surplices, or "rochets for the clerk." Moreover, they furnish evidence that many had been "defaced" as the result of the Royal Visitation "*Anno primo* Elizabethæ."

The returns sent in to Archbishop Parker and reported by him to Cecil, February 28th, 1565, of "varieties in the service," do not so much as mention vestments, albs or tunicles as being known or used *anywhere*.[60]

All the above instances are taken from the period before the issue of the Advertisements; and they shew that the framers and enacters of the Prayer Book, as well as the responsible Ordinaries, had no conception that the law then in force required *or permitted* the sacrificial vestments to be worn by anybody. Whereas if we assume that the Rubric of 1552 was recognised as in force, they all fall into line naturally, with the exception of a certain irregular, partial and inconsistent employment of the cope.

As to that, however, three things deserve to be considered.

---

[59] Jewel, *Defence of Apology*, pp. 176-7.
[60] *Lansdowne MS.* VIII., fol. 16.

First; that the cope was never generally worn, and only on occasions of state when additional pomp might be thought not out of place.

Second; that the cope was neutral ground, involving as it did, no associations with the Mass or the priesthood.

Third; that when the cope was worn at all, it was used in a manner *quite inconsistent with* the Rubrics of the First Prayer Book.

Before the Reformation, the chasuble was regarded as *the* distinctive "Vestment" of the sacrificer: it was specially "blessed," and at each priest's ordination it was placed on him by the Bishop with the words "receive the sacerdotal vesture," and was almost immediately followed by the blessing of his hands to "consecrate hosts which are offered for the sins and negligences of the people."[61] When Sawtre was degraded before being burnt at the stake, the form ran "we pull from thy back the casula (chasuble) and take from thee the priestly Vestment, and deprive thee of all manner of priestly honour."[62] Before the issue of the Advertisements, the Puritan clergy had written to Bullinger in the hope of gaining his authority for their refusal of the surplice and out-door dress; but he replied in terms already quoted, that "the mass vesture, *that is* alb and chasuble," were intolerable, but that the surplice and cap were things indifferent.

In the official translation of Bullinger's letter published by the High Commission in 1566,[63] the word "casula" is printed in the margin opposite "vestment,"

---

[61] Maskell's *Monumenta Ritualia*, III.-209, 212.
[62] Fox, III.-227.   [63] Given above, p. 55.

thus making it perfectly clear what the word "Vestment" in the Rubric of 1549 meant. Lyndwood had described the chasuble as that "with which the priest is clad when about to celebrate mass," while the cope, he said, was used "out of the Mass time" (*extra tempus missæ*).[64] In the Lincoln Pontifical the Bishop was directed to "come to the church in a cope," and at Mass to "*put off the cope* and put on amice, alb," and the rest of the Mass vesture.[65]

The First Prayer Book, as we know from the "Great Debate" held in 1548, was a compromise, in which both parties had an alternative choice of what would harmonise best with their respective theories. Thus under the temporary compromise of 1549, the First Prayer Book of Edward provided for the professors of—

The Old Faith.	*The New Faith.*
"The Mass" (commonly called).	"The Supper of the Lord, and the Holy Communion."
	The Lord's Table; God's Board.
The Altar.	
The Chalice.	A fair Cup "if the Chalice will not serve."
The Corporas; the Paten.	Some comely vessel or plate prepared for that purpose.
The Vestment.	The Cope.
The Tunicle.	The Cope for Bishops.
The Alb.	The Surplice.

And we know in part whence this idea had been derived. For the *Kirchen-Ordnung* of Nuremberg-Brandenberg (from which Cranmer translated his "Catechism" of 1548, and also borrowed largely for the occasional offices of

---

[61] *Provinciale*, p. 252, Edition 1679.
[65] Scudamore, *Notitia Eucharistica*, p. 70.

the First Prayer Book), directed that "the priest is not to wear a chasuble, but a cope only ... lest simple folk should imagine it was intended to celebrate Mass, after the former fashion, without communicants."[66] Hence in the *Greyfriars' Chronicle*, we have the sorrowful record[67] that on July 21st, 1549, Cranmer "did the office himself in a cope *and no vestment*." When Queen Mary's Commissioners visited Cambridge, the fellows and scholars of each college were clad in copes, but the Provost himself "in the ordinary habit in which the celebrants at Mass are clad, *except that* he wore topmost a cope like the rest."[68]

On the other hand, the cope (like the surplice) was a mere choral and out-door processional dress worn by clerks and singers, and even by nuns[69] and children.[70] It had never been worn by the celebrant at Mass.[71] Dr. Gasquet justly observes that

"A cope was not specifically a sacerdotal vestment but might be worn by any cleric. A great number of these clerics were in mediæval England practically laymen, living in secular avocations." Hence "those who desired change would adopt the cope which broke with past ecclesiastical tradition and the universal practice, and enabled them to display their rejection of the sacrificial character of the service."[72]

Migne's *Encyclopédie Théologique*, Vol. VIII., p. 301, article "*Chape*," says: "Il n'est pas d'ailleurs neces-

---

[66] Droop's *Edwardian Vestments*, p. 43. [67] Camden Society, p. 60
[68] Bucer's *Scripta Anglicana*, p. 922. [69] Johnson's *Canons*, II.-93
[70] "Five copes for children." Peacock's *Church Furniture*, p. 220
"Capæ puerorum." Dugdale's *History of St. Paul's*, p. 318.
[71] Rock's *Church of our Fathers*, II.-44, 45; and *Hierurgia*, pp. 436, 439; Bishop Gardiner's *Rationale* of 1540 in Strype's *Ecclesiastical Memorials*, I.-ii.-420; or p. 277 of the *Cotton MS*.
[72] *Edward VI. and the Book of Common Prayer*, pp. 189, 190

saire que la chape soit benite, ce que prouve qu'elle n'est pas proprement un habit sacerdotal."[73]

Hence it was that the Royal Visitors in 1559, being empowered by the statute to "take order" (*i.e.* to give practical directions as to what should be done), connived at a certain indulgence in the matter of cope-wearing, which was designed to soften the blow given to the men of the "old religion" in certain districts, and in Cathedrals or Collegiate churches where pomp had always been a distinctive characteristic. With the traditions and habits of that generation, the cope would seem to lend a certain dignity to the new service, while it was wholly free from "sacrificial" associations. Hence in Elizabeth's own private chapel, at the consecration of Archbishop Parker, and at the communion which was celebrated at the obsequies in honour of Henry II. of France, on September 9th, 1559, copes were worn by the Epistoler and Gospeller, *in defiance of the Rubric of* 1549, which required these persons to wear "albs with tunicles." In this way the "distinctive" dress of the celebrant-"sacrificer" was as it were cheapened, by raising the office of the teacher and preacher to a like symbolic dignity. For, as the *Reformatio Legum* expressed it, "we retain for the Eucharist no greater veneration than for Baptism and the Word of God."[74]

By the Rubric of 1549 a bishop had to wear at "any

---

[73] Compare Maskell's *Monumenta Ritualia*, I.-144. The blessing of the chasuble was "that all clad with this chasuble may have power to perform a sacrifice acceptable to Thee for quick and dead."

[74] De Hæresibus, cap. xix., "nullam relinquimus majorem Eucharistiæ venerationem, quam baptismi et verbi Dei." See above, pp. 89, 90, 104.

other public ministration" the *same* dress as "whensoever he shall celebrate the Holy Communion,"[75] and when a priest officiated, the cope was not put on till "after the Litany ended."[76]

Whereas on September 8th, 1559, "the Archbishop of Canterbury, in his surplice and doctor's hood on his shoulders, who did execute, began the service, assisted by the Bishops of Chichester and Hereford, apparelled as the Archbishop";[77] and on April 23rd of the following year, thirty Court Chaplains in copes "sang the Litany in procession."[77a] Grindal preached at Paul's Cross in "rochet and cymar," on March 3rd, 1560, as did Scory on March 10th, Jewell on March 17th, and Barlow on March 24th, each being in "ys rochet and chimner." So, too, Bishop Scambler on February 21st, 1561.[78] Archbishop Parker, with the Bishops of Lincoln and Rochester, and his own "Suffragan," officiated before the Queen at Canterbury in 1575, in "our chimmers and rochets."[79] No pastoral staff was given to Parker, or used by any of his successors. The surplice used by the Elizabethan clergy from the first at celebrations of Holy Communion was *not even permitted* by the First Prayer Book.

It is clear, therefore, that contemporaneous usage did not recognise the Rubric of 1549 as in any way binding. The cope was used (when used at all) not in

---

[75] *Liturgies of King Edward VI*, Parker Society, p. 157. *Original Letters*, p. 87.
[76] *Edwardian Liturgies*, p. 97.   [77] Strype's *Annals*, I.-189.
[77a] *Bishop Forbes on the Thirty-nine Articles*, Preface XIX., cf. *Hierurgia Anglicana*, p. 152.
[78] Milman's *Annals of St. Paul's*, p. 275.   Machyn's *Diary*, pp. 226-51.   [79] *Parker Correspondence*, p. 475.

compliance with *any* rubric, but on State occasions, as when Elizabeth visited King's College, Cambridge, in 1564, and the Provost "began Evensong, which also was solemnly sung, every man standing in his cope."[80]

On the other hand, the bare toleration of the cope by the authorities was naturally matter of complaint to those advanced Protestants who disliked even the surplice; which abundantly accounts for the cope figuring occasionally among the things which they desired to see "taken away." Their silence as to alb, tunicle and vestment clearly proves that the sacrificial dress had already disappeared.

But, it may be said, "you are forgetting the Ornaments Rubric which appeared in all printed Prayer Books from 1559 downwards till 1662." For convenience of comparison it is here printed side by side with the Statutory Rubric of 1559.

Statutory Rubrics of 1559.	*Elizabeth's alteration.*
The morning and Evening Prayer shall be used in such places of the Church, Chappel, or Chancel, and the Minister shall so turn him as the people may best hear. And if there be any controversie therein, the matter shall be referred to the Ordinary, and he or his deputy shall appoint the place, and the Chancels shall remain, as they have done in times past.	The morning and Evening Prayer shall be used in the accustomed place of the Church, Chappel, or Chancel, except it shall be otherwise determined by the Ordinary of the Place: and the Chancels shall remain, as they have done in times past.
And here is to be no-	And here is to be no-

---

[80] *Hierurgia Anglicana*, p. 150. Nichol's *Progresses of Queen Elizabeth*, pp. 163, 184.

THE ORNAMENTS RUBRIC 123

ted that the Minister at the time of the Communion, and at all other times in his ministration, shall use neither Alb, Vestment, nor Cope: but being Archbishop, or Bishop, he shall have and wear a Rochet: and being a Priest or Deacon, he shall have and wear a surplice only.	ted, that the Minister at the time of the Communion, and at all other times in his ministration, shall use such ornaments in the Church as were in use by Authority of Parliament in the second year of the reign of King *Edw*. VI. according to the act of Parliament set in the beginning of this Book.

It will be seen that the Elizabethan or "fraud-rubric" went beyond the Proviso annexed to the Act of Uniformity (Section 25), which was "set in the beginning" of the Prayer Book of 1559 (see above, p. 97).

1. By requiring that "*the Minister shall use*" the ornaments.
2. By adding that they were to be used "*in the Church*."
3. By specifying "*times of ministration*."
4. By substituting "*as were in use*" for the words "as was in this Church of England."
5. By recognising a distinctive dress for "the Communion," apart from "all *other* times in his ministration."

The change thus surreptitiously attempted will be readily seen by placing side by side the proviso itself, and the fraud-rubric.

Proviso added to Act of Uniformity (1 *Elizabeth, cap.* 2, *section* 25).	*Fraud-Rubric of* 1559 (*substituted without authority for the Rubric of* 1552, *re-enacted by* 1 *Elizabeth, cap.* 2, *section* 3).
"Provided always, and be it enacted, that such ornaments	"And here is to be noted that

of the Church, and of the ministers thereof	the **Minister at the time of the Holy Communion, and at all other times in his ministration**
shall be retained and be in use	shall **use** such ornaments in **the Church**
as was in this Church of England by the authority of Parliament	as were **in use** by authority of Parliament
in the second year of the reign of King Edward VI.	in the second year of the reign of King Edward the VI.
until other order shall be therein taken by [the] authority of the Queen's majesty, with the advice of her Commissioners appointed and authorised under the great seal of England for causes ecclesiastical, or of the Metropolitan of this realm."	according to the Act of Parliament set in the beginning of this book."

But Elizabeth's fraud-"rubric" had no *legal* value whatever. This was clearly laid down by the Privy Council in *Ridsdale* v. *Clifton*, when, after quoting the Proviso (Section 25th) of the Act, they added—

"The authorities whose duty it was to issue to the people, in 1559, a printed Book of Common Prayer, made conformable to the Statute, prefixed to the Book so issued by them a copy, *in extenso*, of the Statute of Elizabeth itself ; and they also *of their own authority, not by way of enactment or order,* but by way of a memorandum or reference to the Statute, SUBSTITUTED a new admonitory note or Rubric for the note immediately preceding the order of Morning Prayer in the Second Book of King Edward.[1]

That note or Rubric, as is pointed out by Bishop Gibson,[2] was *not inserted by any authority of Parliament*. It was meant to be a compendious and convenient summary of the enactment on this subject. If it was an accurate summary, it was merely a repetition of the Act. If it was inaccurate or imperfect, *the Act, and not the note, would be the governing rule*."

We are not concerned to conjecture what Elizabeth's motive may have been. Through life she held the view that Parliament ought to leave to the Crown all Church regulations, and her battle with the Commons as to the enactment of the Thirty-nine Articles has been graphically described by Dr. Lamb.[3] She altered the Homilies, the Articles, and the Canons of 1571 after they had left the hands of their respective framers, so that it was quite in keeping with her individual notions of prerogative to tamper with an authorised text. She *may* have really wished for the ritual of 1549, and this has been confidently asserted by Strype and others : but no particle of contemporary evidence goes to prove this, and it is remarkable that she herself never followed it, though indulging freely in a showy fancy ritual of her own from time to time. We know that in 1559 she was intriguing with the Spanish ambassador, endeavouring to persuade him that she was not far removed from " catholicism," and even pretended to be contemplating a marriage with

---

[1] This was, of course, *ultra vires* : as the Crown could not alter the statutory wording of the Prayer Book, especially with the words "and none other or otherwise" staring them in the face. (See above, p. 106.)

[2] Codex, Edition 1761, p. 296.

[3] *Historical Account of the Thirty-nine Articles*, p. 24. See also Professor Swainson's *Essay on the History of* Article twenty-nine.

Philip himself, or with his "cousin" the Archduke Charles. She *may* have feared that the ornaments would be wasted, and "embezzled" unless their actual use were insisted upon *until* the Visitors could go their rounds, or she *may* have merely wanted to keep a free hand to enable herself to turn either away as seemed most politic. But what is certain is that her Injunctions issued *at the same time with* the Prayer Book, classed "Vestments and copes," with the illegal books and ornaments which the Visitors ordered to be defaced;[81] and we have seen that the thirtieth of these Injunctions was understood by every one at the time to enforce the Rubric of 1552, *i.e.* the standard of the Second Prayer Book, which *alone* was legal in the "latter year of K. Edward." (See p. 38.) Mr. Kennion has even thought that immediately after inserting the fraud-rubrics in lieu of those enacted by Parliament, Elizabeth felt she had made a mistake and gave instructions to her Visitors to remove the distinctive ornaments of the First Prayer Book. On this view, the Injunctions of 1559 were the "other order" contemplated or sanctioned by Section 25 of the Act. (See p. 97.)

We know that she herself regarded the "Orders" printed at the end of the Injunctions of 1559 as the "further orders" contemplated by Section 26 of the Act.

"Her Highness talked with me once or twice in that point, and signified that there was one proviso in the act of the uniformity of Common Prayer, that by law is granted unto her, that if there be any contempt or irreverence used in the ceremonies or rites of the Church by the misusing of the orders

---

[81] *Injunction*, No. 47. See above, p. 36.

appointed in the book, the Queen's Majesty may, by the advice of her commissioners, or metropolitan, ordain and publish such further ceremonies, or rites, as may be most for the reverence or Christ's holy mysteries and sacraments, and *but for which law Her Highness would not have agreed to divers orders of the book.* And by virtue of which law she published *further order* in her injunctions both for the communion-bread, and for the placing of the tables *within the quire*." [85]

The "Order for the placing of the tables" illustrates also Elizabeth's own notion of what the phrase "other order" involved. It recites that in some places "the altars be not yet removed, upon opinion conceived of some *other order therein to be taken* by her majesty's visitors." [86] And it appears on the face of this Order that "in many and sundry parts of the realm the altars of the churches be removed, and tables placed for the administration of the holy Sacrament, *according to the form of the law therefore provided*," i.e. according to the Rubrics of the *Second* Prayer Book which recognised a table only.[87] But it seems to have been thought by some that under the Act of Uniformity the Royal Visitors, being "Commissioners under the great seal for causes ecclesiastical," had power to dispense in particular cases, for local reasons, with a strict observance of the

---

[85] Archbishop Parker to Cecil, Prime Minister, in *Parker's Correspondence*, p. 375. In the original MS. Parker had written "*the* orders of *this* book," Petyt MS. No. 47, fol. 53.

[86] Cardwell's *Documentary Annals*, I -201. Gee and Hardy, p. 439.

[87] Among the Petyt MSS., Vol. 538, 38, p. 29, are "Certeyne reasones to be offered to the Quene's Maties consideration why it is not convenient that the Communion should be ministered at an altar," in which the "Divines" (whom Strype supposes to be the Committee of Revisers, *Annals*, I.-i.-236) urged "that in a great number of places altars are removed and a table set up already, according to the *wordes* of the book now published." Strype had *altered* the title, and changed "wordes" into "rites." The whole paper deserves study.

law:[88] and this accords precisely with what was actually done in some cases as to the cope, and with the explanation given above of the meaning of "other order." Mr. James Parker has indeed endeavoured to account for the anomalous action in regard to the cope by assuming that certain "Interpretations," so called, drafted in 1561, which proposed to use the cope by itself[89] at Communion, and the surplice by itself at other services, may have been tacitly accepted as a valid act of legislation. But this is absurd, for two obvious reasons. First, the proposal was never adopted anywhere by anybody. Second, the document exists only as a draft unsigned by anyone, of unknown authorship, differing widely in the two copies still extant and manifestly not even finished. The version given by Strype is an extremely inaccurate blend of the Petyt MS. with the C.C.C. Cambridge copy. Lord Selborne conjectures that this unfinished draft was a "suggestion for future legislation,"[90] but it was never printed or published and is of no authority whatever. Mr. Parker himself regards these "Resolutions" (as one copy terms them) as "the basis of the first draft of the Advertisements,"[91] and as such they have merely a literary value.

However, the use actually made of the cope was equally irregular and anomalous whatever theory may be adopted: while its official destruction and

---

[88] For six months the Commissioners wielded the sole ecclesiastical jurisdiction of the country.

[89] This is clearly the meaning of the words "That there be used but *only one* apparel; as the cope in the ministration of the Lord's Supper, and the surplice at all other ministrations." Cardwell copies all Strype's blunders.

[90] *Notes on the Liturgy*, p. 12.   [91] *Letter to Selborne*, p. 98.

defacement by the Ordinaries or Visitors in 1559-66 can only be explained on the view that the *legal* rubric forbad the use of these dresses. Thus "the exception proves the rule."

My own view is that the Injunctions of 1559 were but administrative and executive directions intended to enforce the new, or rather the re-enacted Prayer Book of 1552, although the "Orders" appended at the end of those Injunctions may well have been "Further orders" under Section 26. Similarly, the Advertisements of 1566, having Royal authority, would undoubtedly operate as a repeal of the 1549 standard, *if* we are to admit the common interpretation of the meaning of the proviso. But a close scrutiny of all the contemporary estimates points rather to their having been issued under the 26th section, as a "*further* order," *i.e.* by way of *addition to* the standard of 1552. We know from the Spanish State papers, that in 1564 and 1565 the surplice was enforced just as exclusively before the Advertisements were issued, as afterwards,[92] and the Puritan complaints all point to a raising of the legal standard, not to any lowering of it.[93] The Advertisements gave for the first time a legal sanction to the hitherto merely tolerated cope-wearing, and made wearing the hood *compulsory* in cathedrals, while for parish churches the use of the surplice in the occasional offices (other than Baptisms and funerals) was also clearly prescribed. In 1571, long after the Advertise-

---

[92] Hume's *Calendar of State Papers from Simancas*, I-401, 406, 416. See also above, pp. 48-53 and 109-122.

[93] *Zurich Letters*, II -121, I.-158. "Capa, quæ tum lege abrogata est, nunc (July, 1566) publico decreto restituta est." L'Estrange, *supra* p. 81, regarded the Advertisements as a *further* order

ments had been enforced, Grindal wrote to Zanchy saying: "The law itself allows the Queen's majesty, with the advice of some of the bishops, to alter some things. Nothing, however, of the law has been either changed or diminished (*de lege nihil nec mutatum nec imminutum est*), nor, as far as I know, is there a bishop, who does not himself obey the prescribed rules, and also lead and persuade the rest to do the same."[94]

This statement is inconsistent with the notion that a law *requiring* alb, tunicle, and Chasuble ("vestment") had been repealed in 1566 by the power which Grindal here mentioned as reserved to the Queen by the statute. Yet Grindal himself, as his *Register*, p. 110, testifies, was one of the "Commissioners of her Royal Majesty" by whom the Advertisements were published.

Another evidence that the Rubric of 1552 was then recognised as being in force may be found in the pretext constantly put forward by the Nonconformists for disobeying the orders of the Bishops as to the observance of the Liturgy.

In 1583 was published *An abstract of certain Acts of Parliament*, of which there are two copies in the British Museum.[95] On p. 224 the writer says of the Advertisements:—

"The article that the minister shall wear a cope with Gospeler and pisteler agreably, smelleth of superstition, and as far as I can find both against her Highness' Injunctions, and besides the book of Common Prayer."

---

[94] Grindal's *Remains*, pp. 334, 339. Compare Bullinger's Letter, *Zurich Letters*, I.-348.
[95] "T. 2108," and "697, f. 15."

In 1584, Robert Beal, Clerk to the Privy Council, and a statesman of some eminence, presented to Archbishop Whitgift a "book" in MS. in which, discussing the Act of Uniformity, he said:—

"Seeing the statute made 1º of her majesty's reign is penal, and therefore to be literally and strictly understood (and it alloweth but of a book with 3 additions, and not otherwise) if there be no first book, nor ever was with such 3 additions, and not otherwise, then there is no allowance or confirmation of any law: and forasmuch as this book which we have, hath more additions, it is another book, and diverse from that which the law requireth and confirmed. And so hitherto there hath been no book published according to law at all."[96]

Strange as it may seem, it is literally true that no book printed during Elizabeth's long reign ever agreed with that prescribed by statute;[97] nay, more, the several editions differ, so that no two are exactly alike. It was Edward's Liturgy with the alterations made "*therein*," and not any of the varying *printed* books of Elizabeth, which the Act of Uniformity had sanctioned.

Among the Petyt MSS. now in the Inner Temple library is "Certaine motions whereupon a Conference is humbly desired before the Lords of the higher house, and a committee of the lower house," which has never yet been printed. At p. 320[98] it is urged—

"Seeing the statute requireth a book of common prayer with the 3 additions only and not otherwise differing from

---

[96] Strype's *Whitgift*, I.-285.
[97] Clay's *Liturgies and Occasional forms of Prayer set forth in the reign of Queen Elizabeth*, Preface, pp. xii, xiv. James Parker's *History of the Revisions of the Liturgy*, p. xliii.
[98] Petyt MS., 538, 36, No. xxi.

the booke of 5 Ed. VI. forasmuch as themselves in their Advertisements, articles confesse an alteration in the calendar since the 5 year of her Ma^{ts} reign: Whether the prelates have by the law of England any authority to alter the book at all."

At p. 322 there is an inconsistent grumble, asking—

"By what authority *the bishops omit the use of copes and the bearing of their pastoral staffe* which the book of the Q. and 3 Ed. VI. prescribeth, and whereunto the plat of the primo referreth for Rites as well as the minister for ornaments."

Evidently the Puritan draftsmen were more anxious to put the Bishops in the wrong, than to maintain any consistent position, as it is quite untrue that even the printed book of Elizabeth referred to the First Prayer Book for any "rites."

In 1605 appeared "A short dialogue, &c., whereunto are annexed certain considerations."[99] Among these considerations the fifteenth is—

"As for the ceremonies, though the book of Common Prayer used in the late Queen's time require them, yet neither is it the book which is by law established (differing in many things from K. Edward's book, whereas it should differ but in 3 only), as is elsewhere proved, neither doth the statute supposed to establish that book appoint any penalty for the not using of them."

In the same year appeared "Certain considerations drawn from the Canons of the last Sinod,"[100] which at p. 7, observes :—

"The book which the minister of the said church is bound to use should differ from the book of Common prayer authorised by the Act of parliament, 5 and 6 Ed. VI. but in 4 points, that is to say, 'one alteration, &c., and none other or otherwise.'"

---

[99] British Museum, T. 499. [100] British Museum, T. 49,993.

In 1641 the sub-committee appointed by the House of Lords specify among the " Innovations in discipline "—

" By pretending for their innovations, the Injunctions and Advertisements of Queen Elizabeth, which are not in force, but by way of commentary and imposition : and by PUTTING TO the Liturgy PRINTED ' secundo, tertio Edwardi sexti,' which the parliament hath reformed and laid aside."

Dr. Cardwell, who reports this,[101] scarcely seems to have understood the point of this contrast (viz. of Elizabeth's "*printed* book," and its reference to the 2 and 3 Edward VI., cap. i.), with the statutory book of 1552 and 1559, *i.e.* of the " 5 and 6 Edward VI," which contained no such reference till it was " put to " the legitimate text in the " printed " copies.

In 1660, Dr. Cornelius Burges, who had been one of the Lords' sub-committee in 1641, published *Reasons shewing the necessity of Reformation*,[102] in which, after mentioning various ceremonies objected to, he says— " all which were laid aside in 5 and 6 Edw. VI. as appears by the rubrics, and the Act of Uniformity in 1 Eliz. II. compared together, which allows nothing but what was in the book of 5 and 6 Edw. VI., save only the alterations *mentioned in the said Act*." Prynne and Zachariah Crofton adopt Burges' strictures on this point.

At the Savoy Conference in 1661 " exception " was taken to the fraud-rubric of Elizabeth on the ground that —

" Forasmuch as this rubric seemeth to bring back the cope, albe, &c., and other vestments *forbidden by the Common Prayer Book, 5 and 6 Edw. VI* . . we desire it may be wholly left out."

---

[101] *Conferences on the Book of Common Prayer*, p. 273.
[102] British Museum " E. 764 (4);" quoted also in *Hierurgia Anglicana*, p 328.

And, still more explicitly, they objected to the other fraud-rubric as to the "accustomed place," by saying —"We desire that the words of the first rubric may be expressed *as in the book established by authority of Parliament*, 5 and 6 Edw. VI."[103]

It is curious to notice the difficulty in which the bishops and their apologists found themselves when dealing with these objections. Under Elizabeth they were afraid to say that her printed book was a fraudulent misprint, not only because "Great Eliza" had a high-handed way of dealing with ecclesiastics who incurred her displeasure (as Archbishop Grindal and others found to their cost), but, beside this, parties were then so evenly balanced, and the diplomatic pressure of foreign powers upon the Queen of England was so urgent, that every one feared to repel her Majesty lest she should join the enemy's camp. Even the extreme Nonconformists, who were treated with great harshness by the Queen, were always most devoted, in words at least, to the Sovereign. Indeed it was a settled part of their policy[101] to throw all the blame of her action upon the bishops. They frequently taunted the bishops with the fact that the rubric of the *printed* book which they required them to use, gave a verbal sanction to the "mass gear" which neither the bishops themselves nor the conforming clergy ever used.

However telling as an *argumentum ad hominem* that might be, it really furnishes proof that the sacrificial vestments were not in actual use, for the complainants admitted that the bishops were quite as hostile to the

---

[103] Cardwell's *Conferences*, p. 314.
[104] See *Zurich Letters*, I.-235, II.-164; *Parker Correspondence*, p. 237; Strype's *Whitgift*, I.-414

Mass as themselves. More than this, they state explicitly that the sacrificial vestments were discarded by their opponents. Thus the *Answer for the Time*, published in 1566, says—

"What popish ceremonies you reject they are unholy, and what you will receive, that is good and orderly: you reject the vestment and retain the cope: you reject the alb and retain the surplice: you reject the stole and retain the tippet: you reject the shaven crown and retain the square cap" (p. 30).

Robert Johnson, a Puritan minister, and domestic chaplain to Lord Keeper Bacon, wrote to Bishop Sandys—

"You must yield some reason why the tippet is commanded and the stole forbidden: why the vestment is put away and the cope retained: why the alb is laid aside and the surplice used. . . why we may not with as good conscience refuse the surplice, as you refused the cope." (*Part of a Register*.)

"A Petition to her Majesty" was published in London in 1590 in which the petitioners speaking of the ordination of bishops, said "they retain the surplesse, seldom the coape, but they never use their pastoral staves": of the "tunick" they observe "this vesture is scarcely known at this day."[105]

Or, as Archbishop Whitgift in 1574 put it shortly, "all the popish apparel which *they used in their mass* this church hath refused" and "neither do we retain the massing Levitical apparel."[106]

The Act of Uniformity "set in the beginning of the

---

[105] British Museum, "108.6.2," pp. 64, 66. That the pastoral staff never came into use under Elizabeth, see Estcourt's *Anglican Ordinations*, p. 106; Whitgift's *Works*, I.-488; Pilkington's *Works*, pp. 584, 586.
[106] Whitgift's *Works*, III.-550.

book" and referred to by name in the printed "ornaments rubric" of Elizabeth, was the only law then recognised by the courts or the ordinaries, and the only law obeyed by the clergy, with of course the additions made from time to time by subsequent Orders of the Crown or by the Canons of 1604. No change was made in this respect under James, for, as Lord Selborne observes, " those rubrics were not mentioned or referred to in any of the alterations or additions then made, or in the King's Letters Patent or proclamation. The order to reprint the book, with the alterations and additions specifically mentioned, *could not make anything* not so mentioned (and as to which the King had not received the advice required by the statute) *part of the book of Common Prayer, unless it was so before.* The subsequent republication, therefore, of those rubrics did not alter their effect, or their relation to the law."[107]

In other words, Elizabeth's illegal fraud-rubric never became any part of the statutory Prayer Book, though at the Revision of 1661 a modification of the wording of the 25th section of the Act was substituted for it. But the history of that Revision is so absolutely distinct and separate that it ought to be treated in a separate paper by itself.

---

[107] *Notes on the Liturgy*, p. 31.

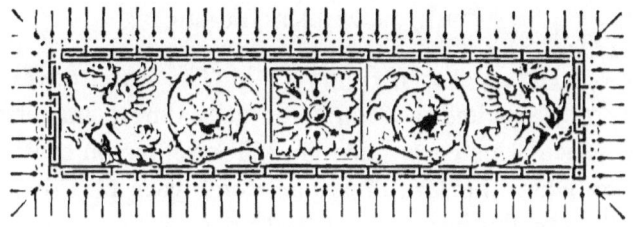

VI

The Ornaments Rubric. No. II. (1662)

ALTHOUGH the Prayer Book was proscribed from 1645 until the accession of Charles II., it did not cease to influence the minds of churchmen. In 1655 appeared (anonymously) the first commentary on it, to which in 1657 Sparrow attached his name, a third edition being called for in 1661. L'Estrange, a layman, published in 1659, his *Alliance of the Divine Offices*, exhibiting, as the title-page intimates, "All the Liturgies of the Church of England since the Reformation." In 1661 Sparrow published his *Collection of Articles*, &c., which included the Advertisements of Elizabeth.

To the men of that generation, these reprints were the only sources of information practically available on a subject which had not as yet interested any large class of students. The Prayer Books of Edward had been burned in every diocese under the proclamation of Philip and Mary in 1555, when the mere possession of a copy endangered the life of its owner under the revived Heresy Act of Henry IV.[1] The scarcity which naturally resulted accounts for the almost universal ignorance which prevailed in the seventeenth century as to what the Use of "the second year of Edward VI." actually implied. L'Estrange, in his preface, and Collier in his history,[2] testify to the difficulty of procuring a sight of the Edwardian Liturgies which had never been reprinted. Even Cosin's son-in-law, Dean Granville, could not get sight of a copy until 1683, when he found it in the Bodleian after he "had searched for it a great while with diligence."[3]

L'Estrange's reprint became the fountain of a new tradition, which will be readily understood from this facsimile of page 63 of the original edition of 1659—as shewn on the next page.

In the first column "Common Prayer" meant, of course, the printed book of King James I. referred to in the Eightieth Canon; and the "Certain Notes" at the *end* of the First Prayer Book were printed by themselves in a column parallel to the (so-called) Elizabethan "Rubric."

It will be seen that these "Certain Notes" (as printed in column 1) required only the surplice and hood for clergymen under the degree of a Bishop. Hence arose a tradition widely prevalent in 1661 that the surplice only was prescribed by the First Prayer Book. Strange as it may seem to us, that view was taken by the compiler of the MS. Notes made in an

---

[1] Cardwell's *Documentary Annals*, I.-167. Even Archbishop Whitgift had not seen a copy. (Strype's *Whitgift*, III.-92.) Very few copies of the First Prayer Book were ever printed. See p. 16.

[2] Collier's *Ecclesiastical History*, V.-282. "The book is very scarce. I grant it may be met with by parts" in L'Estrange.

[3] *Granville Correspondence*, Surtees Society, I.-172.

The Alliance of Divine Offices.

CHAP. III.

The order where Morning and Evening Prayer shall be used and said.

Common Prayer.	2 B. of Edw. 6.

Omitted in the 1. B. of Edw. 6. The morning and Evening Prayer shall be used in the accustomed place of the Church, Chappel, or Chancel, (B) except it *shall be otherwise determined by the Ordinary of the Place.* (C) *And the Chancels shall remain as they have done in times past.*

The morning and Evening Prayer shall be used in such places of the Church, Chappel, or Chancel, and the Minister shal so turn him as the people may best hear. And if there be any controversie therein, the matter shall be referred to the Ordinary, and he or his deputy shall appoint the place. And the Chancels shall remain as they have done in times past.

1. B. of Edw. 6.	The Common Prayer.	2. Book of Edw. 6.

In the saying of Mattens and Evensong, Baptizing & Burying, the Minister in Parish Churches and Chappels annext to the same (E) *shall use a Surplice. And in all Cathedral Churches and Colledges, the Arch-Deacons, Deans, Provosts, Masters, Prebendaries and fellows being Graduates, may use in the quire, besides their Surplices, such hoods as pertaine to their several degrees, which they have taken in any university within this Realm. But in all other places every Minister shall be at liberty to use any Surplice or no. It is also seemly that Graduats when they do preach should use such hoods as pertaine to their several degrees.*

And whensoever the Bishop shall celebrate the holy Communion in the Church, or execute any other publick ministration: he shall have upon him beside his Rochet a Surplice or Alb, and a Cope or Vestment, and also his Pastoral staffe ni his hand, or else born or holden by his Chaplain.

And here is to be noted, that the Minister at the time of the Communion, and at all other times in his ministration shall use (D) such ornaments in the Church as were in use by Authority of Parliament in the 2. year of the reign of King Edw. the 6th. according to the act of Parliament set in the beginning of the Book.

Scotch Liturgy.
And here is to be noted, that the presbyter or Minister at the time of the Communion, and at other times of his ministration, shall use such Ornaments in the Church, as are prescribed, or shall be by his Majesty or his successors according to the Act of Parliament provided in that behalf.

And here is to be noted, that the Minister at the time of the Communion and at all other times in his ministration shall use neither Alb, Vestment, nor cope, but being Arch-Bishop, or Bishop he shall have and wear a Rochet, and being a Priest or Deacon, he shall have and wear a surplice only

interleaved Prayer Book of 1625 which now forms Harleian MS. 7311 in the British Museum.[4] The writer appears from internal evidence to have been a member of Convocation, and makes a variety of suggestions for the (then) forthcoming revision. The same view was taken also by Dr. Cornelius Burges (1660) and Prynne (1661) on the side of the Puritans, as well as by Savage, the Master of Balliol and Chaplain to Charles II., who replied to them.[5] Even Bishop Wren, when he wrote in 1641, held the same view.[6] And the really learned Joseph Bingham, when replying directly to Baxter's attack on the new Ornaments Rubric in the book cited on p. 145 quoted the Rubric from the *end* of the First Prayer Book, and added :—

> "This it was that led Mr. B. into his mistake. He had heard something of albes and other ornaments in use in King Edward's time, but he unluckily put the Bishop's robes upon every private minister: whereas no other ornament belonged to them but only the hood or surplice, the one enjoined, the other allowed or recommended."

He then quotes the Fifty-eighth Canon, and concludes triumphantly, "Where is now the contradiction between this canon and the rubrics? They all speak of surplices and hoods, but of no other ornaments belonging to private ministers."[7] Nor was this peculiar to Bingham.

---

[4] The reference is on p. 45. For some account of this MS., formerly attributed to Cosin, see Cosin's *Works*, V.-xxi., Parker's *History of the Revisions of the Prayer Book*, p. 427. On p. 152 he explains "North side" as designed "to avoid the fashion of the popish priests, who stand with their faces to the East;" and at p. 159 he says "we never use any water in the sacramental wine."

[5] Droop's *Edwardian Vestments*, pp. 65-70.

[6] *Parentalia*, p. 92. Edition 1750.

[7] Bingham's *Works*, VIII.-114.

Dr. C. Burges, who had been one of the Committee of Divines in 1641, writing in 1660, said, "The book of 2 Ed. VI. enjoins only a surplice in parish churches and chappels. See *last page* of that book, where are Notes for explanation." [8]

Archdeacon Sharp, writing in 1753, said:—

"So that the injunction concerning the habits and ornaments of ministers, which is *at the end* of King Edward's first Service Book, with its explanation in the Act of Uniformity by Q. Elizabeth, is the legal or statutable rule of our Church habits at this day." [9]

A very popular book at one time was "The Clergyman's Vade Mecum," by John Johnson of Cranbrook, of which the second edition appeared in 1706. The writer said:—

"There must likewise be in every parish church and chapel, a surplice, which the minister is obliged to use, in saying mattins, evensong, baptizing, burying, etc., in churches and parochial chapels; the minister in other places shall have liberty to use any surplice or no, by a Rubric *at the end* of Ed. VI.'s Common Prayer Book authorized in the second year of his reign, and enforced by the Rubric immediately before Morning Prayer in our present Liturgy" (p. 19).

In the third edition (1709) the writer had at length discovered—

"The occasion of which mistake was, that we looked no further, than to the long rubric at the *end* of that book" (p. 21, note).

Nicholls in 1710 gives only the *final* rubrics from Edward's First Book in *his own* commentary on the

---

[8] *Reasons shewing the Necessity of a Reformation*, p. 12. The chapter is headed "some of the differences and alterations in the present Common Prayer Book from the Book *established by Law*, in quinto and sexto Edw. 6, and 1 Eliz."

[9] *Sharp on the Rubric*, p. 208.

Ornaments Rubric, though he published Cosin's *Notes* in an Appendix.

In our own day Canon Trevor has vindicated this view,[10] urging that the special rubrics at the beginning of the Communion Office of 1549 disappeared together with that special Office just as the "chrysome" and the "chrismatory" disappeared with the Baptismal Office of 1549. The Sacrificial Vestments were never in the Church "BY authority of *Parliament*" in the sense in which the surplice and hood and the eucharistic cope exclusively were: they rested on older canons and rubrics which had no "authority of *Parliament*."

It is highly probable that this belief (whether mistaken or not) made the acceptance of the revised "Ornaments Rubric" a mere matter of course in 1662. No debate or discussion whatever appears to have arisen respecting it in Convocation.[11] The list of "alterations" prefixed to the book in which all the important changes were carefully entered up during the revision of 1661 does not even allude to any change in the wording of the Ornaments Rubric. A footnote to the list, explains: "These are all ye materiall alterations: ye rest are onely verball: or ye changing of some Rubrics for ye better performing of ye service: or ye new moulding of some of ye collects." [12]

The slight regard paid by Convocation to the changes made in the wording of the rubric is fatal to the

---

[10] In his *Disputed Rubrics*, p. 45. Hence Cosin in his younger days had proposed that the rubrics of the Communion Service in Edward's First Prayer Book be "*here* inserted and repeated," viz. at the beginning of the Communion Office. See below, p. 196.

[11] Parker's *History of the Revisions of the Prayer Book*, p. 409.

[12] See the facsimile Black-letter Prayer Book of 1661 published for the Ritual Commission in 1870, p. 4.

contention that Cosin and his brother bishops *designed* to repeal, by means of it, the Injunctions of 1559, the Royal Advertisements of 1566, and the Fifty-eighth Canon, in order to reinstate in 1662 the sacrificial vestments of 1548-9. The Committee of Revision, presided over by Bishop Wren, expunged from the Elizabethan " Rubric" the words which, by differentiating "the Holy Communion" from "all *other* times," might have seemed to imply a distinctive dress for Holy Communion. Wren had himself urged in 1660—

" But what is now fit to be ordered herein, and to preserve those that are still in use, it would be set down in express words, without *these uncertainties which breed nothing but debate and scorn.* The very words too of that Act, 2 Ed. VI., for the minister's ornaments, would be set down, or to pray to have a new one made; for *there is somewhat in that Act that now may not be used.*" [13]

"These uncertainties," and the "somewhat," indicate the thickness of the fog in which all parties found themselves; which was owing to the crooked policy of Elizabeth (or her Council), in tampering with the Ornaments Rubric of 1552, which had been re-enacted in 1559 by the third section of 1 Elizabeth, cap. ii.

The timidity which prevented the Elizabethan bishops from stating publicly that the *printed* Prayer Books issued by the Government were inaccurate and unauthorised as regards their *non-Parliamentary* "alterations and additions" may have been politic, but it seriously embarrassed their successors in office. Before the death of Elizabeth the sacrificial dresses had disappeared so completely that at the Hampton Court Conference the only "ornament of the minister" complained of was

[13] Jacobson's *Fragments*, p. 55.

"the"[14] surplice. In 1641 there appeared a manifesto entitled "The abolishing of the book of Common Prayer by reason of above 50 gross superstitions in it . . being the substance of a book which the ministers of Lincoln diocese delivered to King James I., the first of December, 1605,"[15] in which there is no mention of the Ornaments Rubric nor of any dress save "the" surplice which is coarsely abused as "injoyned in their idolatrous masse."[16] As the same allegation is sometimes made by Ritualists, for a like polemical purpose, it may be well to quote Pugin's comment on the Council of Cologne, A.D. 1260, which directed a *vestis camisialis* to be worn at mass under the alb, which, he says, "can hardly mean the surplice, but rather an under garment of some sort."[17] "The surplice" of the Injunctions, Advertisements and Visitation Articles is described as "large" and "with large and wide sleeves," in contrast with the tight-fitting alb, which was essentially an under garment. The two official apologies, viz. Durel's *Vindiciæ*, dedicated to Charles II.,[18] and Falkner's *Libertas Ecclesiæ*,[19] dedicated to Archbishop Sheldon, both point out that the surplice was neither a "consecrated" nor a Mass ornament.

Laud's unpopular "restorations," however, revived the older complaints which, as in the time of Parker and Whitgift, had always been treated as too unreal to deserve any formal reply. Englishmen knew that neither alb, vestment, nor tunicle had been heard of since the Act of Elizabeth had been "set in the

---

[14] Cardwell's *Conferences*, p. 163.
[16] *Ibid.*, p. 4.
[18] p. 123.
[15] BritishMuseum, E. 178-2.
[17] *Glossary*, p. 222.
[19] Book II., cap. iv., sec. 1-9.

beginning of the book"; while the High Commission was seen day by day enforcing the wearing of "*the surplice*" at Communion in despite of the contrary directions of the First Prayer Book. To maintain the *status quo ante bellum*, it seemed to them unnecessary to make any change; indeed the pride of the Tory-Cavaliers, as well as of the strong Churchmen, opposed any alteration which might seem to admit that their predecessors had ever been in the wrong, or that their opponents had ever been in the right. The exasperations of the recent civil war rendered the Episcopalian clergy but ill-disposed to make concessions.

Hence, at the Savoy Conference, the curt answer was returned, " We think it fit that the rubric continue as it is."[20] The rejoinder of the "Presbyterians," which Cardwell does not print, spoke of the ceremonies of 1549 as "absolute,"[21] *i.e.* obsolete: and in 1690 Baxter admits that—

"We know not what was then in use". "We meet with few Conformists that know what was then in use. And we see that all those that subscribe or consent to this, yet use them not."—"We must know what it was, and *whether no act of Parliament have since reversed that which then was used.*"[22]

If Baxter, the leader at Savoy, knew nothing about the "Vestments," it is not likely that at that time anyone else knew much more.

Wiser counsels afterwards prevailed. It seems to have struck somebody that by adopting "the very

---

[20] Cardwell's *Conferences*, p. 351.
[21] Bayne's *English Puritanism*, p. 305.
[22] *English Nonconformity*, second edition, chapter XX., Point XVII. The proofs of Cosin's ignorance will be found below at pages 177 to 190.

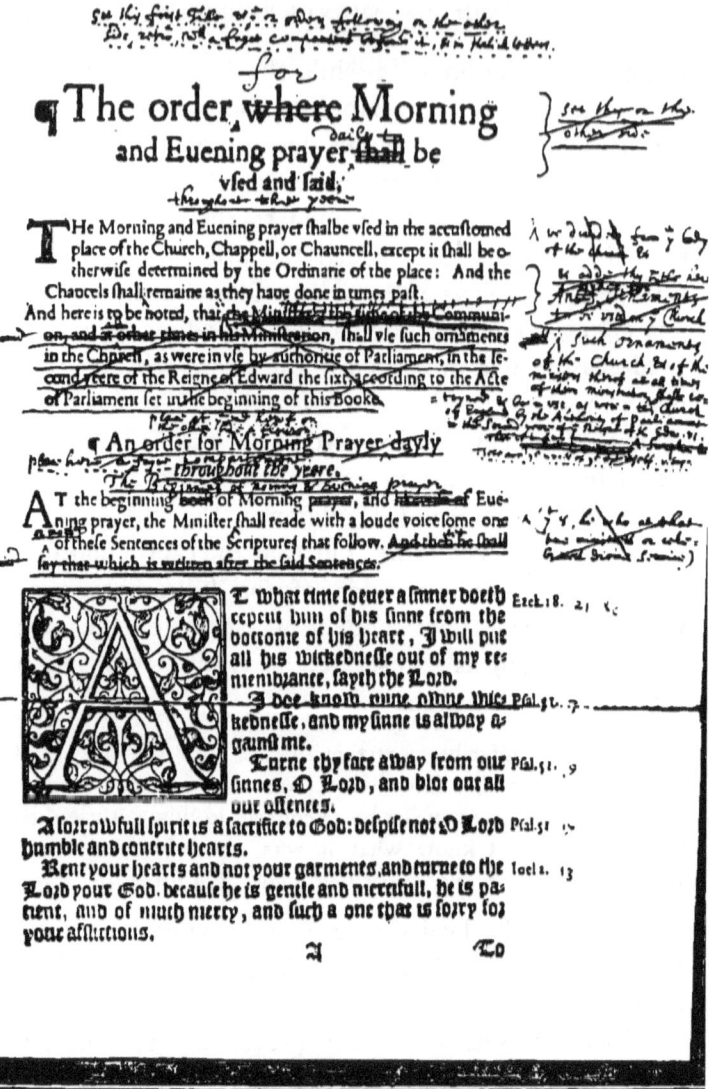

¶ The order for Morning
and Euening prayer daily be
vſed and ſaid,

THe Morning and Euening prayer ſhalbe vſed in the accuſtomed place of the Church, Chappell, or Chauncell, except it ſhall be otherwiſe determined by the Ordinarie of the place: And the Chancels ſhall remaine as they haue done in times paſt.
And here is to be noted, that the Miniſter at the time of the Communion, and at other times in his Miniſtration, ſhall vſe ſuch ornaments in the Church, as were in vſe by authoritie of Parliament, in the ſecond yeere of the Reigne of Edward the ſixt, according to the Acte of Parliament ſet in the beginning of this Booke.

¶ An order for Morning Prayer dayly throughout the yeare.

AT the beginning both of Morning prayer, and likewise of Euening prayer, the Miniſter ſhall reade with a loude voice ſome one of theſe Sentences of the Scriptures that follow. And then he ſhall ſay that which is written after the ſaid Sentences.

T what time ſoeuer a ſinner doeth Ezek.18. 21
repent him of his ſinne from the
bottome of his heart, I will put
all his wickedneſſe out of my remembrance, ſayth the Lord.
I doe know mine owne wickedneſſe, and my ſinne is alway againſt me. Pſal.51. 7
Turne thy face away from our ſinnes, O Lord, and blot out all our offences. Pſal.51. 9
A ſorrowfull ſpirit is a ſacrifice to God: deſpiſe not, O Lord Pſal.51
humble and contrite hearts.
Rent your hearts and not your garments, and turne to the Ioel 2. 13
Lord your God, becauſe he is gentle and mercifull, he is patient, and of much mercy, and ſuch a one that is ſorry for your afflictions.

A   To

FROM THE "DURHAM BOOK" SHEWING THE FIRST STAGE IN THE REVISION OF 1661.

And the & and in thy Title here
~~Communi~~
naments
in the se-
the Acte

{ ~~An Act of Uniformity~~
~~for & into the Church~~ }

: Such ornaments
of the Church, & of the
ministers thereof at all times
of their Ministration shall be
retained and be in use in this Church
of England by the Authority of Parliament
in the Second year of K. Edw. VI.
~~that is to say~~ ———— A footnote to
———————————— be
set out yt would of it itself, v. infra.

ENLARGEMENT OF THE DRAFT "ORNAMENTS RUBRIC" SHEWN ON LAST PAGE.

words" of the statute, they might obviate the objection of irregularity which undoubtedly did attach to Elizabeth's "fraud-rubric." Clarendon tells us that—

"The bishops had spent the vacation' [which lasted from July 30 to Nov. 20, 1661] 'in making such alterations in the Book of Common Prayer as they thought would make it more grateful to the dissenting brethren."[23]

The result of the labours of this informal Committee are embodied in the "Durham Book," of which an account is given at page 191.

The above photographic reproduction of a page of this book, together with the enlarged facsimile of the new wording, will shew the steps by which the present form of the rubric was reached. First, it had been proposed to insert as a heading, "Of Ornaments to be used in the Church," which was after corrected into "An order for Ornaments," &c. Lastly, this was struck out again. Then the word "all" (carelessly omitted by the Jacobean printers) was inserted before "times of ministration" with the object of retaining the rubric unchanged ; as, indeed, had been threatened at the Savoy. But, after debate, this has been again changed by striking out all the words peculiar to Elizabeth's fraud-rubric (thus getting rid of any allusion to a distinctive dress for the Holy Communion) and by substituting the words of the Proviso (sec. 25 of Elizabeth's Act) with the (after ?) addition of the words "that is to say . . . ." The blank left was doubtless intended to be filled up afterwards: but after further debate a line was dashed through the row of dots, and the words "A Surplice, &c.," were filled in. Com-

---

[23] *Life*, Vol. II., p. 118.

paring this with the Visitation articles of the Bishops which were published during the next twelve months, the "&c." clearly meant "with tippet and hood according to his degree." The Revisers could not have intended to lump the Mass Vestments under a mere "&c." as appendages to "A Surplice."

Underneath the new rubric were written (with the dotted line under to shew that it was a mere direction to the printer, and not to be printed), the explanatory words, "these are the words of the Act itself *v.* supra," *i.e.* the Act of Elizabeth, "set in the beginning."

The rubric thus recast appears to have been adopted by Convocation *without debate*.[21]

It may be regretted that the intention to enumerate the lawful ornaments was not carried out, but it was probably found to be more difficult than at first sight appeared. The "magpie" of the bishops did not rest upon the "Ornaments Rubric" either for its scarf or its chimere, which were really portions of the outdoor dress, retained in service time by custom alone. Similarly the customary "tippet" or scarf of the "inferior clergy" was a portion of their outdoor attire, though specially extended to non-graduates by the Canons of 1604; while the *compulsory* use of the hood rested on the Advertisements and Canons alone. Lastly the dress of the preacher might have to be prescribed, and all these would be difficult to weld into a borrowed sentence professing to relate in some way to an Act of "Parliament in the second year of

---

[21] Mr. James Parker has shewn that on November 22nd between the hours of 8 and 10 A.M., the Book was read as far as the end of the Litany, involving the change of over three thousand words.—*History of the Revisions of the Prayer Book.* p. 409.

Edward VI." Beside, the wearing of copes having been ordered by the Canons of 1604, still in force, would also have to be recognised; and this, as we have seen, pp. 117-122, was a totally different "Use" from that of the First (or any other) Prayer Book. Cosin was present, and it is possible that he may have aired the theories which in his younger "Notes" he had copied from the "Survey"; and if so, it might be found convenient to evade their discussion. But there is no evidence that Cosin at any time communicated his earlier theories to any of his contemporaries; whereas Sparrow[25] and Wren[26] are known to have held a view opposite to his.

A more interesting inquiry is, in what sense were the words "retained and be in use" taken over from the old Act, in the revision of 1661? It is not probable that the antiquarian learning of the revisers would suffice to make them understand the restricted meaning of the older language; while Parliament would assuredly enact the newly introduced words in their modern sense, as if speaking from 1662. Mr. Justice Coleridge in *The Queen* v. *The Justices of Kent* (2 Q. B., p. 691) says "words used in a consolidation act may have a different meaning from that of the *same words* when used in any one of the acts comprehended." The Parliament of 1662 could not order to be "retained" ornaments which had long ceased to exist. It must be remembered that on the accession of Charles, the Prayer Book had immediately regained its legal status; for, as the Preface to the present book reminds us, the "laws had never been repealed." During the long

---

[25] See pp. 81, 199. [26] See p. 198.

interval from May 29th, 1660, to August 24th, 1662, the Liturgy with its appropriate "ornaments" had been restored and in actual use. In the British Museum alone there are seven separate editions of the Prayer Book (beside an Ordinal of 1661) issued during those two years which preceded the publication of the revised book; and Mr. Parker mentions some others. "A whole year before the Act of Uniformity commenced," proceedings were taken against a Mr. Oliver Heywood, of Coley, in Yorkshire, who was suspended *ab officio* for not reading the old service.[27] The word "retained" then, would be understood, in 1662, to mean the perpetuation of what (had long been and) then was in actual and accredited existence. This is proved, moreover, by the fact that the Canons of 1604 (the fifty-eighth of which ordered the surplice *at Communion*) were reprinted in 1660; and again in July, 1662, they were "published for the due observance of them by His Majesty's authority."[28] Nearly every Ordinary asked for the "Book of the Canons" at the ensuing Visitation.

The intention of the legislature is shewn beyond doubt by the proposal of the House of Lords to give the King power to dispense clergymen from wearing "the surplice," which was rejected by the Commons on the ground that it was incongruous "at the time you are settling *uniformity*, to establish schism."[29] Again, in 1667-8, two relief bills were brought in, each making "the surplice" optional, and both alike ignoring the reputed "ornaments" of 1549.

---

[27] Kennet's *Chronicle*, p. 722.   [28] *Ibid.*, p. 725.
[29] Swainson's *History of the Act of Uniformity*, pp. 45, 59.

Yet the Lord Keeper, the Lord Chief Justice, and Lord Chief Baron, all of whom had been parties to the passing of the Act of Uniformity, were among the promoters of this "relief."[30]

After 1662, as well as before it, the Act of Elizabeth remained, as it still remains the primary law of Ornaments.

This was recognised in a variety of ways.

In the "Durham Book," the Act was numbered "1" in the Table of Contents, and its title was completed by the addition of the words "made in the first year of the reign of Queen Elizabeth." In Cosin's writing appear several proposed amendments of the wording of the Act, which were afterwards erased, but Sancroft has written against the erasures "stet," as if desiring to have them reconsidered; and the same passages are marked "q" in his Bodleian fair copy. The proposal was dropped, and indeed it was inherently absurd: yet it shews how the continuity of the Act was taken for granted. On the other hand, the proclamation of James was struck out by the revisers, and his action, having been *ultra vires*, was completely ignored in the subsequent statute.

On January 24th, 1662, the House of Bishops "discussed of and about the Act of Parliament concerning the Book of Common Prayer,"[31] which may mean whether the Act of Elizabeth should be retained in the Prayer Book already subscribed by the Convocations, or not. At any rate this statute, unlike every other on the statute book, was subscribed by every member of Convocation and has the full

---

[30] Thorndike's *Works*, Anglo-Catholic Library, V.-301-8.
[31] *Synodus Anglicana*, p. 98, Appendix.

"spiritual" authority of the "sacred synod" added to that of the Crown and Parliament! On Tuesday, April 15th, 1662, the Commons also debated as to making "the Act of Primo Elizabethae for enjoining it to be used" apply to the revised book.[32] That Act remains therefore in full force and is an essential part of the Prayer Book to this day, and it has been invoked as "the governing rule" in all the ritual suits which professed to deal with ornaments.

It deserves to be remembered also that the House of Commons desired to enact Edward's *Second* book, and caused it to be searched for, but in vain. Failing that, they next selected a book of 1604[33] in order to get behind the supposed Laudian alterations. That book of 1604 was, accordingly, read three times and sent up to the Lords who also read the Bill relating to it a first time and then waited for the Convocation Book, which, however, the Commons refused to adopt until a Committee of their own House had minutely scrutinised it to see what the alterations were. This jealousy of Laudian changes (such as Cosin's "Notes" had suggested, and Convocation had rejected) is in itself proof that it was not the intention of Parliament

---

[32] *History of the Revisions of the Prayer Book*, p. 470.

[33] In the British Museum, numbered "C. 25,;H. 13," is a copy of the edition thus adopted. It is identified by the "two" prayers which had to be partly "taken out" and partly "obliterated" because they had been printed (without authority) on the back of the last leaf which contained the end of the Commination Service and the word "Finis." Mr. Wayland Joyce fancied that the Commons proposed to enact Sternhold and Hopkins (!), not having observed that these last were by a different publisher and are printed on different paper, though accidentally bound up with the British Museum copy. His statements about the language of the Earl of Dorset on this point are simply untrue (*Acts of the Church*, p. 241) and his account of the action of the various Committees is altogether inaccurate.

in 1662 to go back an entire century, and to render the Canons of 1604 inoperative and inconsistent with their new book.

But the crucial test is to see what was *done* by the responsible Ordinaries when the Act of Uniformity was recent and while the framers of both the rubric and the Act were looking on as keenly interested spectators, under the vigilant criticism of the disestablished nonconformists. We are able to call as witnesses nearly *every Bishop who sat on the bench* at the time of the last Revision of the Prayer Book.

At the head of these, stands the aged

ARCHBISHOP JUXON whose Articles, issued in 1663, were overlooked in the Report of the Ritual Commission.[34] The Primate asked—

"Doth your Parson, Vicar, or Curate, saying public prayers, ministering Sacraments, or other Rites of the Church, wear a decent Surplice with a hood (if he be a graduate) agreeable to his degree in the University?"

ARCHBISHOP FREWEN had issued in the year 1662, Articles for the diocese and province of York which also escaped the Ritual Commissioners. He asked—

"Have you . . . a decent Surplice, one or more, for your Parson, Vicar, Curate, or Lecturer, to wear in the time of public ministration?" Again, "Doth he wear *the* Surplice while he performs that office, *or other* offices mentioned in the Common Prayer Book?"[35]

Next to these we may place the Bishop who presided both at the "Savoy Conference" (owing, perhaps, to the accident that he was himself then

---

[34] A copy is in the British Museum, "5515. c. 54."
[35] *Archdeacon Harrison on the Rubrics*, p. 176.

"Master of the Savoy") and in Convocation (owing to the great age of Archbishop Juxon). The Ritual Commission give no Articles of Archbishop Sheldon's, but Cardwell publishes his "Letter concerning the King's Directions to the Clergy,"[36] 1670, in which Archbishop Sheldon charges his clergy that—

> "In their churches they do decently and solemnly perform the Divine Service by reading the prayers of the Church, as they are appointed and ordered in and by the Book of Common Prayer, without addition to or diminishing from the same, *or varying, either in substance or ceremony* from the order and method, which by the said book is set down, wherein I hear and am afraid too many do offend; and that in the time of such their officiating, they ever make use of, and wear *their priestly* habit, *the* surplice and hood."

WREN deserves to be mentioned next, because at his house, "Ely House," an important stage of the revision was perfected, and to him is due a larger number of alterations than to any other of the Bishops. (See p. 193.) In 1641, he prepared for Parliament a statement that Queen Elizabeth's Advertisements "are authorised by law, 1 Eliz. c. ii., sec. penult."[37]—words which almost decide the meaning of Sancroft's "*these are the words of the Act itself sec. penult. ut supra.*" Nothing is more likely than that these words were dictated by Wren as Chairman of the Committee meeting at "Ely House." In 1662 Wren simply repeated the language of his former Articles of 1636.

> "Doth your minister and curate, at all times . . . in administering the Holy Sacraments . . . and all other offices

---

[36] Cardwell's *Documentary Annals*, II.-278. Compare Bishop Gibson. *Synodus Anglicana*, p. 242. [37] *Parentalia*, p. 75.

of the Church, duly observe the orders and rites prescribed, *without omission, alteration,* or addition of *anything?* And doth he, in performing all and *every* of these, wear *the* surplice duly, and never omit the wearing of the same, nor of his hood, if he be a graduate?" [38]

Cosin had asked as Archdeacon in 1627—

"Doth he .. when any sacrament is to be administered or any other rite or ceremony of the Church solemnised, use and wear *the* surplice, without excuse or pretence whatsoever? And doth he never omit the same?" [39]

After the New Prayer Book had been enacted he visited his diocese in 1662, asking

"Have you a large and decent surplice (one or more) for the minister to wear at *all times of his public ministration in the Church?*

"Have you .. a hood or tippet for the minister to wear over his surplice, if he be a graduate?

"Doth he always at the reading or celebrating any divine office in your church or chappel, constantly wear *the* surplice, and other his ecclesiastical habit *according to his degree?* And doth he never omit it?" [40]

Both in 1662 and in 1668 Cosin's only question under this head to his Cathedral staff was

"Does every one that is bound to come to church put on his habit of surplice, tippet and hood according to his degree?" [41]

HACKET, Bishop of Lichfield, in 1662, asks—

"Hath he read the Book of Common Prayer as it is enjoined by the late Act of Uniformity, .. and did, and doth he, wear *the* surplice while he performed that office, and other offices mentioned in that Common Prayer Book?" [42]

---

[38] *Second Report of the Ritual Commission,* pp. 559-8. cf. 561, foot-note.
[39] Cosin's Works, II.-8, 9.
[40] *Second Report of the Ritual Commission,* p. 601.
[41] *Granville Correspondence,* Surtees Society, I.-256, 270.
[42] *Second Report of the Ritual Commission,* p. 609.

IRONSIDE, Bishop of Bristol, 1662, asks—

"Doth your minister, when he readeth publique prayers or administer the sacrament, wear a comly surplice *with sleeves*? And if he be a graduate, such hood as by the orders of the University is agreeable to his degree?"[13]

EARLE [?], Bishop of Worcester, 1662—

"Have you a fair surplice and other *ornaments, according to his degree*, for your minister to use in his public administrations, only for outward decency, order, and distinction?"[14]

***

The next series of Visitation Articles has a special history of its own. On June 21st, 1661, the Upper House of Convocation appointed a committee to prepare a standard book of Articles; and on February 2nd, 1662, this task was further relegated to Cosin. On March 8th, 1662, Cosin, "according to the order given to him and the charge committed to him, introduced and delivered into the hands of the Lord President" (Sheldon) his draft Articles, and "it was unanimously agreed that the same Articles should be sent to the Lord Archbishop of Canterbury' (Juxon) 'for his perusal and due consideration of them, and for his emendation, reformation, and correction of them."[45] On June 26th, 1662, Skinner, Bishop of Oxford, wrote to Sheldon to inquire about them, saying, "I well hoped to have seen that uniform book of Articles (viz. for Visitations) before this day, resting assured that no pretences could take of [f?] your lordship's resolution

---

[13] *Second Report of the Ritual Commission*, Appendix, p. 614.
[14] *Ibid.*, p. 604. See Note 52, below.
[45] *History of the Revisions of the Prayer Book*, p. 463. Lord Selborne's *Notes*, p. 53. Swainson's *Rubrical Question*, pp. 33, 113. Droop's *Edwardian Vestments*, p. 76, note.

from what so much concerns the honour and peace of the Church." [46]

It seems probable that Cosin's Articles, quoted above, represent the draft as originally sent to Juxon, and that the series published by the Ritual Commission, p. 615, are the same Articles after their correction by Juxon. Morley was confirmed Bishop of Winchester on May 14th, 1662, just five days before the statute enacting the new Prayer Book received the Royal Assent.

MORLEY's Articles were also used by nine other bishops in 1662, viz. Bishops PIERS, KING, WARD, CROFT, SANDERSON, LLOYD, SKINNER, LANEY, and LUCY, as well as by various archdeacons in 1662, and by other Ordinaries in after years. This gives special importance to their "uniform" inquiry.

"Doth your minister at the reading or celebrating *any* Divine office in your church or chappel wear *the* surplice, together with such other scholastical habit as is suitable to his degree?" [47]

HENCHMAN, Bishop of Salisbury, however, preferred to issue Articles of his own. He asked, in 1662,

"Doth your Minister reading Divine service and administering the Sacraments and other Rites of the Church, wear *the* surplice *according to the Canons?*" [48]

Those last words are very important, and may be compared with Bishop Juxon's Articles of 1663 before mentioned. Juxon asked—

"Art. XXII. Doth your Parson, Vicar, or Curate reade in

---

[46] Tanner MS. quoted in *Cosin Correspondence*, Surtees Society, II.-xvi.

[47] *Second Report of the Ritual Commission*, Appendix, pp. 616-vii.

[48] *Ibid.*, p. 611. Kennet, p. 771, shews that Henchman's Visitation was in September, 1662.

your parish-church or chapel the Canons of the Church upon some Sundays or holy days in the afternoon before Divine service; so dividing the same that one half may be read one day and the other half the other day?"

Cosin, Henchman, Ironside, and the twenty-two Ordinaries cited in the *Ritual Commission Report*, p. 615, insist on each Parish having "the Book of the Canons."

It is clear therefore that they knew nothing of the theory that the Canons of 1604 could have been repealed by the later Act of Uniformity.

REYNOLDS, in November, 1662, merely asks—

"Have you a *large* Surplice for the use of the Minister in his public Administrations?" [49]

GRIFFITH, Bishop of St. Asaph, asks in general terms whether the Minister duly observes the Orders, Rites and Ceremonies "as in the said Book of Common Prayer is enjoyned?" But he asks for catechising "*before* Evening Prayer," shewing that he held the Fifty-ninth Canon to be still in force and unrepealed in 1662.[50]

NICHOLSON, Bishop of Gloucester, at his Visitation in 1661, had asked—

"Doth your Minister, at the reading or celebrating of *any* solemn divine office in the church or chapel wear *the* Surplice"[51]

He calls it a "*comely large surplice*." But his later articles have not been met with.

GAUDEN, Bishop of Exeter (afterwards Bishop of Worcester), in his "Considerations touching the

---

[49] *Second Report of the Ritual Commission*, Appendix, pp. 619-vi.
[50] *Ibid.*, pp. 607-11.
[51] *Harrison on Rubrics*, p. 176.

Liturgy," [52] describes the ceremonies "*retained*" as "the cross (in Baptism), surplice, standing up at the creed, or kneeling at the Lord's Supper."

DUPPA died, March 26th, 1662, before issuing any Articles: and the bishopric of Sodor and Man was vacant till 1665.

STERNE, of Carlisle, ROBERTS, of Bangor, FEARNE, of Chester, and WARNE, of Rochester, are the only missing links in this episcopal catena. There is no reason to think that they differed from the rest of their brethren.

However, from *Carlisle* diocese, we can produce [53] the Visitation Articles of Bishop

RAINBOW. As Dean of Peterborough he had taken part in the Revision, and signed the MS. Prayer Book in 1661. As Bishop of Carlisle, he asked in 1666 for "the Canons," and a "surplice for the Minister to wear at *all* times of his public ministration." Again, "Doth he make use of *the* surplice when he reads Divine service, or administer the Sacraments" (plural).

Bishop Warner, of Rochester, was succeeded by DOLBEN, who (as Proctor for Christ Church, Oxford) had also been an active reviser in 1661. In 1664, being then Prolocutor, Dolben was one of those appointed by Convocation to translate the new Prayer Book into Latin. His "primary" Visitation Articles as *Bishop of Rochester* in 1668 are therefore of the first

---

[52] p. 19. There is a copy in the British Museum, E. 2949: as Earle was not consecrated till November 30th, 1662, it is possible that the Articles assigned to "John, Bp. of Worcester," were Gauden's. Kennet, p. 728, places the Visitation of Worcester in July.

[53] British Museum, "5155. b."

rank as evidence.⁵⁴ He, too, asks for "the book of the Canons," and whether the minister "doth read the Canons once a year as directed." Also, "Doth he perform *all* his ministrations with decency, gravity, and reverence, wearing his surplice *with a hood* (if he be a graduate in the University) as he is directed by authority and the laudable customs of the Church?"

GUNNING, who had been a Savoy Commissioner, asked in 1679 for "a *large* and decent Surplice for the Minister to wear at *all* times of his public Ministration."⁵⁵

₊

In the Lower House of Convocation in 1661 the three most influential and active members were Archdeacons Pory, Pearson, and Sparrow.

PORY, in August, 1662, asks—

"Have you a comely decent Surplisse *with sleeves* for the use of your Minister in saying the public prayers, or ministering the sacraments, and other rites of the Church; together with an university hood according to the degree of your said minister?"⁵⁶

He refers by name to "the Advertisements of Q. Elizabeth."

PEARSON, when Bishop of Chester in 1674, inquired—

"Doth he make use of *the* Surplice when he reads divine service or administers the sacraments?"⁵⁷

SPARROW republished in 1661, 1664, 1668, 1672 (as Bishop of Exeter), 1676, and 1684 (as Bishop of Norwich), the following statement:—

---

⁵⁴ British Museum, "5155, c. 61."
⁵⁵ *Second Report of the Ritual Commission*, Appendix, pp. 651-8.
⁵⁶ *Ibid.*, p. 625, 627-3.   ⁵⁷ *Ibid.*, p. 642.

"The Minister in time of his ministration shall use such ornaments as were in use in the second of King Edward VI., *Rub*. 2, *viz.* : a Surplice in the ordinary ministration, and a cope in time of ministration of Holy Communion in Cathedral and Collegiate Churches, Queen Elizabeth's Articles set forth in the seventh year of her reign."[58]

Archdeacon BASIRE had taken part in the revision. His Visitation Articles[59] vouch for the Use of the diocese of *Durham* under the vigilant *régime* of Bishop Cosin. Several times he refers to "the *late* Act of Uniformity." He asks for "*the* surplice and other ornaments appointed *according to his degree* in time of officiating."

One other witness of the highest authority may be cited, viz. Sancroft, who as secretary during the *first* stage of the revision entered up the final changes in the so-called "Cosin's Book," at Durham. The "Bodleian Book" embodying the *second* stage of the revision, is exclusively in Sancroft's handwriting.[60] The MS. additions in the black-letter book of 1636 (which was photozincographed for the Ritual Commission) were also made by Sancroft. Lastly, in the manuscript "annexed" to the Act of Uniformity (in nine places) the *final* alterations in the known handwriting of Sancroft are believed to have been ordered by the King in Council. Thus it will be seen that Sancroft was "in at" the revision of the Prayer Book at every stage of that revision from first to last.

---

[58] *Rationale*, p. 387. The edition of 1684 (the year before his death) instead of being the "second" as Lord Selborne calls it, was the eighth. And as the 1664 edition was modified in some points, the persistence of the above quotation was not due to accident or oversight.

[59] British Museum (" 698. b. 27 ").

[60] Press mark "Arch. D. Bodl. 28."

Now it happens that in the Bodleian Library beside the Prayer Book of 1634 referred to above (and at p. 196) there is another Prayer Book, dated 1684, containing MSS. notes also by him. On the fly-leaf opposite the "Ornaments Rubric" Archbishop Sancroft has written—

"*Ornaments of the Ministers. Dr. Grove's Persuasive to Communion with the Church of England,* 27. *A Letter to a friend relating to the present Convocation, p.* 10."

In the two publications here named the *only* "Ornament" to which any reference is made in either is the surplice.

For a knowledge of this fact we are indebted to Mr. Kennion, and it has since been verified independently.[61]

Two years before this Prayer Book of 1684 had been printed, Sancroft, as Archbishop, had inquired in his Visitation,

"Doth your Parson . . . publicly administer the Holy Sacraments of Baptism *and the Eucharist* . . . in such manner and form, as is directed by the Book of Common Prayer, lately established, and the Act of Uniformity therewith published, without addition, *diminution,* or *alteration?* And doth he in those his Ministrations wear *the* Surplice, with a Hood or Tippet befitting his Degree?"[62]

As to the bishops themselves, who must be supposed to have been craving for the "vestments" if they contrived the rubric in a ritualistic spirit, not one ever adopted the dress prescribed by the First Prayer Book. They adhered to the same "episcopal surplice" (as Parker's register calls the Rochet) as had been worn

---

[61] Grove's *Persuasive.* Second Edition. London, 1685 p. 25, and Vol. II., p. 46.

[62] *Second Report of the Ritual Commisson,* Appendix, p. 654.

by Grindal and Sandys. (See p. 121.) Durel in his *Vindiciæ* describes (chapter xv.) the "episcopalis ornatus" in the following terms—

"Primò enim episcoporum vestitus excogitatus est *diversus ab eo quo utuntur Ecclesiæ Romanæ pontifices*. . . . Nam positâ togâ, qui eorum vestitus communis superior est, tunicam ex lino byssino manicatam laxamque, quæ paululum infra genua dimittitur, sumunt, eique superinduunt aliam nigram holosericam absque manicis atque anterius apertam, adeo ut byssinæ manicæ et ipsa tunica byssina per anteriora, conspiciantur," p. 123.

In all the long line of witnesses adduced there is not one who could have been ignorant of the meaning of the newly revised rubric. Nor is there the smallest discrepancy in their testimony. Hence we learn with certainty that—

(1.) "*A Surplice, &c.*," meant a surplice with a tippet or hood, "*pro cujusque gradu.*"

(2.) "*The*" surplice is always spoken of as the one universally recognised dress.

(3.) No distinction whatever between the Holy Communion and any "*other* times in his ministration" was recognised or tolerated by any Ordinary. No alb, chasuble, dalmatic or tunicle is anywhere recognised, nor, in fact, did any such then remain in any church so as to be "*retained.*"

(4.) The "*Act itself, v. supra,*" viz. 1 Elizabeth, cap. ii., was regarded as THE standard, of which the newly framed rubric aspired to be an abridgement, *in virtue of* its employment of the "words of the Act itself, *sec. penult.*" But the Act 1 Elizabeth, cap. ii., was also printed as *part of* the Prayer Book, into which it was now for the first time incorporated; *the authority of*

Convocation being superadded to its ancient Parliamentary sanctions. Hence the Elizabethan Statute has Synodical authority equal to that of the rest of the Prayer Book, and is now (with the Canons of 1604) the *supreme* legal standard for the "Ornaments of the Minister." See above, p. 125.

(5.) So far from any dual standard of "Maximum" and "Minimum" being tolerated, the Visitation Articles everywhere insist upon the absence of *any* "diminution" or "variation" from the statutory standard.

(6.) It has been suggested indeed that the revising bishops wished to open a door for the reintroduction of the abrogated Mass gear, and for that purpose craftily omitted the concluding words of section 25, viz. "*until* other order shall be therein taken," &c.

But that hypothesis would not only blast their character for honest dealing with the Nation and the Parliament which trusted them; it would further shew that they were fools as well as knaves, seeing that the statute *containing the omitted words* remained the *primary* authority, and would supplement any defects in their inaccurate summary. The true reason for the omission of the words "*until . . . shall be*," &c., was that they had ceased to be appropriate, seeing that a century had elapsed since the contemplated "other order" *had*, in fact, *been* "taken." Hence the removal from the Elizabethan rubric of the words "*at the time of the Communion, and all* OTHER *times*," and the substitution of "*at* ALL *times*," words by no means synonymous with "at the *several* times of their ministration." Men like Bishop Reynolds would have been no parties to a wretched trick of the kind suggested above. Cosin, the only man who ever gave ground for suspecting him of having wished it, will be vindicated in the next chapter. He never wore alb, tunicle, or chasuble, nor in any public or official act performed by him as "bishop," did he ever recognise any standard for Ornaments higher than that of the Canons. The theory and practice of the Ritualists was not even recognised in the Church of England at the time when the Ornaments Rubric assumed its present shape.

To appreciate the cumulative force of the above evidence it must be borne in mind that the Visitation Articles were the official interpretation of the Ornaments Rubric, given at the time by the very men who had taken part in the recent framing of it. By the Rubric of Edward's First Prayer Book it would have been *illegal* for "the celebrant" (unless he were a bishop) to wear a surplice: yet the surplice (often described as "large" and with "large sleeves") was required as compulsory from ALL the clergy. No "distinctive dress" for holy communion is ever hinted at; "both the sacraments" are put in this respect on the same footing. The hood is required as a dress of *ministration*, yet the combination of hoods with chasubles would be too absurd for even ritualists to attempt. If the ritualistic interpretation were correct, the Ornaments Rubric of 1662 would operate as a repeal *pro tanto* of the Canons of 1604 which had no "authority of *Parliament*," and were of course of older date. Yet every Ordinary required the Canons of 1604 to be procured, directed them to be read, and adduced them as binding *precisely where they conflict with* the rubrics of 1549. It is simply impossible to imagine a more complete consensus of authoritative opinion or a clearer proof of the intention of the legislature.

VII

The Ornaments Rubric. No. III
THE GREAT "COSIN" MYTH

DOWN to the year 1708, no single Anglican writer admitted that the Eucharistic vestments (alb tunicle, and chasuble) of the First Prayer Book had ever been required by law, since the Elizabethan settlement of religion in 1559. That theory had, indeed, been broached after a fashion, in certain anonymous pamphlets arguing against conformity or subscription, though chiefly as an *argumentum ad hominem* against the Bishops. But no printer's name or date appeared on any of these wild polemical squibs. On the other hand the responsible defenders of "the religion established by law" invariably treat the plea as artificial, unreal, far-fetched, and undeserving of any serious reply.

But in the opening years of the eighteenth century a change came over the Church of England. Some unpublished "Notes" attributed to Bishop Cosin, and written or copied by him more than half a century before, fell into the hands of Dr. Nicholls, who published them about forty years after Cosin's death. The effect was marvellous. Though Nicholls himself adhered to the older view which prevailed at the last revision of the Prayer Book in 1661, viz. that the reference in the "ornaments rubric" was to the *general* rubrics at the END of the First Prayer Book of Edward VI. (which prescribed only a surplice and hood for clergymen under the rank of a bishop), yet his contemporaries at once adopted, though only as a speculative theory, what may be termed the "Ritualistic" interpretation. Thus John Johnson in the *third* edition of his *Clergyman's vade mecum*, published in 1709, and Wheatly (who did not even know, any more than Baxter did, the difference between a "cope" and a "vestment") in 1710, Collier (1714), and Neale (1732), were the first of a long line of followers who "took over" without any attempt at criticism the supposed "new light." Lord Selborne says[1] Cosin's "Notes" became the "fountain-head of a new tradition": so that Gibson (1713), Burns (1763), and Cardwell (1839) copied the *ipsissima verba* of Cosin's reputed "Notes" without so much as a pretence of original research.

Cosin himself had learned what now forms the "Ritualistic theory of the ornaments rubric" from a polemical tract by an anonymous Puritan lawyer, published in 1606 under the title of *The survey of the book of Common Prayer*, the views advocated in which Cosin for the most part sought to combat. But it was not till 144 years after Elizabeth had "taken order" that this notion found any lodgment among the clergy.

In our own day, the authority supposed to attach to Cosin's views has greatly increased. The subject is

---

[1] *Notes on some passages in the Liturgical History of the Reformed English Church*, p. 28.

presented commonly in this form:—" Bishop Cosin was a man very learned in liturgical matters, his influence was paramount at the last revision of the Prayer Book in 1661, and we may with confidence reason from the views expressed in his 'Notes' to the 'mind of the Church' as expressed in the Prayer Book, at least so far as regards the changes introduced into the Prayer Book in 1661."

No part, however, of that estimate is correct; on the contrary it deserves to be called "The great Cosin Myth," because it involves and rests upon a long train of fallacies.

In the first place, as we shall see, Cosin was *not* learned, according to the modern standard of Prayer Book learning. It could hardly have been otherwise. For, as Canon Robertson (the historian, and editor of Heylin) remarks, "The divines of Charles the First's reign appear to have had exceedingly little traditional information—the line of historical and antiquarian investigation was as yet unopened. The earliest histories of the Reformation (after Foxe), by Fuller and Heylin,—the earliest regular commentaries on the Prayer Book by Sparrow and L'Estrange,—were not published till the time of the Usurpation."[2] When Cosin was a young man (he was only twenty-four when the first series of " Notes " was written up) he began to make " notes " in the margin of a " large paper " folio Prayer Book dated 1619, which he had interleaved to serve as a commonplace-book. These notes are in Bishop Cosin's earlier—" very fine and minute "—hand-

---

[2] *How shall we Conform?* p. 117.

writing and appear to have been copied by him for the most part from a similar Prayer Book printed in 1617, the Notes in which had been made by "a friend or Chaplain" of Bishop Overall, conjectured to be a "Mr. J. Hayward of Coton," of whom nothing is known. In one of the "Chaplain's" notes (as Bishop Hickes, the non-juror, pointed out), Bishop Overall is spoken of as *then* Bishop of Norwich. Now, as Overall died on May 12th, 1619, and the book in which Cosin copied the "Notes" was not printed before March, 1619, at the earliest, it seems pretty certain that Hickes' book of 1617 was the *original*, and Cosin's merely *a copy*, as Mr. James Parker justly infers.[3] Nicholls (who did not attribute this "First Series" to Cosin), says "nine parts in ten" are the same in both books,[4] from which it follows that only a tithe of these notes are of Cosin's own making. Unluckily Hickes' book is not now extant, so that we cannot tell *which* were the additions made by Cosin himself to the "Chaplain's" entries. Oddly enough, these very *same* Notes have again and again been attributed to Bishop Overall, though the "Chaplain" says in one of them, "I have heard my Lord Overall preach it a hundred times." Such is the value of "tradition"!

Now, it is precisely this "First Series" of Notes, the authorship of which is unknown, that contains the most strongly Romish pronouncements for which "Bishop Cosin's" authority is ever claimed. Mr. James Parker

---

[3] *History of the Revisions of the Prayer Book*, p. 324 and 326 note "h." Canon Meyrick in his *Letters to the Bishops on the Neo-Eucharistical System* (Rivingtons, 1886), disputes the handwriting of this "First Series," and denies that Cosin even *copied* this "Series" which he merely annotated.

[4] Cosin's *Works*, Anglo-Catholic Library, Vol. V., p. xiii., note. The page references in this paper are made throughout to this edition.

(who is concerned to magnify the influence of Cosin to the utmost) says, "The notes in this book perhaps, on the whole, have the most direct bearing of any upon the alterations Cosin made in the Rubrics."[5] Yet he admits that "few of the notes seem to be original"[6] and that the book "affords but very few notes which seem to have suggested any corrections in the Offices."[7] And it is from this same "First Series" that we often see quoted long extracts from the Jesuit Maldonatus, which Bishop Cosin is alleged to have "adopted as his own" by merely copying them at second hand, for future use, into his "Notes."

It seems worth while, therefore, to test in some detail the value of this

"FIRST SERIES."

The compiler, whoever he was, had undoubtedly a great admiration for Maldonatus, whom he describes as "their greatest divine that I meet with."[8] From that Jesuit polemic the writer accepted the practices of Chrism, and the blow upon the cheek in Confirmation, which "being so significant," he says, "it were better we had them: neither were it any fault, for aught I see, if any man should use them in our Church," though he admits that "we omit" them.[9] From the same source he mentions "another custom of the Christians, now also used among many, that they touched their eyes, their nose, their temples and forehead, with the Sacrament before they did eat it, as being confident that there was such virtue and force in it, that it would make all their senses the more happy by it, and less subject to evil desires. And these

---

[5] *History of the Revisions of the Prayer Book*, p. 366.   [6] *Ibid.*, p. 325.
[7] *Ibid.*, p. 367.   [8] Cosin's *Works*, V.-163.   [9] *Ibid.*, p. 149.

things men did and do naturally, more than out of any injunction."[10]

The *genuine* Cosin, by the way, repudiated these same practices as being "new fashions brought in, without any example of the Apostles." See "Third Series" of the "Notes," p. 486.

His juvenile loyalty to Maldonatus reached its highest point, perhaps, when he gravely wrote, "we are so disposed that we would rather go wrong with so many and great authors than speak that which is true with the Puritans."[11] It is hard to say whether the folly or the wickedness of that frank avowal is the more amazing; but it is clear that the writer (whoever he was) was "keeping a diary" intended for no other eye than his own or that of some familiar spirit. The "Anglo-Catholic" editor (Dr. Barrow) shows that the authorities quoted are often spurious,[12] while the quotations themselves are commonly inaccurate,[13] and he points out in the Preface that "statements respecting ecclesiastical antiquities, are derived from works which are of little or no authority, and cannot be relied on as matter of historical truth."

When the writer of these Notes had occasion to allude to the past history of the Prayer Book, he blunders amusingly. For instance, at pp. 21 and 38 he tells us that the Act 5 and 6 Edward VI., cap. iii.,

---

[10] Cosin's *Works*, V.-111.   [11] *Ibid.*, p. 120.
[12] See notes on pp. 64, 74, 87, 101, 103, 105, 110, 113, 121, 128, *bis*, 130, 131, 133, 167, 172.
[13] *Ex. gr.* pp. 91, 95, 109, 124, 139, 141, 150, 157, 164. Other blunders *not* noted by Dr. Barrow are such as the mistake of "the Council of Venice" [Venetum] for that of Vannes [Veneticum], a mistake of some four hundred years. Compare *Works* V.-9, with Dr. Stephens' *Notes on the Common Prayer*, I.-305.

repealed by 1 Mary, cap. 2, was "*not since revived.*" Whereas, it had been revived in May, 1604, by the passing of 1 James I., cap. xxv., during Cosin's own lifetime, only a few years before the annotation was made. In the same passage he suggests that some particulars in Queen Elizabeth's published Order of 1561, for the new Calendar, may have been due to the printer's pleasure and "ignorance." (So also at p. 17 and elsewhere.)

At p. 47 he suggests that the introductory sentences, exhortation, confession, and absolution, were added to Morning and Evening Prayer in Edward's Second Prayer Book, "in imitation of the Liturgy and Mass of the Church of Rome"! At p. 91 he quotes the language of 1 Elizabeth, cap. ii., as though it had re-enacted the *First* Prayer Book of Edward. At p. 93 he gravely observes, "The author of the Homilies wrote them in haste," evidently fancying that the two books (which have a perfectly separate history) were written by one man.

At p. 114 he suggests that the transposition of the "prayer of oblation" in the Communion Office of 1552 was due to the "printer's negligence," and he adds, "the Consecration of the Sacrament being ever the first, it was always the use in all Liturgies to have the Oblation follow." That statement is utterly erroneous. The Oblation always *preceded* the Prayer of Invocation.[14]

At p. 170, he says a communion at funerals "was appointed in King Edward's Service (before Calvin's

---

[14] See Hammond's *Ancient Liturgies*, Preface, pp. xxvi.-xxviii. Professor Cheetham's Article on "Canon of the Liturgy" in Smith's *Dictionary of Christian Antiquities*, p. 271.

letter to the sacrilegious Duke of Somerset got it yielded) that there should be a celebration of the Sacrament at the burial of the dead." The "Anglo-Catholic" editor in his footnote, points out that Calvin did *not* speak of the burial service; and that the date of his letter was October 22nd, 1548, *i.e.* five months before the *First* Prayer Book of Edward was printed. He might have added that Somerset fell from power before the First Prayer Book was four months old, and he never regained his former influence, but was beheaded, January 22nd, 1552, before the commencement of the session in which the Second Prayer Book was enacted, with which "the sacrilegious Duke" had nothing whatever to do. Now all these blunders occur in *one* series only of the "Notes;" and they illustrate the truth of Mr. Droop's criticism that "the references, not very numerous, which Cosin makes in his Notes to what had happened during Elizabeth's reign, and the earlier part of the sixteenth century, show that he had only a very limited and superficial acquaintance with the history of that period."

It is evident that the writer of the Notes was some youthful pioneer on a new and untrodden path of inquiry, fresh from reading Maldonatus whom he quotes at inordinate length, and simply recording his own first impressions, and accumulating stores for after-sifting and adjustment. As the "Anglo-Catholic" editor observes, "Cosin used his interleaved Prayer Book very much as a commonplace-book," and "left them incomplete"; Dr. Barrow is "disposed to think that *all* the Latin notes (except some short ones, and others that are manifestly Bishop Cosin's own) are extracts." Bearing in mind the above data, it will be seen that Bishop Cosin's responsibility for the "First Series" of notes is of the very slightest. In some instances we can prove that on second thoughts he modified or rejected the views originally drafted by the unknown compiler. For instance, at p. 43 (on the supposed contradiction between the Ornaments Rubric and the 58th canon) Cosin has added in a *later* hand [15]—"*But* the Act of Parliament, *I see*, refers to the canon, and *until* such times as other order shall be taken." Thus, as Lord Selborne expresses it, "at some time afterwards, not ascertained, he corrected this last passage, as having been written in forgetfulness of the statutory power"[16] to "take other order." Unfortunately Nicholls, who first published these Notes, and whose edition was the *only* one available till 1855, *omitted* this "later" correction, and thus contributed to build up the erroneous "tradition."

So again, on p. 118, after a long random defence of the application of the title "sacrifice" to the Lord's Supper, there comes a wiser after-thought *added in the margin*—"Not in strictness and rigour of speech; for so, was there never sacrifice, nor never shall be any, but Christ's alone." So, on the Te Deum, his Editor interjects—"these statements are corrected in the *next* series of notes" (p. 64).

But it must not be inferred that where no such footnote has been added, Cosin necessarily adopted,

---

[15] Both Dr. Barrow, p. 43, and Mr. James Parker, *History of the Revisions of the Prayer Book*, p. 130, agree as to this.

[16] Selborne's *Notes on the Liturgy*, p. 27. So when Bishop Andrewes had written, "Mention is there made of cope, surplice, tippet, hood, pro cujusque gradu;" Cosin added, "I.C. I find not that." p. 44.

still less retained, the views contained in these crude jottings. For example, on p. 131, the "Notes" say—"upon the words of consecration, the Body and Blood of Christ is really and *substantially* present, and so exhibited and given to *all* that receive it. . . . But yet there remains this controversy . . whether the Body of Christ be present only in the use of the Sacrament, and in the act of eating, and not otherwise. They that hold the affirmative, as the Lutherans, *in Conf. Sax.*, and all Calvinists, do seem to me to depart from all antiquity, which place the presence of Christ in the virtue of the words of consecration and benediction used by the priest, and not in the use of eating of the Sacrament." Not a hint is given either in these "Notes," or by the Editor, that these were *not* the mature views of Bishop Cosin. Yet in his *History of Transubstantiation*, written in 1656, *intended for publication*, and published with Cosin's expressed permission, in 1675, by his executor, Dean Durel, he defends the Lutheran teaching on this very point,[17] and says, "We deny that the elements still retain the nature of Sacraments when not used according to Divine institution, that is, given by Christ's ministers, and received by His people; so that Christ in the consecrated bread ought not, *cannot be kept and preserved* to be carried about, because He is present *only* to the communicants."[18] In his Second Series of the "Notes,"[19] he says, "Though the bread and wine remain, yet the consecration, the *Sacrament of* the Body and Blood of Christ, do not remain longer

---

[17] Brewer's edition, p. 29, n.
[18] *History of Transubstantiation*, Ed. Brewer, p. 61.
[19] Cosin's *Works*, V.-357.

than the holy action itself remains for which the bread and wine were hallowed; and which, being ended, return to their former use again?"

And, again, after referring to his *History of Transubstantiation*, he says, "that the body and blood is neither sensibly present—nor *otherwise at all* present but only *to them* that are duly prepared to receive them, and in the very act of receiving them and the consecrated elements together, to which they are sacramentally *in that act* united."[20]

Thus, to sum up the evidence as to this "First series of Bishop Cosin's (?) Notes"—their authorship is unknown; only "one part in ten" is alleged as traceable to him; it was not until 1855 that they were *for the first time* attributed to Cosin by Dr. Barrow solely on the ground of handwriting; which is no proof of authorship. When examined minutely in detail they prove to be crude and incomplete annotations by some hot-headed partisan, ignorant as to the history of the Prayer Book upon which for purposes of *private* study he was making such illustrative comments as his reading from day to day happened to suggest. Such of the "Notes" as can with certainty be referred to Cosin himself, are in the nature of additions demurring or hesitating as to some of the conclusions of the original Annotator. Few of them can be shewn to represent Cosin's matured views. It was a grievous wrong and injury both to Bishop Cosin and to the Church of England when Nicholls in 1709-10, nearly forty years after poor Cosin's death, published these private memoranda. For, what statesman or

---
[20] Cosin's *Works*, V.-345.

theologian could bear to be thus made responsible for the "sins of his youth"? Which of us has not by him in some secret drawer an "essay" or a "notebook" which he would feel heartily ashamed to see published with his name to it, though it may have represented truly enough the fervid and confident dogmatism of his hot youth?

THE "SECOND SERIES" of the NOTES was made in a Prayer Book of 1638, "wherein be inserted leaves of white paper through the whole book, for my own notes and observations upon it, both doctrinal and practical." There is no question that this is Cosin's. The authorities cited are "nearly all different from those used in the former volume."[21] The inaccurate citations are much fewer.[22] He speaks much more respectfully of Calvin as "laude suâ dignum,"[23] and warmly of Luther as "the man of God, Doctor Martin Luther, ever to be observed as our preceptor,"[24] and of the "Protestants in Germany whose example we also in England have for the most part followed."[25]

In these Notes Cosin rejects the sacrifice of the Mass,[26] the Elevation[27] and Adoration of the Host,[28] Purgatory,[29] and expresses himself as to the ritual of consecration in a way which illustrates the meaning of the words "before the people" in the rubric before the Prayer of Consecration. He says: "Our Lord willed the blood to be received apart, and as separated from the Body, and willed the blessed bread, which is

---

[21] Parker's *History of the Revisions of the Prayer Book*, p. 369.
[22] Cosin's *Works*, V.-235, 240, 351.   [23] *Ibid.*, p. 306.
[24] *Ibid.*, p. 374.   [25] *Ibid.*, p. 302.   [26] *Ibid.*, pp. 333, 343, 347.
[27] *Ibid.*, p. 340.   [28] *Ibid.*, p. 342.   [29] *Ibid.*, p. 373.

the communion of the body of Christ, to be broken, and the wine poured into the cup to be poured out, that thus the Passion and Death, and the sufferings of the body, and the outpouring of the blood, might be represented and reproduced, not only to the mind, but *to the very eyes also*, by signs and actions of this sort."[30] "The character of the later part at least of this second series of notes is to oppose the Anglican view of doctrine to the Roman, and there is a controversial tone in them which is in marked contrast with that of the former series," says Dr. Barrow.[31] Cosin's ignorance of liturgical matters comes out in the statement that the Injunctions put forth in July, 1547 (*i.e.* the first year of Edward VI.), "were set forth *about* that time, and mentioned *or* ratified by the Act of Parliament here named" (*i.e.* in the words "authority of Parliament in the *second* year of the reign of K. Ed. VI."). For, as Dr. Barrow[32] and Mr. James Parker[33] both admit, "it cannot be said that these Injunctions are directly either mentioned or ratified by it, as Cosin implies." Again,[34] he regards the First Prayer Book, (which was not printed till March, 1549) as having been "in use" in the second year of Edward, *i.e.* 1548. But this "Second Series" of Notes need not detain us, since even controversialists have not ventured to build anything upon them. Mr. James Parker says : "It has not been easy to find many passages in the 1638 Notes bearing upon the rubrics at all, and, even where they do so, they seem to have influenced his alterations but little."[35] We pass on, therefore, to

[30] Cosin's *Works*, V.-343.   [31] Preface, p. xix.   [32] *Ibid.*, p. 231.
[33] *History of the Revisions of the Prayer Book*, p. 132.
[34] Cosin's *Works*, V.-305.
[35] *History of the Revisions of the Prayer Book*, p. 369.

The "Third Series,"

which is perhaps the oldest of the three. It consisted of an octavo MS., printed by Nicholls in 1709-10, but now lost. It seems to have been commenced after the Hampton Court Conference in 1604, and the latest event referred to is " the 17th of Charles I.," *i.e.* 1642. Mr. Parker says "it is not possible to say that any one note especially influenced a correction in Cosin's corrected copy." Dr. Barrow conjectures that this "Series" was made about 1640. They are chiefly historical, and, as such, illustrate the slenderness of Cosin's information. At that time he had not so much as seen a copy of Edward's First Prayer Book, but had access only to the notoriously inaccurate translation of Aless. This leads him into making a number of absurd conjectures, attributing to Bucer divers changes which never happened, and explaining the origin of others which existed only in his own re-translation.[36] To Bucer, who was his pet aversion, he attributes[37] the declaration on kneeling, or "black rubric," with which Bucer had nothing to do, its history commencing after Bucer's death. See p. 254. To Bucer again, he imputes Cranmer's Catechism, which notoriously had a different origin, and had been published in England at least nine months before Bucer's arrival.[38] He states[39] that Nowel's Catechism "was never received by any public authority," although Convocation in 1562, and again in 1571,

---

[36] Cosin's *Works*, V.-416, 445, 446, 489, 497.
[37] *Ibid.*, p. 479.
[38] See *Original Letters*, pp. 381, 643. Yet Cosin speaks of it as later in date than the Catechism of 1549.   [39] *Ibid.*, p. 491.

had revised it, and, so recently as 1604, had required it to be taught in schools.[40] As to the Ornaments, he fancied that under the First Prayer Book a priest might wear "his surplice" at Communion![41] and that "albs *or* tunicles" were alternatives offered to the assistant clergy;[42] while a Bishop might wear "Rochet *or* Alb."[43] He imagined that under that book "the people go up to offer at the altar, *and besides* go to put somewhat into the poor man's box;"[44] the fact being, of course, that the only money offering then made by the people at "the offertory" was to the box.[44a] He repeated[45] the mistake mentioned above, as to the Injunctions of 1547 having *Parliamentary* authority in 1548: also (p. 437) as to the Duke of Somerset getting the Second Prayer Book "confirmed in Parliament," which did not meet until after the Duke's head had been taken off. He says[46] the "new book was set out in the 5th and 6th years of King Ed. VI., *a little before the Protector was beheaded.*" The Protector was beheaded January 22nd, 1552, Parliament met the day *after* that event, the Act of Uniformity passed April 14th, and the "new book" was printed in August, 1552, to come into legal use November 1st, 1552—*i.e.* eight months later than Cosin's reckoning. At p. 441 he has a

---

[40] Cardwell's *Synodalia*, pp. 128, 291, 495. Dr. Grove's Preface to the *Little Catechism*, p. xvi., or Dr. Corrie's Preface, p. v., *Parker Society*.
[41] Cosin's *Works*, V.-417.   [42] *Ibid.*, p. 440.
[43] *Ibid.*, p. 439.   [44] *Ibid.*, p. 459.   [44a] See p. 94, *supra*.
[45] *Ibid.*, p. 440. Probably Cosin never saw these Injunctions, for Sparrow's reprint had not yet been published, and Cosin never quotes the crucial words "lights *before the Sacrament.*" Hence Wheatly fancied the two lights were for use at Evening Service.
[46] *Ibid.*, p. 474.

characteristic passage on altar-lights. He says, "In the latter end of King Edward's time they used them *in Scotland itself*, as appears by Calvin's epistle to Knox, and his fellow-reformers *there* anno 1554." The blunders in that sentence are exquisite. *First*, 1554 was not "in King Edward's time." *Second*, Knox was not "in Scotland." Knox had remained in England from 1549 until Edward's death; and there was no public Protestant service in Scotland until 1558 at earliest. *Third*, the letter in question was *not* written to "Knox," but to Dr. Cox, afterwards Bishop of Ely. *Fourth*, so far from its "appearing that they used" altar-lights, both parties wrote to Calvin to tell him that he had been misinformed. Cox wrote: "As for lights, we never had any;"[47] while the Puritans eagerly disclaimed the authorship of the slander.[48] "By cause that Maister Calvin in his letter maketh mention of lights, some might gather he was untruly informed that in the English Book lights were prescribed, the *contrary* whereof appeareth by the description before." By the time he wrote his "Second Series," Cosin had learned that Knox was at Frankfort (though he still fancied that altar-lights were "used" there, and were so "represented" in the letter signed by Knox, which does not so much as hint at them), but he still assumes that the Ornaments of the First Book were retained in 1554.[49]

It is instructive to notice that Dean Durel, the personal friend and literary executor of Cosin, published his *Vindiciæ* in 1669, three years before Cosin's

---

[47] *Original Letters*, p. 757.
[48] *Troubles at Frankfort*, p. liv., or Gorham's *Reformation Gleanings*, p. 347.   [49] Cosin's *Works*, V.-306.

death, and pointed out this very blunder (in mistaking "Knox" for "Cox") as a Puritan falsehood. From this we may safely infer, either that Cosin did not let his intimates know of the crude theories embalmed in his private "Notes" *which were never designed for publication:* or else, that before he died, Cosin had outgrown these mistakes, for the sake of which, his professed admirers now usually quote these Notes. Durel says, "Denique ex Calvini epistolâ ad Coxum (non Knoxum prout mendose vulgò legitur) datâ, qui pro Liturgiâ Anglicanâ stabat, manifestum est, in eâ liturgiæ descriptione quam a Puritanis acceperat, quorundam mentionem factam, Luminum scilicet, *quae usurpata non sunt in Ecclesia Anglicana*, ex quo prodiit Edwardi regis Liturgia posterior."[50]

Durel's *Vindiciæ*, which was written partly in vindication of "the Bishop of Durham" (Cosin) against the Puritans, being published some years after the last revision, is a much more reliable "authority" as to the requirements of the new Prayer Book, than Cosin's "Notes."

Durel, Chaplain to the King, and Dean of Windsor, was entrusted in 1662 with the duty of translating the Liturgy into French, and was probably acting under the authority of Convocation when making his Latin translation of it. Both versions had been published before the *Vindiciæ* was written. The proof sheets of this last work were submitted to Sancroft before publication, and also to the Judge of the Prerogative Court; and the work itself was dedicated to the King. Its statements are a complete refutation of the theory

[50] *Vindiciæ*, p. 97; cf. 489.

once privately embodied (but never acted upon) by Cosin. Thus after enumerating the Mass garments (amice, stole, alb, girdle, maniple, chasuble), he adds that the English Reformers "when they came to the correction of abuses in Church vestures . . . desired these to be reformed in such wise that the whole entire theatrical mass-gear (such as before described) has been clean removed from the Church of England (Choragium missaticum universum . . . ab ecclesiâ Anglicanâ penitus sublatum est)."[51] He repeats this on p. 156, saying the Reformers " were not of opinion that a *distinction* of dresses should be retained *from the first:*" and in proof of this he refers to the Thirtieth Injunction of 1559 as ordering the surplice.[52] Lastly, he described the Bishops' "magpie" as "differing from that used by the prelates of the Roman Church," and "plainly not the same as is used by the bishops of the Roman Church."[53] This published and quasi-official Vindication of the Church of England against the Nonconformists proves that the theory secretly embalmed in Cosin's private "Notes" had not even been made known to the public in 1669: and those "Notes" having been made prior to the Revision, most of them long before it, cannot be evidence of anything beyond the first-thoughts (or wishes) of a student at the time when he jotted them down for after consideration.

Such blunders as those above enumerated would not now be perpetrated by a pupil teacher who professed to have any knowledge whatever of the history of the Prayer Book, and they are not merely erroneous in

---

[51] *Vindiciæ*, pp. 124, 125. [52] *Ibid.*, p. 127. [53] *Ibid.*, pp. 125, 159 f.

themselves, but imply unfamiliarity with the Ecclesiastical history of the period. At p. 454, Cosin informs us that the collects at the end of the Litany, which were all printed in Edward's Second Prayer Book of 1552, were "added only by virtue of the Queen's injunctions of 1559," which, however, do not in any way refer either to the "Collect for the Queen" or to any other collect.

There are one or two passages in this "Third Series" worth quoting, as throwing light upon the rubrics. On the title of the Church Militant Prayer, for instance, he says, "Those words 'militant here upon earth,' were added *to exclude* the prayers that were used in the ancient Liturgies, and in the former edition of this Liturgy, 2 Ed. VI."[54] And "in like sort, *because* the very term of 'offering' and 'sacrifice' though well used of old, and in a far different meaning from that sense wherein the Papists used them, seemed nevertheless to sound their meaning, and therefore to give offence, *it is altered* into another expression of 'Christ's precious death' only."[55]

Cosin's "Considerations." (1640?)

Together with the above Three Series of Notes, both Nicholls and Dr. Barrow (the "Anglo-Catholic" editor) print also a list of "Particulars to be considered, explained, and corrected in the Book of Common Prayer," which Cosin is believed to have drawn up with a view to an expected revision in 1640. The suggestions are numbered from 1 to 67, as far as the

[54] Cosin's *Works*, V.-464.   [55] *Ibid.*, p. 471.

end of the Communion Service, and there follow 24 unnumbered ones at the end. More than half of these proposed changes were ultimately adopted either in substance, or in part, at the last revision of the Prayer Book; but of these many were merely typographical; others related to the substitution of the then "new version" of King James' Bible; others relate to technical objections as to the legality of changes made in 1604 by the authority of the Proclamation and Letters Patent of King James. Twenty-eight of Cosin's "Considerations" found no place in the so-called "Cosin's corrected" Prayer Book (the "Durham Book" to be mentioned hereafter), yet fourteen of these were ultimately adopted. Many are to be found also in the perfectly independent suggestions of Bishop Wren, and of the ".Puritans" at the Savoy Conference. In "Consideration" No. 29 he states that Queen Elizabeth's Injunctions appointed the Litany to be said "in the midst of the *choir*,"[56] though the Eighteenth Injunction of 1559 merely spoke of "the midst of the *Church*." In No. 61 Cosin repeats the very grave error of stating that in "Ancient Liturgies" the oblation came "after" consecration. In No. 47 he imputes to the First Prayer Book of Edward a direction which is only found in the Scotch Liturgy of 1637. To that same Scotch Liturgy are due also his "Considerations" numbered 28, 40, 46 and perhaps 13.

We come now to a much more interesting inquiry, viz. as to the true character and importance of what has been called

---

[56] Cosin's *Works*, V.-509.

"The Durham Book"

CONTAINING THE FIRST DRAFT OF THE REVISION OF 1661.

Our knowledge of the above "Notes" is derived from the editions published by Nicholls (1710) and the Anglo-Catholic edition of Cosin's works, Vol. V. (1855). But there is another book connected with Bishop Cosin's name which is of vastly greater importance than any of the above. This is practically inaccessible to the public except through Mr. James Parker's *History of the Revisions of the Book of Common Prayer*, 1877. It is a Prayer Book printed in 1619, and now in the Durham Library, which it is most important to distinguish from that other "Prayer Book of 1619," previously mentioned as containing the "First Series" of Notes, and which also is in the Durham Library. The latter has, according to Dr. Barrow (p. xvi.), the press mark "c. I. 2," but the press mark of the more valuable and important book is "D. iii. 5." It has never been published by its custodians the Warden and Fellows of Durham University, as its importance surely demands. For the sake of distinction we shall speak of it henceforth as "The Durham Book." Its appearance is thus described by Mr. James Parker. "This book of Bp. Cosin's was evidently prepared for the printers, for on the fly-leaf, in the Bishop's own handwriting, we find" a series of "directions to be given to the printer."[57] Next, in Sancroft's handwriting comes a revised version of these "directions." On a third leaf "inserted, but evidently belonging to the

---

[57] *History of the Revisions of the Prayer Book*, p. 94

book," comes "the rough draft of the form of assent of Convocation to the corrections, together with notes how the signatures are to be attached."[58] As this form (given by Mr. Parker at p. 445) was settled after a four hours' debate on December 19th, 1661,[59] it throws light on the nature and date of the work. Throughout, "though the writing of Bishop Cosin when erased is not always legible, the greater part is very clear. Still many of the pages have a very confused appearance, not only on account of the obliteration of the text and the marginal additions, but from these marginal additions being in many cases struck through and others added in their stead."[60] "There are a great many entries, in different styles of writing, and evidently at different times, though all undoubtedly by Cosin himself; and these constitute a great proportion of the whole of the corrections in the book. The rest are in one hand, apparently written at or about the same time, and sometimes over Cosin's writing, and all by Sancroft."[61]

Mr. James Parker chooses to entitle this book "Cosin's Corrected Copy, 1640-61," a date purely arbitrary and intended to establish a theory that the whole book was in the first instance a *private* revision by Cosin. Mr. Parker thinks "the book was brought to the provisional committee with none but Cosin's writing in it."[62] Yet, even so, it would not follow that Cosin had been compiling these amendments for twenty-one years. Mr. Parker says,[63] "There are *good*

---

[58] *History of the Revisions of the Prayer Book*, p. 95.   [59] *Ibid.*, p. 90.
[60] *Ibid.*, p. 96.   [61] Parker's *Letter to Lord Selborne*, p. 110.
[62] *Letter to Selborne*, p. 110.
[63] *History of the Revisions of the Prayer Book*, p. 385.

grounds for supposing that the corrected copy was commenced as early as 1619"; but though he italicises the words "good grounds," he gives no hint as to their nature. It is more reasonable to suppose that— just as Article XXVIII. was said to be of Bishop Geste's "own penning," not in the sense of authorship, but because he may have acted as clerk at the revision in 1563 of the Edwardine articles, which Archbishop Parker had previously altered and re-drafted [61]—so, the "Durham Book" was commenced about 1660, and contains merely the minutes of the revision of 1661 in its *preliminary* stage, embodying the results of the informal Committee which sat during the abortive Savoy Conference, but earlier than the formal meetings of the bishops "at Ely House."

It has been calculated that "of the corrections finally made in the revision of 1661, about ninety out of every hundred are due to the suggestions which are found in Bishop Cosin's corrected copy," *i.e.* this very "Durham Book." On the Parkerian hypothesis that the Durham book was compiled, in private, by Cosin, during the years from 1640 downwards, it would follow that his individual influence upon the revision of 1661 had proved overwhelming. Mr. Parker fancies, for instance, that the Ornaments Rubric, as shewn in our photograph, "had been made probably some *twenty years before* the Savoy Conference was thought of."[61a] That would take us back to 1641 when Wren, Sanderson, Hacket, and Warner—all of whom took part as bishops in the subsequent revision of 1661—were even then engaged (together with Archbishop Ussher and Bishop

---

[61] See Lamb's *History of the Thirty-nine Articles.*
[61a] *History of the Revisions of the Prayer Book*, Preface, p. 15.

Williams) in advising a committee of the House of Lords as to possible emendations of the Prayer Book. At that time (1641), as Izaak Walton tells us in his *Life of Sanderson*, Sanderson "and two others did meet privately twice a week at the Dean of Westminster's house, for the space of five months or more"—to " draw up some such safe alterations as he thought fit in the service book, and about some of the ceremonies that were least material for satisfying their consciences."[65] It is *possible*, therefore, that Cosin's " Considerations," mentioned above at p. 185, may have been *begun* about this time : the " First series " of Notes contains some references to books published in 1656 : his Second series mentions his *History of Transubstantiation*, written in 1656 : and the " Considerations," Mr. Parker thinks, were probably revised by him in 1661, " as there are additions in a later hand."

If Mr. Parker's theory were correct, therefore, Cosin must have been busy making the " Durham Book " *at the same time* that he was compiling the First and Second series of Notes and the " Considerations." And, if that were true, it would follow that we should find marked up in the Durham Book the changes which were at that very time being indicated by Cosin as desirable, in his " Notes " and " Considerations." Yet if we analyse the "Particulars to be considered, explained, and corrected in the Book of Common Prayer" (which for the sake of brevity we have spoken of above as the " Considerations "), we shall find that they were dealt with in the Durham Book (and subsequently) just as though after a discussion they

---

[65] Sanderson's *Works*, Jacobson's edition, V.-300.

had been rejected, modified, postponed or adopted by a Committee on precisely the same footing as other private suggestions made by other of the Revisers in 1661.

If the reader will take the trouble to prefix consecutive numbers to the suggestions as printed in Cosin's *Works*, V.-502-525, the following table will show what became of these "Considerations."

OUT OF COSIN'S NINETY-ONE "CONSIDERATIONS,"

66 (a) 14 were *never entered in the Durham Book* nor finally accepted.

(b) 16 others—*not entered in Durham Book*—were accepted at some *later* stage of the Revision.

(c) 8 were modified [by the Committee?] *before* being entered.

(d) 8 were in part accepted, and in part rejected.

(e) 22 were entered in Durham Book and finally accepted.

(f) 21 were entered in Durham Book but ultimately declined.

(g) 2 erased *after being entered* in Durham Book, were accepted at some *later* stage.

---

66 (a) viz. Nos. 17, 21, 31, 78, 88, all of which related to James I.'s revision in 1604; and 5, 26, 27, 33, 34, 62, 67, 74.
(b) viz. Nos. 1, 7, 8, 9, 10, 11, 12, 13 in part, 14, 15, all of which related to calendar; and 24, 35, 42, 53 (at very last stage), 75, 85, 86.
(c) viz. Nos. 6, 22, 28, 43, " Savoy Concession," 48, 49, 68, 71.
(d) viz. Nos. 4, 29, 47, 50, 51, 69, **87**, 90.
(e) viz. Nos. 3 (in part), 4 (except latter part not proposed), 20 (in part), 25, 36, 38, 39, 40, 41, 46, 52, 55, 57, **59, 65, 66**, 72, 73, 77, 83, 89, 91.
(f) viz. Nos. 2, 16 (in part), 19, 23, 30, 32, 37 (after proposal had been *changed* [by Cosin?]), 44, **45**, 54, **56**, 58, **60, 61, 64,** 76, 79, 80, 81, 82, 84.
(g) viz. Nos. 18 in " Sancroft's " Bodleian book only, and 70.

The Nos. in "**Clarendon**" type alone possess any doctrinal significance.

Some of Cosin's most cherished hobbies, it will be seen, were ignored entirely in the Durham Book. Thus the Proclamation of King James at which Cosin gibes in every one of his "series" of private memoranda, was nevertheless left intact both in the Durham Book and in Sancroft's "Fair Copy," which is now in the Bodleian. Again, many other changes which Cosin advocated, and which were in fact ultimately adopted, found *no* acceptance at this stage of the revision. The transfer, for example, of the passage about "Judas," from the "third" Exhortation in the Communion is *not* indicated, though *other* changes in the same Exhortation are duly entered in the Durham Book. There are in fact but three entries which from internal evidence seem to suggest that Cosin had devised them privately out of his own head. These are the very curious emendations of the Act of Uniformity, 1 Elizabeth, cap. ii., against which Sancroft has written "stet" after erasing the alterations;[67] a rather wordy but very Protestant address on Confirmation which Mr. Parker thinks was designed as a Preface to the Confirmation office, but of which "no notice appears to be taken" by erasure or otherwise in the "Fair Copy" made by Sancroft;[68] and a proposed verbal Oblation *after* consecration, *which was decisively rejected*.

With these possible exceptions, the rest of the Durham Book must be referred (*pace* Mr. Parker) to the post-Restoration period. This is proved by the fact that many entries *in Bishop Cosin's handwriting*

---

[67] *History of the Revisions of the Prayer Book*, p. 109.
[68] *Ibid.*, p. 260.

THE ORNAMENTS RUBRIC

in the Durham Book were taken from Bishop Wren's suggestions framed in 1660. Bishop Jacobson published these Notes of Wren's in his *Fragmentary Illustrations of the History of the Book of Common Prayer*, 1874 (Murray): and in the preface evidently written after the Restoration, but before the Savoy Conference to which it points, Wren speaks of "the loud clamours which for *these fifteen years* have been taken up in general terms against the Book by the several factions." Bishop Jacobson points out that 1645 was the date of the parliamentary ordinance against the Prayer Book: and "fifteen years" from 1645 brings us to 1660.

The date of Wren's Notes being thus fixed, we proceed to show that his suggestions were considered, and in several instances adopted into the text of the Durham Book *as originally written by Cosin*. If this can be established it proves, *first* that Cosin's handwriting is evidence merely that he was at one time acting as secretary to a committee, and *secondly*, that for the most part (at least) the Durham Book was not earlier than 1660. Let us examine, then,

BISHOP WREN'S NOTES EMBODIED IN THE "DURHAM BOOK."

Bishop Wren is described by Lord Clarendon as "very learned, and particularly versed in the old liturgies of the Greek and Latin Churches"; and after the Restoration no Bishop stood higher than he in the estimation of the Prime Minister who habitually consulted him as to the exercise of the Royal Patronage.

In May and June, 1661, Committees of Convocation met at his house—"Ely House"—to discuss the new Forms of Prayer for May 29th, &c., Sancroft acting on these occasions as secretary.[69]

In the next Convocation (November 21st, 1661) a Committee of eight Bishops was ordered to meet "at the palace of the Lord Bishop of Ely"; and Wren was also on the committee for revising the new Preface. In his *Notes on the Ornaments Rubric*[69a] Wren had written :—

"But what is now fit to be ordered herein, and to *preserve* those that *are still in use*, it would be set down in express words, without those uncertainties which breed nothing but debate and scorn. *The very words too of that Act 2 Ed. VI.*, for the minister's ornaments, would be set down, or to pray to have a new one made; for *there is somewhat in that Act that now may* NOT *be used*."

In accordance with this suggestion the present text of our Ornaments Rubric appears in the Durham Book, differing from the preceding rubric (1) By abolishing the previous distinction between the "time of the Communion and [at] all *other* times in his ministration": (2) By introducing the word "retain" so as to fulfil Wren's requirement "to *preserve* those that are *still* in use": to which, in Cosin's handwriting was added in the Durham Book, "*that is to say* . . ." This was clearly intended to fulfil Wren's wish to have the Ornaments of the Minister "set down in express words." And lastly, over the row of dots Cosin has "written in with darker ink than the rest

---

[69] D'Oyly's *Life of Sancroft*, p. 112.
[69a] *Fragmentary Illustrations of the Book of Common Prayer*, p. 55.

and so at a different time"[70] "*A Surplice, &c.*" Underneath the rubric thus altered, Sancroft has further written, "These are the words of ye act itself, v. supra," and this explanation appears also in Sancroft's "Fair Copy" in the Bodleian. See above, p. 147. Sancroft has added in the Bodleian "Fair Copy," "*see. penult ut supra*" as a reference to the 1 Elizabeth, cap. ii., the Act of Uniformity which then was always, as it is still by law required to be, printed "supra."[71] So Wren in his parliamentary defence had written "those Injunctions' of 1559 'are allowed by the Queen's Advertisements, Cap. I., Art. 3, and those Advertisements are authorised by law, 1 Eliz. c. 2, sect. penult."[72]

Bishop Sparrow, who was both a Savoy commissioner and a member of Convocation (being appointed on several important committees) at the last revision, and whose book on the liturgy was then the only commentary published by a clergyman, also understood this "sect. penult" in the same sense, viz. as relating to the Advertisements; as also did Heylin and L'Estrange.[73]

---

[70] *History of the Revisions of the Prayer Book*, p. 129. The meaning of the "*&c.*" is clearly explained by Bishop Sparrow (who, *after taking part in the revision* of 1661, republished his explanation in 1664 and 1668), in these words—"such ornaments as were in use in the second of Edward VI., viz. a surplice in the ordinary ministration, and a cope in time of ministration of the Holy Communion in Cathedral and Collegiate Churches.—Q. Elizabeth's Articles set forth in the 7th year of her reign." The Visitation Articles cited above prove this. See pp. 154-162.

[71] *History of the Revisions of the Prayer Book*, p. 129.

[72] Wren's *Parentalia*, p. 75.

[73] *Rationale. Alliance of Divine Offices*, p. 104. *History of the Reformation*, II.-408-10. See pp. 81, 82, above.

Now Cosin's own private suggestion had originally been that *at the beginning of the Communion office* "HERE is to be inserted and *repeated* the order *there* appointed, as well concerning the ornaments of the church, as of the priest or bishop, and other ministers that celebrate the Holy Communion."[74] When "distinctive" vestments for Holy Communion were in use they were thus prescribed *at the beginning of the Communion office* in the First Book of Edward: but in the Durham Book, no trace of this proposed Cosinian revival is to be seen.

Hence it is clear that the influence of Wren prevailed over that of Cosin (if we are to believe that Cosin still held his juvenile theory), even in the re-construction of the Ornaments Rubric, as drafted in the Durham Book. Yet Mr. Perry coolly urges that

"Cosin having proposed to use the language of the act, it follows that whatever he understood the act to mean, that he must have intended the rubric to mean; and as *his form was adopted* by the revisers in 1662, it is most reasonable to believe that they adopted it in his sense."[75]

Apart from the circumstance that Cosin had in the meantime changed his mind, the above recital of the facts of the case will show the untenableness of this "great Cosin Myth." Mr. Blunt [*Annotated Prayer Book*, p. 3], says that the words "after me" in the close of the Exhortation at Morning Prayer "were erased by Bp. Cosin." But this had been previously urged by Wren.[75a] Mr. Parker has not noticed this alteration, which was disallowed by the Committee.

---

[74] Notes, Second series, p. 305. [75] *Perry on Purchas Judgment*, p. 93.
[75a] *Fragmentary Illustrations of the Book of Common Prayer*, p. 55.

In Wren's Notes, p. 64, we have a suggestion for a new Thanksgiving with this title—

"*A Thanksgiving for the Restoring of Public Peace.* O Eternal God, our Heavenly Father, Who alone makest men to be of one mind in an house, and art the God of peace and unity in every Nation, we bless Thy Holy Name for this gracious change among us, and that it hath pleased Thee with so high a hand to appease those seditions and tumults, which by the subtlety of the Devil were raised up and long fomented among us, and so to subdue the oppositions of men of evil minds, as that, through Thy grace, we may now assemble in peace and safety, to offer up unto Thee this our sacrifice of praise and thanksgiving, through JESUS CHRIST our LORD. Amen."

Now if anyone will compare this with the Thanksgiving "for restoring public peace at home" in our present Prayer Book, he will see that Wren's is manifestly the first draft of this new collect which appears in the Durham Book *in Cosin's writing, but altered* into its present form, except that the words "grant to all of us grace" were written by Cosin "grant us all grace." Yet Mr. Parker claims, on the strength of the handwriting, that "the prayer was composed by Bp. Cosin himself"! He omits to explain how a prayer written by Wren in 1660 came to appear in "Cosin's corrected copy, 1640-61." Again, the existing prayer "In the time of any common plague or sickness" *first* appeared among Wren's suggestions, 1660 (p. 63), thus:—

"O Almighty God, Who in Thy wrath in the wilderness didst send the first Plague upon Thine own people, for the obstinacy of their rebellion against Moses and Aaron ; and also in the time of King David, didst slay, &c. . . That like as Thou didst then accept of an atonement and didst command the destroying Angel to cease from punishing," &c.

In this shape, with hardly any change, it appears also in the Durham Book, in Cosin's handwriting.[76]

In the Visitation of the Sick, Wren suggested the introduction, into the rubric before the absolution, of the words "if he perceive that he doth humbly and heartily desire it," which accordingly appear (in their present form) in the Durham Book.[77]

In the same office Wren proposed to insert into the collect which follows the Lord's Prayer, the words "strengthen him by the comforts of Thy Blessed Spirit; and when it pleaseth Thee to take him from hence." The words as now read appear accordingly in the Durham Book "written by Cosin, but very hastily, and re-written by Sancroft," says Mr. Parker,[78] which is just what would be likely to happen upon a change of secretaries, while Cosin was writing from dictation. For the Commination service, Wren proposed[79] to add to the title the words "a denouncing of God's judgments against sinners." This appears to have been edited by the committee, who added the words "*anger and*" before "judgments," and so Cosin entered it in the Durham Book.[80] Wren had written[81] "that collect for Easter Tuesday, 'Almighty Father, &c.,' would be reserved for the Sunday after Easter, and the collect for Easter Day to serve for all this week." Both changes were adopted in the Durham Book, Cosin having erased the previous collect, and

---

[76] *History of the Revisions of the Prayer Book*, p. 158.
[77] *Ibid.*, p. 287. *Fragmentary Illustrations of the Book of Common Prayer*, p. 96.
[78] *History of the Revisions of the Prayer Book*, p. 283.
[79] *Fragmentary Illustrations of the Book of Common Prayer*, p. 98.
[80] *History of the Revisions of the Prayer Book*, p. 302.
[81] *Fragmentary Illustrations of the Book of Common Prayer*, p. 68.

written in the margin "print this for the next Sunday."[82]
Of course, many of Wren's suggestions (like Cosin's)
failed to find acceptance; but it is curious to note that
(just as happened also to Cosin's "Considerations")
suggestions which were thrown out in the first stage,
and consequently were *not* entered in the Durham
Book, were often adopted at a later stage by subsequent
committees of revision. For instance, the insertion of
"the Conversion of St. Paul," and of "Barnabas,"
into the Kalendar, though suggested by Wren,[83] did
not appear in the Durham Book.[84] The adoption of
St. Matthew xxvi. as a second lesson proper to the
sixth Sunday in Lent, and of Acts ii., "to begin at
verse 22," for Easter Day at evening prayer, and of
I John v., for Trinity Sunday at evening prayer,
though ultimately adopted, gained no footing in the
Durham Book. Many changes which were afterwards
disallowed, but which did appear in the Durham Book,
were also due to Wren. Wren proposed for Ash
Wednesday, which previously had no proper Psalms,
those which we still retain; to these Cosin had added
Psalm xxiii. in the morning, and Psalm lxix. in the
evening. But his own pen (or that of Sancroft) has
in the Durham Book reduced the list so as to correspond with Wren's.[85] The title of the second collect
was altered into "for peace *and defence*" at Wren's
suggestion,[86] but the pen was afterwards drawn through
the addition.[87] The Septuagesima collect received the

---

[82] *History of the Revisions of the Prayer Book*, p. 170.
[83] *Fragmentary Illustrations of the Book of Common Prayer*, p. 50.
[84] *History of the Revisions of the Prayer Book*, p. 121.   [85] *Ibid.*, p. 119.
[86] *Fragmentary Illustrations of the Book of Common Prayer*, p. 50.
[87] *History of the Revisions of the Prayer Book*, p. 146.

addition of "with Thee O Father and the Holy Ghost ever one God" in the Durham Book, which is manifestly a variation upon Wren's suggestion, "with Thee and the Holy Ghost ever one God,"[88] which was ultimately preferred. In the Baptismal service Wren suggested a rubric: "Let us pray, *all the congregation shall kneel down*"; this reappears in substance in the Durham Book, though only to be rejected. Again, "these children *severally* have covenanted," appears in the Durham Book from Wren,[89] the order of the words being, however, transposed. At private baptism, Wren inserted "to every one of these questions shall answers be directly given by those that bring the child, as far as they know." This appears *verbatim* in the Durham Book, except "must" for shall, "answer" for answers, and the omission of the last five words. The insertion of "or unto marriage" after "communion" in the final rubric of the Confirmation service, by Wren,[90] clearly occasioned the insertion of "or unto matrimony" in the Durham Book.[91] "Speaking directly unto the persons that stand before him," wrote Wren, and these very words are inserted in the Durham Book.[92] In the Burial service Wren proposed to insert "the lesson being ended, they shall kneel down and the priest shall say."[93] This was entered in the Durham Book, the word "being" alone omitted, but the rest literally transcribed. At the close of the Burial office, Cosin

---

[88] *History of the Revisions of the Prayer Book*, p. 166. *Fragmentary Illustrations of the Book of Common Prayer*, p. 67.
[89] *Fragmentary Illustrations of the Book of Common Prayer*, p. 88.
[90] *Ibid.*, p. 93.   [91] *History of the Revisions of the Prayer Book*, p. 276.
[92] *Fragmentary Illustrations of the Book of Common Prayer*, p. 93. *History of the Revisions of the Prayer Book*, p. 279.
[93] *Fragmentary Illustrations of the Book of Common Prayer*, p. 97.

had written in the Durham Book "the blessing of God Almighty," &c. Whereas Wren had proposed 2 Corinthians xiii. Mr. Parker says of the former "but it is erased, and this' (*i.e.* Wren's suggestion) 'is substituted for it in Sancroft's hand."[94]

⁎

On the face of it, then, the Durham Book appears to be the record of a progressive revision by a committee to which *Cosin himself acted as secretary*, until (after the Savoy Conference) Sancroft was permanently installed as secretary to the revisers. An indication of this is furnished by the changes successively made in the first rubric of the Communion office. The rubric stood before revision, "*So many as intend to be partakers of the Holy Communion, shall signify their names to the curate overnight, or else in the morning before the beginning of Morning Prayer, or immediately after.*" In his forty-third "Consideration" Cosin had urged this rubric as a reason for allowing a space of time between Morning Prayer and Communion. But in the Durham Book, in Cosin's handwriting appears, *first*, an erasure of the words "overnight, or else in the morning," and instead of them is written "*two days before at the least.*" This again is erased, and in its stead "*some part of the day before.*" These successive emendations in Cosin's handwriting are quite different from his own expressed wish, and were evidently made by him *as the secretary* to the committee. Then, last of all, in this same Durham Book, comes the final emendation *in Sancroft's handwriting*—"At least sometime the day before," which was the actual wording of the Savoy

---

[94] *History of the Revisions of the Prayer Book*, p. 298. *Fragmentary Illustrations of the Book of Common Prayer*, p. 97.

"Concession" No. 5, as given by Cardwell.[95] Cosin was a Savoy Commissioner, and we know that seventeen "concessions" were made by the bishops at the Savoy during the first fortnight of July, 1661. These concessions are all found in the "Durham Book," and several of them are in the *ipsissima verba* as then agreed upon.[96] These entries are in Sancroft's handwriting,[97] and they illustrate the nature of the "Durham Book" as being in fact the minute book of a committee of revision. Many of the entries in Cosin's writing are at variance with his own "Considerations," which, as we saw, dated after 1640, and with his "Second series" of Notes which could not be earlier than 1638, at which date the Prayer Book containing them was printed.

For instance, in his "Consideration" No. 20 Cosin had written that the absolution "is no prayer to God," yet in the Durham Book he wrote "shall answer here and at the end of all *other* prayers, Amen." Many other suggestions in the "Considerations" are altogether *absent* from the so-called "Cosin's corrected copy," *i.e.* the "Durham Book." Nay, some, such as 63 and the parallel proposal 72 to *tighten* the rule as to private baptism[98] were altered in the opposite sense, being *relaxed* by alterations which appear for the first time in this (so-called) "Cosin's corrected copy, 1640-1661." If we compare still further the text of the Durham Book with the three series of Notes described above, we shall be struck by the variances of the latter

---

[95] *History of the Revisions of the Prayer Book*, p. 179.
[96] See Cardwell's *Conferences*, p. 362.
[97] *History of the Revisions of the Prayer Book*, pp. 179, 181, 263, 266 276, 280, 294, &c.   [98] *Ibid.*, p. 231, 249, 250.

from the Durham Book which Mr. Parker chooses to fancy was of even date and of the same authorship.

What is more likely than that when Charles II. by his "Declaration" of October 25th, 1660,[99] publicly promised a revision of the Prayer Book, Cosin should have procured a copy of the 1619 book (if he had it not by him) to serve as a basis for the coming revision? Mr. Parker's sole pretext for assuming that Cosin privately elaborated entries in this book during a protracted gestation of twenty-one years is that the "Durham Book," in which they were made, was printed in 1619! But there were two "good reasons" for Cosin's selection of that book. First, because being page for page uniform with the "First series of Notes" it would facilitate reference from one to the other as the revision progressed. Next, having been printed before the rise of Laud who was suspected and openly accused of having tampered with the text of the printed Prayer Books, the "1619" book would obviate any such delay as the scrutiny of such objectors might otherwise occasion. We know that the House of Commons manifested great jealousy of supposed Laudian alterations, which led them to select a copy of the Prayer Book printed in 1604.[100]

Probable Date of the Durham Book.

On July 24th, 1661, the very last day before the Savoy Commission expired, Bishop Cosin brought in a paper "as from a considerable person,"[101] urging the Puritans to propose in writing "what they desire in

---

[99] Cardwell's *Conferences*, p. 294, and *Documentary Annals*, II.-246.
[100] Cardwell's *Conferences*, p. 376.
[101] *Ibid.*, p. 265. Baxter's reply is printed in *Reliquiæ Baxterianæ*, p. 341

point of expediency"—adding, "let that then be received from them, and speedily taken into consideration and judgment of the Convocation."[102] Heylin, who was also a Savoy Commissioner, urged that the business of the Conference was "only to prepare matter for a convocation,"[103] and Dr. D'Oyly in his *Life of Sancroft*,[104] says: "the episcopal divines who met on this occasion, were satisfied in the result of the discussions, that some alterations in the Book of Common Prayer were expedient, and they in consequence determined to bring the matter before Convocation." Nicholls in his preface (p. x.) agrees with the statement of Dr. Cardwell that "the bishops had *already* made preparations for such changes as they deemed expedient in the Book of Common Prayer."[105] But the Royal Licence to Canterbury Convocation, enabling it to revise the Prayer Book, was not read till November 21st, nor that to York till November 30th, 1661, although the House of Commons had already read, FOR THE THIRD time, their Bill for Uniformity, and had sent it up to the House of Lords as early as July 10th. The Commons repeatedly expressed their impatience at the delay of the House of Lords to give effect to their bill, and the Bishops became seriously alarmed lest the matter should be hurried through Parliament before they had completed their revision.

How are we to explain the delay? Lord Clarendon tells us that "the bishops spent the vacation" (*i.e.* from July 30th to November 20th, 1661) "in making

---

[102] *History of the Revisions of the Prayer Book*, p. 80.
[103] Barnard's *Life of Heylin*, p. 180.   [104] p. 111.
[105] Cardwell's *Conferences*, p. 369.

such alterations in the Book of Common Prayer, as they thought would make it more grateful to the dissenting brethren."[106] But it is probable that the Durham Book and Sancroft's "Fair Copy," now in the Bodleian, represent a *still earlier* stage of the revision conducted by the episcopal delegates at the Savoy, *during* the sessions of the Savoy Conference itself,[107] and embodying among its *latest* "corrigenda" the results of that conference. To take the last point first. The seventeen "Concessions" made at the Savoy by the bishops were announced to their opponents on July 14th.[108] Every one of these Concessions, except the second (which, however, was ultimately conceded, and is really trivial), was entered, in Sancroft's writing, into the Durham Book, and for the most part in the very words used on July 14th. They *always* appear *as the last* of several successive alterations. This would seem to indicate that the Durham Book was completed about the date of these "Concessions," when the finishing touches were being put in. Even Sancroft's Bodleian "Fair Copy," which is later than the Durham Book, does not contain the "Prayer for the High Court of Parliament to be read during their session," which had been introduced into Convocation on May 31st,[109] and appeared *verbatim*, exactly as we now have it, title and all, in the printed

---

[106] *Life*, Vol. II., p. 118.
[107] Lucy, Nicholson and Griffiths spoke at the Savoy Conference although not Commissioners [Kennet's *Register*, p. 508]. Griffiths was on four Committees and Nicholson on two Committees of Convocation connected with the Revision.
[108] Cardwell's *Conferences*, pp. 263-4.
[109] *History of the Revisions of the Prayer Book*, p. 83

form for June 12th, which was drawn up by a Committee of Convocation "at Ely House," on June 7th.[110] Of course, no trace of it exists in the (earlier) Durham Book, shewing that its revised version of the "Occasional Prayers" had been completed *before* the new Prayer for Parliament had been settled. The new office for Baptism of Adults, settled on May 31st, had no place in the "Durham Book," though a direction there to the printer to "print in a new leaf," and an inaccurate recital of the title of the new Office, both imply a knowledge that some such Form was then being prepared. In the Sancroft's Bodleian "Fair Copy," the new Form was written on two sheets of paper which were an after insertion.[111] Another indication of age is found in the circumstance that Sancroft's Bodleian "Fair Copy" contains an alternative form of the "Canon" in the Communion service on a separate leaf, inserted into the printed book, and preceded by a marginal note, viz. "what follows from hence to the end of the distribution is somewhat otherwise methodized in the paper "B," and *both left to censure.*" Paper "B," which is of some length, is headed "Another method of the consecration, oblation, address, and distribution."

Sancroft was not a member of Convocation, but simply the clerk, and as such he has recorded the fact that these two alternative forms were "both left to

---

[110] Clay's Book of Common Prayer illustrated, Preface xxvi., *History of the Revisions of the Prayer Book*, p. 83. The Royal Order for its publication is dated June 10th. There is a copy in the British Museum having the press-mark 472. a. 12. An earlier form, not identical, dated 1640, is B. M. E. 203, and is copied correctly in Blunt's *Annotated Prayer Book*.

[111] *History of the Revisions of the Prayer Book*, p. 257.

censure," presumably by some provisional committee, the members of which were divided in judgment. Yet in the Durham Book we find this important memorandum of the "censure" to which the rival drafts had been "left." "*My Lords the Bishops at Ely House ordered all in the old manner.*" This has been added by Sancroft at some *later* time and shews that the revision recorded in the Durham Book was prior to the meetings "at Ely House" where the subsequent "censure" took place. If these "Ely House" meetings were the same of which Lord Clarendon speaks as being held prior to November 20th, 1661, it increases the likelihood that the Durham Book was completed by the end of July. For we know that the Northern bishops (Cosin being one) first sat with the Southern on June 21st,[112] and that Cosin spoke at the Savoy Conference on July 24th. Cosin went to Durham in the second week of August,[113] leaving his Chaplain, Sancroft, in town during his absence till, on September 6th, in answer to an urgent appeal from Sancroft, Cosin writes—"since my Lord of London [Sheldon] and Ely [Wren] will have it so, I shall make all the haste I can to be at London upon the beginning of November." He accordingly returned to town on October 31st, leaving an interval of but twenty days before the book came before Convocation for its final and hasty revision. It seems probable that Cosin's "handwriting" must have found its way into the Durham Book *before* he left town, and that Sancroft's later emendations may have been made during Cosin's absence when Sancroft

---

[112] Gibson's *Synodus Anglicana*, p. 210.
[113] *Cosin Correspondence*, Surtees Society, I.-21.

superseded Cosin in the Secretariat. This would, of course, explain and account for the unbeneficed "Chaplain" being left behind in town at Cosin's formal and stately entry into his new diocese, as well as for the change of handwriting in the Durham Book.

It is probable that Wren and Sheldon were urgent for Cosin's return in order that he might take part in that important debate when "the bishops at Ely House" decided *against* the restoration of the "oblation," *before* Convocation met. For (as Mr. Parker and Mr. Milton for once agree), the bishops *did not meet at Ely House during the sittings of Convocation*, when the formal revision was gone through after November 21st.[114] Dr. Cardwell, in his *History of the Conferences*, p. 371, and Canon Swainson in his *History of the Act of Uniformity*, p. 15, also agree that the bishops abandoned their original intention to meet at Ely House, during *that* period; and as the time spent by the Upper House was far too brief for any debate of such magnitude and importance—(two hours at most being then spent on the entire Communion office—as Mr. Parker calculates [115]—we may regard it as almost certain that the second stage of the revision took place between October 31st and November 21st, and was begun "at Ely House," after the completion of the Durham Book. The Durham Book therefore must be dated sometime between October 25th, 1660, and October, 1661. That it dates from "1640"

---

[114] *History of the Revisions of the Prayer Book*, p. 407. Mr. Milton, *Church Perplexities*, p. 207, disposes of the objections raised by Lord Selborne.

[115] *History of the Revisions of the Prayer Book*, p. 409.

is "a fond thing vainly invented" by Mr. James
Parker.

*_**

Fortunately we may deal with Mr. Parker's facts
without accepting any of his inferences and deductions.
Lord Selborne, Canon Swainson, and the Rev. W.
Milton have each carefully investigated the same facts,
and all agree in rejecting Mr. Parker's conclusions
from those facts. Lord Selborne holds that the
Durham Book prior to Sancroft's corrections repre-
sents the result of a revision made by the bishops
between July 30th and November 20th, 1661.[116] Canon
Swainson, who calculates that the so-called "Cosin's
corrected copy," *i.e.* the Durham Book, "contains
almost two hundred suggestions which emanated from
Bp. Wren," thinks the Durham Book was prepared for
the bishops at Ely House: and Mr. Milton regards
the Durham Book as containing the results of the
revision which ensued as the result of the Savoy
Conference.[117] He dates it, therefore, as prior to
July 24th, 1661. No student has accepted Mr. Parker's
theories, which are merely intended to link the worthless and partially spurious "Notes" of Mr. Cosin with
the great reputation of Bishop Cosin, who *did not
become "bishop" till the age of sixty-six.* In any case
the influence of Cosin on the Revision of 1661 has
been grossly exaggerated. Lord Selborne observes,
"The influence which Cosin personally exercised over
the work of revision cannot be measured as Mr. Parker
seems, in part at least, to measure it, by the number
of changes entered into his 'book,' which were

---

[116] *Notes on the Liturgy*, pp. 44, 47.   [117] *Church Perplexities*, p. 163

ultimately adopted. Very many of these changes—whatever may have been their origin—were verbal and trivial. Many others of greater importance were (in one stage or other of the work of Convocation), rejected, and of these, some of the most considerable may be inferred, from their agreement with passages in Cosin's 'particulars' or 'Notes,' to have been suggested by him. Contemporary writers, such as Baxter and Burnet, ascribed the prevailing influence to Sheldon, Morley, and Henchman, who, above all other bishops, possessed the confidence both of the king and of Lord Clarendon. Neal, in the next century, wishing to note for reprobation those who were reputed by the Puritans to have been the chief authors and promoters of the Act of Uniformity, mentions the same three names, with seven others; of which Sparrow's is, but Cosin's is not one."[118] Canon Swainson, in his *Rubrical Question of 1874*, points out that Cosin was not placed on the more important Committees of Convocation, that his very name was unknown to the clerk (who repeatedly left a blank for it), and that "almost every proposal [by him] of any important alteration was rejected" (p. 113). Mr. Bulley, in his *Tabular View* (p. 142), says "many were inserted, but the *most material* were omitted." These REJECTED Amendments proposed by Cosin occupy no less than *forty-one pages* in the *Cosin Correspondence* published by the Surtees Society. Vol. II., pp. 39-80. See also Cardwell's *Conferences*, p. 392.

---

[118] *Notes on Liturgy*, p. 48. Baxter describes Cosin at the Savoy Conference in these words: "Bp. Cosin was there constantly, and had a great deal of talk with so little logic, natural or artificial, that I perceived no one much moved by anything he said."—*Reliquiæ Baxterianæ*, p. 363.

The result of our inquiry is that the so-called Cosin's *Notes* had no more to do with the revision of the Prayer Book in 1661 than the private diary of some statesman who took part in the passing of an Act of Parliament has to do with the interpretation of the Act. If the diary in question had been kept while the politician was trimming his first feathers as a political fledgling, the cases would be still more parallel. And if some busybody were to publish the diary, laying bare the youthful indiscretions of a man who became afterwards famous, we should have the exact counterpart of the hard fate of "Bishop" Cosin. Charity bids us draw the veil of oblivion over these youthful indiscretions of one who lived to learn, by bitter and personal experience, the banefulness of Romanism in his actual contact with its workings in Paris. Mr. Keble,[119] and Neal the Historian of the Puritans,[120] admit that Cosin changed his doctrinal views. He came back to England a wiser and a better man. If we take for evidence his official acts and his public utterances rather than the back-stairs revelations of his too-officious post-mortem "friends," we shall find that Cosin uniformly and consistently abstained from employing the Ritual of the "First Prayer Book of Edward VI.," that he enforced the ritual of 1552 where it *conflicted* with that book, and that (with one temporary and doubtful exception) he never adopted any one of the "six points" of modern Ritualism.

---

[119] *Eucharistical Adoration*, p. 139.
[120] The Doctor was "softened in his principles by age and sufferings." *History of the Puritans*, II.-388. See also Droop's *North Side of the Table*, p. 34. Brewer's *Memoir*, p. xxvii., and Canon Elliott's *North Side of the Table*, p. 40.

VIII
"The Breaking of the Bread"

THIS is the earliest and most frequent title given in Scripture to the Lord's Supper. The Revised Version does not bring out the full force of the definite article "*the*"[1] bread, in Acts ii.-42. "We must bear in mind that in the East, and throughout Holy Scripture, there is no such thing as "bread," distinct from "loaf." We are accustomed to cut "bread" from the "loaf," as we cut "meat" from a "joint," or "flesh" from the "body"; and this difference of idiom in rendering the same Greek word, ἄρτος, has created great confusion of ideas in many passages, but in none more, perhaps, than in our Saviour's institution of the Holy Eucharist. Owing to the custom of baking in large earthenware jars buried in the earth, "a loaf" in the Holy Land is of the size and shape of a large bun, or of what is commonly called a "tea-cake." The crust of it is no thicker, and is broken or torn, together with the crumb, and eaten with it, as we do a bun; whence the expression

---
[1] Although Bishop Middleton "On the Greek Article," p. 183, long ago called attention to the point.

"breaking bread" which occurs so frequently in Holy Scripture. Now, ἄρτος, and Syriac "*lehem*," like "panis," "pain," &c., means "a loaf"; and "bread" —only in the general sense of "meat" or "food," but never *as distinct from* "loaf." A number of such loaves always form a part of each day's provision; therefore did the disciples reason among themselves, " because we have taken no loaves" (plural). (St. Matthew xvi.-7.)

So also is the point lost in Matthew iv.-3, "Command that these stones be made loaves," every stone a "loaf" and not "bread" (Authorised Version). This is proved by the parallel passage in St. Luke iv.-3, " Say to this stone that *it* become a loaf." [2] Again, ἄρτοι προθέσεως (Matthew xii.-4) are "shew-loaves," a limited number, and not "bread" in general. Thus our Saviour at His supper did not take "bread," but He took "a loaf." He then gave thanks, or blessed it, and brake it, saying, "Take, eat, this is My body" (not "my flesh"), "which is," &c. It is evident that a square bit of bread-crumb divided into regular pieces, or a wafer, give no idea whatever of the symbol intended in the "breaking of a [*the*] loaf." [3]

"The bread, or loaf, which our Saviour used in celebrating the Sacrament, was whole and unbroken; for He took bread, and blessed it, and broke it. He did not break it before, but after it was sanctified.[4] The Apostle Paul proves the unity of Christians from

---

[2] In St. Matthew vii.-10, the superficial resemblance of a stone to a loaf (like that of a serpent to a fish), is used to illustrate the mockery of sham sympathy in contrast with the love of the Father.

[3] Malan's *Two Holy Sacraments*, p. 142.

[4] Palmer's *Origines Liturgicæ*, II.-77. The "breaking," however, like the distribution, occurred *before* He said, "This is my body." See St. Matthew xxvi.-26.

the unity of that 'bread,' of which they were all partakers." (1 Corinthians x.-17.)

"The Pentecostal Christians continued steadfastly in the 'breaking of bread,' and on the first day of the week 'the disciples came together to break bread.' The breaking of the bread is even set forth as parallel to the 'blessing' of the cup (1 Corinthians x.-16). If the breaking of the bread had not greater prominence at the first than it has in most liturgies, it is difficult to understand how the rite should ever have been named after it."[5]

Ignatius, in his Epistle to the Ephesians (cap. xx.) speaks of "breaking one loaf": and the newly-discovered "Teaching of the Apostles" (cap. ix.) directs the thanksgiving at the Eucharist "concerning the fragment" (using the same word as in Mark vi.-43, &c.), to be made in these words, "as this broken piece was scattered over the hills, and having been brought together became one, so let Thy Church be brought together from the ends of the earth," &c.[6]

This symbol of the unity and fellowship—"communion"—of the faithful by their joint participation at the Covenant Feast is paralleled by St. Paul with the fellowship which the Jews and Pagans also had with their respective deities by "part-taking *with* (not 'of') the altar" upon which a portion of the previously sacrificed victim had been offered to the deity.

Not, of course, that any worshipper, Jewish or Pagan, degraded his altar into a cooking stove (as

---

[5] Sadler's *Liturgies and Ritual* in *The Church and the Age*, p. 296.

[6] Horneck's *Fire of the Altar*, 1619, similarly says, "See here, O my soul, the bread which is broke. Is it not the Communion of the body of Christ? *See how many pieces* are here, which all make but one loaf" (p. 73). Compare Cardwell, *Documentary Annals*, II.-50, second edition.

some seem to fancy) by allowing a worshipper to eat any portion which had once been placed *upon* the altar: for *this* portion was supposed to be consumed by the god to whom it was offered, and whose own private "table" the altar was therefore reputed to be. Where animal sacrifices were required, the demand for animals became so great, that the only chance, for a poor man at least, of tasting "butcher's meat"[7] practically depended upon the sacrificial feasts which followed, and whose value as Covenant rites rested upon the *previous* acceptance of the offering upon the altar, with which they were closely connected, but from which they were altogether distinct. Thus it was that the notion of part-taking *with* the Deity, and so of holding intercourse and "communion" with Him, made it a matter of "conscience" to refuse to share the viands of an alien Covenant Feast, even though the Christian might "know that an Idol is nothing in the world" (1 Corinthians viii. and x.-18, 28). The "one loaf" was an apt symbol of the one Bread of Life,[8] inasmuch as part-taking of it made all the participants "one body," as deriving their common nourishment from one Federal Head.

The "One"-ness of the loaf it was, which made the "breaking" of it so full of symbolic meaning. As Hooker[9] expressed it, "that saving grace which Christ

---

[7] "The Mishna says that the altar was intended to sustain men's lives. The Rabbins describe it as the town's shambles, surrounded with all the appurtenances of a slaughter-house, such as rows of beams, with hooks, supporting a multitude of carcases in process of being flayed, &c.—*Sepher Middoth.*" (Street.) Compare Proverbs vii.-14, xvii -1.

[8] St. John vi.-48-58, the same word being translated "loaf" in the earlier verses of the chapter. [9] *Ecclesiastical Polity,* V.-lvii.-5.

originally is or hath for the *general* good of His whole Church, by Sacraments He *severally* deriveth into every member thereof."

It is a striking proof, therefore, of the worthlessness of "Catholic tradition" as a voucher for primitive usage,[10] that the so-called "ancient liturgies" ALL lack the *ritual* "breaking" which appears as a peculiarity in our English Prayer Book. To find a precedent for it Sir W. Palmer had to go to the "Alexandrian Liturgy as used by the Coptic *Monophysites*," *i.e.* to an obscure and heretical sect: and he adds, "I am not aware that any other Liturgy, except the English, prescribes a breaking of bread during the Benediction."[11] Mr. Scudamore[12] bears the same witness: and even the "Annotated Prayer Book" of Mr. Blunt[13] says that, "though apparently 'most agreeable with the institution of Christ,' [it] is peculiar to the English rite."

In 1881 Mr. Christopher Wordsworth (with Canon Perry, Mr. James Parker, Dr. Littledale, Mr. J. Fuller Russell, and other Ritualistic "authorities") published a Directorium called "Ritual Conformity" in which they testified[14] that "any breaking of the bread at this period of the service was then [1661] a novelty, and is now peculiar to the English Liturgy."

The "catholic" (*i.e.* Mediæval and Western) substi-

---

[10] "Throughout east and west alike, the officiating clergy, and they *alone*, receive in the ordained manner. To the laity the Bread and Wine are *nowhere* given into the hands; worse still, they are in the East given not even separately but mixed; saddest of all, and most fearful to think upon, in the Roman West the Wine is never given at all." (Freeman's *Principles of Divine Service*, II., Part ii.-367.)
[11] *Orig... s Liturgic.*, II.-145.   [12] *Notitia Eucharistica*, p. 610.
[13] Vol. II., p. 187   [14] p. 7

tute for the broken loaf of Scripture was the wafer. Honorius of Autun, A.D. 1130, says "because *from the people not communicating*, it was unnecessary that so large a loaf should be made, it was settled that it should be moulded or made, like a denarius,"[15] and these tiny wafers ("nummuli") with unconscious irony are compared to the pieces of silver of that disciple who betrayed his Master!

Not only was "the breaking of the loaf" absent from the Sarum and other missals, it was positively forbidden by the Ritualistic Rabbis. Thus John de Burgo, an Englishman, writing A.D. 1385, said "the sign of a fraction is *not* to be made here,"[16] and the Sarum Manual published under the authority of Cardinal Pole in the reign of Queen Mary (A.D. 1554) said, "here the Host ought *not* to be touched by way of fraction, as some silly (*fatui*) touch it, and do ill."[17]

The previous edition of 1543 (Rothomagi, fol. lxxix., dorso) contained the same direction "hic non debet tangi hostia modo fractionis sicut aliqui fatui tangunt et male faciunt": and Mr. Pearson in his translation of the Sarum Missal,[18] interpolates at "He brake," the words—"Here let him touch the host, but *not* to break it, as some do; for although the order of the words seems to imply that Christ brake before consecrating, tradition teaches the contrary."

It is clear, therefore, that it is from no (so-called) "Catholic" source that the Anglican rite of "breaking the bread" is derived. On the contrary it is Protestant both in its origin and its history. For,

---

[15] *Notitia Eucharistica*, p. 856.
[16] *Ibid.*, p. 607
[17] *Ibid.*
[18] Edition 1868, p. 311

going back afresh to the fountain-head of Scripture in despite of all intervening usage is the very essence of "Protestantism."[19]

Yet in the sixteenth century the English Reformers were confronted with this difficulty, that the manual acts of "taking the bread into the hand," &c., were liable to be perverted into a pretext for elevating the Host; and to minds nurtured in life-long superstitions, even the priest's touching the elements seemed to savour of magical or mechanical notions :—"basely *objecting* and binding ourselves to the earthly elements" as the Homily[20] on the Sacrament expressed it.

Hence Bucer urged the discontinuance of the manual acts of the First Prayer Book, "lest by this practice men would think that the minister said these words *to the bread and wine* and not to the communicants."[21] In the Second Prayer Book of Edward *all* manual acts of a merely ritual kind were discontinued.

The Romanizers then took a different line. One section of them, viz. the honest ones, represented by Bishop Scot,[22] declared that no consecration was effected by the revised Communion Office ; the other, or "Ritualistic" section, are described in the following extract from Bishop Middleton's Injunctions, issued in A.D. 1583 :—

"Whereas, heretofore in sundry places, it hath been a foolish use amongst a sort of ignorant blind priests and ministers,

---

[19] See Bishop Hooper's *Works*, II.-465.
[20] N.B.—This is the *only* recognition of an "objective" presence by the Church of England : but much stress cannot be laid upon it, since about an equal number of the editions issued by Jugge and Cawood in the reign of Elizabeth read "*abjecting*."
[21] See Cosin's *Works*, V.-478.   [22] Cardwell's *Conferences*, p. 113.

that at the saying of these words immediately going before the distribution of the sacramental bread and wine : ' Who, in the same night he was betrayed,' &c., they would take the bread and wine in their hands, lift it up, and shew it unto the people : whereupon hath ensued horrible idolatries, and religious adoration of the sacraments themselves, or *rather*²³ of the bread and wine, as by kneeling, knocking of the breast," &c. . . . "For the avoiding whereof it is decreed, that no persone, vicar, or curate, whatsoever, hereafter shall handle, lift up, or shew unto the people, the bread and wine, but shall let it lie still upon the table, until the distribution thereof, and *then* to break it, receive it himself, and distribute it unto others, according to the orders of the book, without any addition or detraction."²⁴

If such caution were needed a quarter of a century after the second book of Edward had been reinstated, we need feel no surprise that the leading Anglicans felt afraid to revive even the Scriptural rite of "taking and breaking": especially as the use of wafers lingered in some churches down to the close of Elizabeth's reign. For, it is obvious that the cracking or snapping of a single wafer out of many could be no symbol of the Unity of Christ's Church, as shewn by the distributed "fragments" of the "One loaf" of primitive times.

It was to the school opposed to Laud and Andrewes that we owe the restoration of the Scriptural usage. The Directory, which in 1644 was substituted for the Book of Common Prayer, contains the following Rubric :—

"*The minister, being at the table, is to take the bread into his hands, and say,* . . . .

---

²³ Note here the distinction between "Sacraments" and the mere consecrated elements, as pointed out in the Catechism.—See *my Misprinted Catechism*, p. 10. (J F. Shaw. Price One Penny.)

²⁴ *Second Report of the Ritual Commission*, Appendix, p. 426.

"According to the holy institution, command, and example of our blessed Saviour, Jesus Christ, I take this bread, and having given thanks, I break it, and give it unto you." [25]

Again, in the substitute which Baxter proposed for the Communion Office, we read:—

"*Then let the minister take the bread and break it in the sight of the people, saying:*

"The body of Christ was broken for us, and offered once for all to sanctify us: behold the sacrificed Lamb of God, that taketh away the sins of the world." [26]

At the Savoy Conference, among the "exceptions to the Book of Common Prayer," we have this remark:—

"We conceive that the manner of the consecrating of the elements is not here explicit enough, and the minister's breaking of the bread is not so much as mentioned."

And, it is curious to note how grudgingly the "concession" was made.

"We are willing," said the bishops, "that the manner of consecrating the elements be made more explicit and express, and to that purpose those words be put into the Rubric, 'Then shall he put his hand upon the bread and break it,'" &c. [27]

Yet in the original draft of the revised Rubric (as it stood in the so-called "Bishop Cosin's Book," now contained in the Durham Library) the provision for

---

[25] Bulley's *Tabular View*, p. 190.
[26] Hall's *Reliquiæ Liturgicæ*, IV.-70.
[27] Cardwell's *Conferences*, p. 321, 363. Bishop Kennett, in his *Register*, I.-585, attributes the change to the Puritans.

breaking the bread "*before the people*" was not admitted. The draft Rubric ran:—

"*When the priest hath so ordered the bread and wine placed upon the table, as that he may with the more ease and decency take them into his hands, standing up, he shall say as followeth.*"

This, in Cosin's own handwriting, was the original suggestion. But, in committee, successive alterations were made which are extremely interesting. At present we shall only notice those which bear upon the "breaking." First, then, the words "take them into his hands" were changed into the more explicit words "break the bread, and take the cup into his hands." Then, after the interlineated words "break the bread," the important words "before the people" were inserted *by continued interlineation*. This was doubtless done upon the urgent request of the Puritans, who made a great point of the act of breaking the bread being seen by the people. The writing shews that this was a *distinct* addition and final concession; for the words "before the people" were *not inserted at the same time* as "break the bread," for, at the time that alteration was made, the word "cup" was inserted above the line. But in the after addition of "before the people" the word "before" ran over the interlined word "cup," which had then to be written in the margin instead,[28] as the subjoined facsimile (produced by photography) shews—

---

[28] This fact, which may be verified in the Photograph, is concealed in Mr. Parker's *History of the Revisions of the Prayer Book*, p. ccxiii., which also makes "break the bread" and "before the people" to form *two separate* half lines.

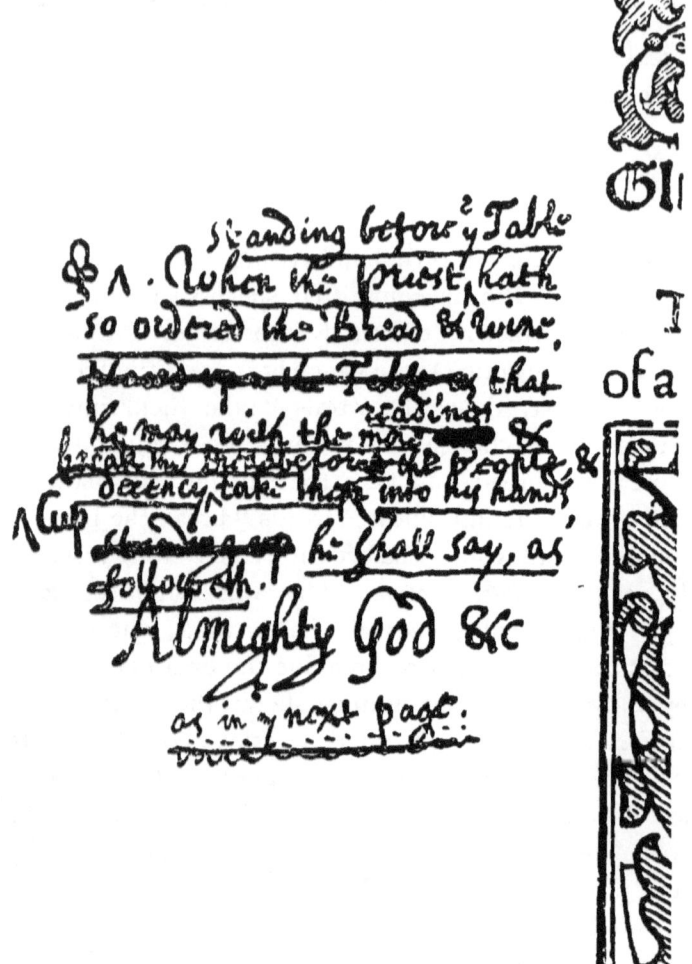

These facts, patent on the pages of Cosin's book, shew that "before the people" cannot mean, as some suppose, publicly in the church, as opposed to privately in the vestry, because the ordering of the act in this part of the service rendered the latter impossible.[29] That is to say, the side Rubric, "And *here* to break the bread," secures publicity for the rite; and its equivalent appeared in Cosin's *original* draft of the Rubrics.

Though it is impossible to shew by ordinary type the erasure of the word "Cup" in the fifth line, the following reproduction of the "Cosin" Rubric from the Durham Book may perhaps make these successive changes clearer; the old English lines representing the original text, and the square brackets indicating erasures subsequently made by a stroke of the pen; while the Italic type shews the newer insertions; and the Roman type the *final* addition.

> "When the Priest ₍*standing before yͤ Table*₎ hath
> so ordered the Bread & Wine,
> [placed upon the Table as] that
> he may with the more ₍*readines*₎ [ease] &
> break the Bread before the People &
> ₍*ACup*₎ decency ₍take the[m] into his hands₎,
>
> [standing up] he shall say, as followeth":—

***

It is fair, however, to recognise that from the other side also, there was a readiness to revert to the Scriptural command "do this," of which the Catechism of Trent itself admitted that it referred to what the Lord

---

[29] Milton's *Church Perplexities* (J. F. Shaw), p. 180.

"did"[3] at the institution of His Supper. The "breaking" thus solemnly "done" before their eyes, was a symbolic rite of which, unless the first communicants had been observant and attentive eye-witnesses, no authentic record could possibly have reached us. Happily, no eastward position or sacrificial vestment intervened to convert *that* "outward and *visible* sign" into a "dumb and dark ceremony." Compare St. Luke xxiv.-43.

Hence, Cosin himself in the memoranda which he made of "particulars to be considered," said the breaking of the bread before the people is "a needful circumstance belonging to this sacrament";[31] and Bishop Wren in his very similar memoranda, suggested that "the Rubric be thus—

Then the priest standing before the table shall so order and set the bread and wine that, while he is pronouncing the following Collect, he may readily take the Bread and break it, and also take the Cup, to pour into it (if he pour it not before)," &c.[32]

And in 1641, he repelled the blame thrown upon him for having altered certain pews so as to face eastward, by saying "the people would the better hear and *see* what the minister said and *did* in his administration."[33]

Ephraim Udall, a writer of the opposite school, in

---

[30] "Nam quod Dominus faciendum præcepit, non solum ad id quod egerat; sed etiam ad ea quæ dixerat referri debet." (*Cat. ad Parochos.*, II.-IV., 19, p. 185. Ed. Lugd., 1675.) The Lutheran liturgies contained no Ritual fraction. Yet Calixtus at the close of the sixteenth century is quoted by Cosin as urging that the death and passion of Christ are represented "not only to the mind but to the eyes also"—"Ipsis quoque oculis"—by the breaking of the bread, &c. (Nicholls' *Appendix*, p. 48.)

[31] Nicholls' *Appendix*, p. 63.

[32] Bishop Jacobson's *Fragmentary Illustrations*, p. 81.

[33] *Parentalia*, p. 78.

his *Communion Comeliness* (written in the same year, 1641), urges the same argument, "if the people be not brought to the Table *within sight* and hearing, to what end are the sacramental actions of breaking the bread?" &c.

But the meaning of the new Rubric is placed beyond all doubt by the fact that the Welsh Prayer Book (which equally with the English, was authorised by Convocation and by the Statute of Uniformity), renders the words "before the people" by "*in sight of* the people." This was expressly pointed out by the Bishops of St. Asaph and St. David's, who sat as assessors in the Folkestone case.[34]

Bishop Gauden, who was one of the Anti-Puritan Divines at the Savoy Conference, published a devotional work called *The Whole Duty of a Communicant*, which received the imprimatur of Mr. (afterwards Archbishop) Sancroft, who acted as secretary during every stage of the revision in 1661. The following direction will shew how these competent witnesses understood the language of a Rubric which was penned by the latter. "At the time of the consecration *fix your eye upon the elements* and at the actions of the ministers . . . we ought joyfully to meditate after this manner," &c.[35]

Dr. Gunning, another Savoy Commissioner, inquired as Bishop of Ely, in 1679, whether the minister doth "break the bread, and lay his hand upon *all* the bread, and . . . upon *every* vessel," &c. (*Second Report of the Ritual Commission*, Appendix, p. 648), questions which

---

[34] See Dr. Stephens' Speech, p. 117, or p. 501 of Mr. Perry's Report.
[35] Cited in *Perry on Kneeling*, p. 318. Gauden was also the author of the re-introduction of the Black Rubric in 1662. (Burnet, *History of his Own Times*, Vol. I., p. 183.)

imply that the churchwardens witnessed the prescribed rites, which they then had to swear to.

In addition to the testimony of Wheatly, Nicholls, Bishop Mant and Professor J. J. Blunt, among commentators on the Prayer Book, Dean Howson cites many devotional allusions to "*seeing*" the bread broken, from Bishops Beveridge, Wilson, Ken, Kidder, as also from Horneck, *The Whole Duty of Receiving* (1685), and other writers.[36]

Dr. Littledale in his *North Side of the Altar*, p. 25, cites Archdeacon Yardley's *Rational Communicant* as a witness that the position "before the Altar" held its ground in 1728, "in spite of innovations." The quotation given related to the Prayer of Access; but Dr. Littledale omits to quote Yardley's remarks two pages later, which had *direct* reference to the Prayer of Consecration, viz. :—

"*He doth not stand before* the Altar as the Romish priests do, nor like them, pronounce the words in a low voice, to countenance their pretended miracle of transubstantiation, and to make the people gaze with wonder on those who are thought to perform it in that secret manner, but the priest in the Church of England says the prayer with an audible voice, as in the Primitive Church, that the people may hear and join with him, and stands so as he may with readiness and decency break the bread before the people, and take the cup into his hands ; that they may *observe* and meditate upon *those actions* which are *significant* and proper to this rite." [37]

⁎

---

[36] See Howson's *Before the Table*, pp. 67-72, 95, 169-175, published by Macmillan. Bishop Patrick and others are cited in Mr. B. Shaw's speech in Folkestone Case, pp. 65-74.

[37] Yardley's *Rational Communicant*, p. 96, cited in Droop's *North Side of the Table*, p. 41 (Hatchard's), and in Elliott's *North Side of the Table* (Parker & Co.), p. 94. It is obvious that "Decency" in breaking the Bread *must* have reference to the spectators.

Although, as Hippolytus says, all modern celebrations are designed "to bring to mind that ever memorable and first divine table of the mystical Lord's Supper,"[38] yet a merely *ritual* "breaking" fails to reproduce literally the action of our Lord. "Breaking bread" was constantly used in the New Testament for the distribution of viands at the common family meal, and among pious Jews was always accompanied by "Eucharist" (Matthew xv.-36), *i.e.* "blessing" or "giving thanks to God." The usage of "the Last Supper" differed in nothing from this. The "breaking" took place (not, of course, when the Evangelist recorded the fact in the words "He brake it," but) when our Lord was about to give to each disciple his own separate "broken-fragment." So Bishop Jewel quotes from the "Hierarchies" of Dionysius the Areopagite, the words—" The priest, uncovering the bread that came covered and in one cake or loaf, and dividing the same into many portions, and likewise dividing the unity of the cup unto all, mystically [συμβολικῶς] and by way of a sacrament he fulfilleth and divideth unity:"[39] and so late as the twelfth century it was usual " while the priest was making the solemn fraction and communicating himself, for the deacons and minister to break the other *hostiæ* into convenient pieces for communicating the people. (See Bocquillot, p. 288, and Humbert, there quoted.)"[40]

---

[38] Εἰς ἀνάμνησιν τῆς ἀειμνήστου καὶ πρώτης ἐκείνης τραπέζης τοῦ μυστικοῦ θείου δείπνου. Migne, p. 265.

[39] Jewel's *Works*, Parker Society, I.-115. Bishop Hooper urged that the Minister "as he giveth the bread, let him break it after the example of Christ." *Early Writings*, pp. 61, 180, 534.

[40] J. D. Chambers, *Divine Worship in England in the XII.-XIVth Centuries*, p. 232. See article "Fraction" in Smith's *Dictionary of Ecclesiastical Antiquities*, p. 688.

But at the original institution, the bread was broken and distributed *before* the Lord said of it "this is My body which is (given) for you." As Tertullian said, "*Acceptum* panem et *distributum discipulis*, corpus illud suum fecit, 'hoc est corpus meum' dicendo, id est figura corporis mei."[11]

No ritual outpouring was ever known, for no thought of a "libation" ever came in. The only "outpouring" in the Eucharist was, as St. Augustine said, "into the mouths of the faithful." And the dramatic "stabbing" of the Greek Church was a mere afterthought conceived in very childish taste. From the very first the ceremony of "breaking" was utilitarian and manward, for purposes of distribution, and not sacrificial or emblematic of the destruction or death of the covenant victim. And the essential sacramental "action" was after all not any ritual "breaking" but "eating and drinking" of that bread and wine which "the Lord hath commanded to be *received*."

---

[11] *Adv. Marcion*, IV.-40.

IX

The First Book of Homilies

AT the close of the year 1539 the murderous "Six Articles" Act was in full swing, and the Lutherans of North Germany had finally given up all hope of any possible alliance with Henry VIII. on Protestant lines. Melancthon then wrote to the English monarch (on November 1st) an indignant remonstrance, saying—

"I am pained that you are becoming the minister of another's cruelty and godlessness. I am pained that the doctrine of Christ is being restrained, vicious rites established, and lusts strengthened. I hear that men of excellent learning and godliness, Latimer, Shaxton, Cranmer, and others are held in custody; for them I pray courage becoming Christians. And although nothing better or more glorious could happen to them than to meet death in the confession of such manifest truth: yet do I not wish your Royal Highness to be stained by the blood of such men, I do not wish the lights of your Church to be extinguished, I do not wish such concession to be made to the godlessness and venomous pharisaic hatred of Christ's enemies, I do not wish pleasure to be afforded to the Roman Anti-Christ, who . . hopes by the aid of the Bishops to regain easily that possession from which he was driven by your honourable and godly counsels. He sees that the Bishops are for a time complying with your will, but that they are joined to the Roman Pontiff."[1]

---

[1] Dr. Jacob's *Lutheran Movement in England*, p. 156.

Henry had by that time got all he could out of the plunder of the Monasteries, and was thenceforth free to follow his own personal tastes, so that, being still a papist both in *doctrine* and ritual, though not in discipline, he felt discontented with the "Institution of any Christian Man" drafted by Cranmer, from which he had always most cautiously withheld any *direct* royal approval.[2] That is why the earlier formulary of 1537 was termed the "Bishops' book": and why the "King's Book," of 1543, which originated from a *Royal* Commission, and was issued by his Majesty, was a much more Popish production. It could hardly have been otherwise while the recent Act of the Six Articles brandished its lighted faggots before the eyes of the draftsmen.

From that Convocation which met on January 20th, 1542, the first book of *Homilies* originated. On January 27th in that year the archbishop mooted the drawing up of Homilies at a joint meeting of the two Houses. On April 3rd the subject was discussed, and a twelvemonth later, on February 16th, 1543, we find the final entry in the records of Convocation: "there were produced the Homilies composed by certain prelates of divers matters: the which books were delivered to Mr. Hussey to be kept." "Kept" they certainly were, but, in prison. Not until July 31st, 1547 (still under the unrepealed Act of "the Six Articles"), did they see the light. The presumption is that Henry had refused to authorise their publication. For, when Bishop Gardiner, in the reign of Edward, formally refused them, it was on this very ground—[3]

---

[2] See Cranmer's *Works*, Parker Society, II.-337, note, 469.
[3] Strype's *Memorials of Cranmer*. Ecclesiastical History Society's Edition, II.-18 (under date June 10th, 1547).

"I have received this day letters from my lord of Canterbury, touching certain homilies, which the bishops in the Convocation holden A.D. 1542, agreed to make for stay of such errors as were then by ignorant preachers sparkled among the people; for other agreement there had not then passed among us. Since that time God gave our late sovereign lord the gift of pacification in those matters, which, established by his Highness' authority, in the Convocation, *extinguished our devices*, and remaineth of force with your Grace."

In another letter to the Protector,[4] Gardiner wrote—

"I have eftsoons received other letters from my said lord of Canterbury, requiring the said homilies by virtue of a Convocation holden five years past, wherein we communed of that which took none effect then, and much less needeth to be *put in execution* now, nor in my judgment cannot without a new authority from the King's Majesty that now is, commanding such a matter to be enterprised."

Gardiner's plea rested on the objection that the teaching of the newly published Homilies was contrary to "the King's book," *i.e.* the "*Necessary doctrine and Erudition*" which had been "established by his Highness' authority" on May 29th, 1543. No doubt, the allegation was quite true. The "King's book" which Mr. Tyrrell Green seeks to pass off as a genuine Church of England formulary, taught that "justification may be forfeited or lost, recovered again by the sacrament of Penance, and increased to an indefinite extent by fastings, alms-deeds, works of charity, and general obedience to the commandments of God, until final justification be attained in the day of Judgment. In the matter of Justification, therefore, the teaching of 'the King's Book' is in substance, and, to some extent, in detail, the same as that which was afterwards made an Article of Faith by the Council of

---

[4] Strype's *Memorials of Cranmer*. Ecclesiastical History Society's Edition, II.-19.

Trent."[5] Indeed, so Romish was its teaching, that Bishop Bonner re-issued the book with but trifling alterations, under Mary.[6] One of Gardiner's arguments may make the modern reader smile. He urged that since King Henry had gone to heaven, the doctrine of "the King's Book" must needs be right!

"Specially considering it is agreed our late sovereign is received to God's mercy. And though some would say, he had [his errors] and saw not perfectly God's truth; yet for us, it were better to go to heaven with one eye after him, than to travail here for another eye with danger to lose both . . . For our sovereign lord is gone from us to heaven, *in his way*."

These courtly flatteries of the royal bigot, which extended even beyond the grave, explain the ascendancy which Gardiner gained over Henry during the later years of his reign.

In reviewing the evidence as given above, it seems probable that the Homilies which it had taken the bishops a twelvemonth to prepare, and which were ready for publication in 1543, were suppressed by King Henry acting under the advice of Gardiner. On the other hand, it seems pretty certain that four at least of the series must be dated from the reign of Edward. Gardiner repeatedly refers to the celebrated Homily of Salvation as being Cranmer's, and, apparently, as recently compiled[7] by the Primate. This Homily, it will be remembered, has an authority greater than any other, being specially referred to and incorporated in Article XI. on "Justification," as "declaring more largely" the doctrine which every clergyman now pledges himself to maintain. The Homily against

---

[5] Dr. Corrie's *Concise History of the Church and State of England*, p. 89. (Hatchards.)
[6] *Ibid.*, p. 98.   [7] See Foxe, VI.-45, 49, 55.

"Strife and Contention" is attributed by Dr. Wordsworth[8] to Latimer who, in 1542, was in hiding to save his life, having resigned his bishopric; so that it is highly improbable that he would be employed, in 1542, to prepare any official declaration of doctrine.

Becon was the author of the one against "Adultery",[9] and that against "Swearing" is, at least, based on his *Invective*, published in 1543: but as Becon was at that time "made to recant and burn his books"[10] it is hardly likely that Convocation would then have employed him as a writer. These four must presumably have been added in 1547 by Cranmer to the drafts "kept by Master Hussey."

The names of the writers of the Homilies on "Declining from God," and "Obedience," are unknown. Cranmer himself is credited with four or five, viz. those on the "Reading of the Scriptures," "Salvation," "Faith," "Good Works," and probably "Against the fear of death."[11] Two men of the "Old Learning," as it was called, wrote respectively the one on the "Misery of Mankind," which was by Archdeacon Harpsfield, and that on "Christian Love" which was by Bonner and his chaplain. The former of these was reprinted by Bishop Bonner during the reign of Queen Mary, viz. in 1555. It is verbatim the same with the Edwardian Homily, except that the texts are quoted in Latin, and the following significant changes have also been made. In the "Second part"[12]

---

[8] *Ecclesiastical Biography*, III.-188.
[9] Becon's *Works*, II.-643. It was published by himself in 1560-4.
[10] Becon's *Works*, I.-Preface, viii.
[11] Cranmer's *Works*, Parker Society, II.-128.
[12] p. 16 of the 8vo. edition of the Society for Promoting Christian Knowledge.

the words in Italics were left out (by Harpsfield?) from the sentence—

"Let us know our own works . . . *nor challenge any part of justification by our merits or works.*"
It would be interesting to know whether these words had been *added* in 1547[13] by Cranmer to the original Homily of 1542. They certainly mark the dividing line between England and Rome: the true watershed of Romish heresy. On page 18, Cranmer's edition reads—

"He is that High and everlasting Priest, which hath offered Himself *once for all upon the altar of the cross, and with that one oblation* hath made perfect for evermore them that are sanctified. He is the *alone* Mediator between God and man."

In Bonner's revised version of 1555 the words here italicised were left out, and instead of them we read—
"offered Himself *to God when He instituted the sacrament of the altar, and once for all, in a bloody sacrifice done upon the cross, with which oblation He*" (folio 12): and, no less significantly, the word "*alone*" is blotted out before "Mediator."

On the last page of the Homily the following paragraph has been erased by Bonner—

"Hitherto have we heard what we are of ourselves; verily, sinful, wretched, and damnable. Again, we have heard how that, of ourselves and by ourselves, we are not able either to think a good thought, or work a good deed: so that we can find in ourselves no hope of salvation, but rather whatsoever maketh unto our destruction. Again, we have heard the tender kindness and great mercy of God the Father toward us, and how beneficial He is to us for Christ's sake, without our merits or deserts, even of His own mere mercy and tender goodness. Now, how these exceeding great mercies of God, set abroad in

---

[13] The Homily Of Salvation is said to have been taken from Melancthon s *Loci Communes.* Compare Jacob's *Lutheran Movement in England,* p. 335.

Christ Jesus for us, be obtained, and how we be delivered from the captivity of sin, death, and hell, it shall more at large, with God's help, be declared in the next Sermon. In the mean season, yea, and at all times let us learn," &c.

All this, save the last three words, is omitted by Bonner, who alters the latter into " Let us *now* learn," &c. It can perhaps never be cleared up whether Cranmer, as editor, had added to the original text of Harpsfield's Homily of 1542; or whether Bonner had erased words which had been written there from the first. But what is not by any means uncertain is that between the two versions there is a wide gulf fixed : that no "continuity of doctrine" can connect the Church of England, as reformed, with the Mediæval system ; and that modern " Ritualists " elect to stand with Bonner rather than with Cranmer as to the precise points involved in the above changes. Bonner would indeed have been much aggrieved had he been told that he was *not* " Undoing the Reformation."

***

It is a pity that the original Edwardian Preface to this First Book of Homilies is not now reprinted with them, as it would explain the character of the Notice which still appears at the end of the book—" Hereafter shall follow Sermons of Fasting, &c.," [14] a notice which was in fact merely a continuation of the Royal Preface, and concluded with " God save the King." In all the nine editions put forth during the last six months of 1547, and in Grafton's edition of June 21st, 1548, this Preface directed a Homily to be read " every Sunday in the year *at High Mass*, when the people be most

---

[14] Cranmer (*Answer to Gardiner*, p. 53) and Ridley (*Works*, p. 196) expressly repudiated the phrase " under the forms of bread and wine," which occur only in this *Royal* Notice of 1547. In several editions, though not in all, the Notice appeared on a separate page. See below, p. 245

gathered together." For, during those two opening years of Edward's reign, the Latin Mass continued to be said, and up to Christmas Eve in 1547, people were even thrown into prison under the *still unrepealed* " Act of the Six Articles." It was not until the First Prayer Book came into use, on June 9th, 1549, that the Mass was finally supplanted. The change was instantly marked by an *alteration in the wording* of the Preface, which in Oswen's edition of the Homilies, dated at Worcester, October 8th, 1549 ("they be also to sell at Shrewsbury") ran thus—" At the celebration of *the Holy Communion*, in such order and place as is appointed in the book of Common Prayer." This alteration is but another proof that the Mass and the Communion were not supposed to be convertible terms, but direct opposites, and it illustrates also the unfairness of the reasoning in the Lambeth Judgment which was based on the notion that no breach in *doctrinal* " continuity" ever took place at the Reformation ! The Preface now usually printed with the Homilies, dates only from 1560, and directs a Homily to be read " every Sunday and holy-day in the year, at the ministering of the Holy Communion, or *if there be no Communion ministered that day*, yet after the Gospel and Creed, in such order and place as is appointed in the Book of Common Prayer."

But it is important to remember that the "Advertisement" which is still printed at the end of the First book of Homilies was not a theological document proceeding from any "spiritual" authority, but only an "Erastian" announcement of what the Government of that day *proposed* in 1547 to issue, a promise which was never fulfilled. The Homilies themselves were sandwiched, as it were, between these two, just as the

Canons of 1604 lie embedded in the middle of the Royal Letters Patent, or the Thirty-nine Articles between the Royal Preface of one Monarch and the "Ratification" of another. Had this always been recognised, the theological importance sometimes attributed for polemical purposes to this belated "Advertisement" would have been seen to be misplaced.

∗

Before the Jesuits in the Council of Trent succeeded in getting their Pelagian theory of Justification passed by the Italian and Spanish votes, in despite of the more Evangelical views of Cardinals Pole, Contarini, and Cajetan, "Justification by faith" continued to be taught, even within the Church of Rome, as it had been of old by St. Paul, and by St. Clement of Rome. Canon Jenkins, in his interesting book on *Pre-Tridentine doctrine*, has called attention to the close correspondence of Cranmer's *Homily on Justification* with the commentary of Cajetan on Romans iii. There are two facts, apparently not then known to Canon Jenkins, which lend plausibility to this conjecture. The first is that in the MS. *Notes on Justification*, now in the library at Lambeth, there is a list at the end (though *not* printed in the Parker Society edition of Cranmer's *Remains*, p. 203), of the authorities relied on by the compiler of those Notes, giving the Greek and Latin writers in two groups, the last name being "Cajetanus." The other fact is mentioned by Mr. Burbidge (*Liturgies and Offices*, p. xxv.), viz. "that Cranmer's own copy of Cajetan's commentary on the New Testament, 2 vols. folio, Paris, 1532, is now at the British Museum, 1277. d. 1."

Thus we certainly know that Cranmer had read Cajetan and noted his testimony in the matter of justification. Canon Jenkins gives in parallel columns some illustrations of the close similarity of thought, if not of language.

If we choose to suppose with Canon Jenkins that this was the immediate source of the Homily, it is of course possible that it might have been written in 1542, and if so the motive for suppressing the First Book of Homilies becomes obvious. Gardiner's dislike found expression in his letter to Somerset of November 12th, 1547, in which he said:—

"As for my Lord of Canterbury's Homily of Salvation, it hath as many faults, as I have been weeks in prison . . . and is handled *contrary to the teaching of the Parliament*."

This latter suggestion was an adroit reference to the Parliamentary authority supposed to attach to the "*Necessary Doctrine and Erudition*" of 1543 from the Acts 32 Henry VIII., cap. xxvi., and 34 and 35, Henry VIII., cap. i. And it very possibly led to a repeal of those Acts, during the following month, viz. by the passing of the 1 Edward VI., cap. xii., on Christmas Eve, 1547, which (by repealing also the Six Articles Act) left Convocation thenceforth free to acquiesce in any reforms which Cranmer could persuade them to assent to.

But it seems more probable that Melancthon's *Commonplaces. De Vocab. gratiæ*, furnished the quarry from which this Homily was dug, as Bishop Fitzgerald points out in his *Lectures on Ecclesiastical History*, II.-215.

HOMILY.	MELANCTHON.
"This sentence that we be justified by faith only, is not so meant that the said justifying faith is alone in man, without	"When Paul says that we are justified freely through faith, he does not mean that contrition does not exist in

true repentance, hope, charity, dread and the fear of God, at any time and season. But this saying that we be justified by faith only, freely and without works, is spoken for to take away clearly all merit of our works; . . . and therefore wholly to ascribe the merit and deserving of our justification to Christ only. . . . Justification is not the office of man, but of God; for man cannot make himself righteous by his own works, neither in part nor in whole. . . . The true understanding of this doctrine, we be justified freely by faith without works, or that we be justified by faith in Christ only, is not that this our own act to believe in Christ, or this our faith in Christ which is within us, doth justify us, and deserve our justification unto us (for that were to count ourselves to be justified by some act or virtue that is within ourselves); but the true understanding and meaning thereof is, that although we hear God's word and believe, although we have faith, hope, charity, &c., we must renounce the merit of all such virtues." those that are converted, or that the other virtues do not follow, yea, rather he means that they are present; but he excludes the condition of merit or worthiness on our part; he denies that contrition or any virtues of ours are the causes of our reconciliation, and he testifies that the cause thereof is the merit of Christ the Mediator. Nor is the meaning of our divines different when we say that we are justified by faith only. Nor does that word 'only' exclude contrition or other virtues from being present in him who is justified, but denies that they are the causes of our reconciliation, and transfers the cause to Christ alone. So that this saying, 'we are justified by faith in Christ,' is equivalent to this, that we are justified for the sake of Christ, and not for our own deservings. Faith is itself a work, like love, patience, chastity, and as these are infirm and weak, so is faith; so that we are not said to be justified by faith because faith is a virtue of such dignity as to deserve justification, but because there must needs be some instrument in us by which we lay hold upon the Mediator who intercedes on our behalf."

X

The Second Book of Homilies

THE history of the Second Book is quite distinct from that of the First. Edward's Homilies continued to be reprinted separately down to the year 1623, when both books were, for the first time, included in one volume. At least three editions of that " First " (Edwardian) book of Homilies had been issued under Elizabeth before any publication took place of the later set. The earliest of these reprints was probably issued before February, 1559, because in it alone are found the words " Supreme Head," as applied to Elizabeth in the " Exhortation to Obedience." " Supreme Head " had been the legal title of Henry VIII. and of Edward VI. under the 26 Henry VIII , cap. i. That title was used also by Mary in the writs which summoned her first Parliament;[1] but it was disliked both by Papists and by Puritans. Sandys tells us that " Mr. Lever wisely put it into the Queen's head that she would not take the title of Supreme Head " (Letter to Parker,[2] dated April 30th, 1559), and the word "wisely"

---

[1] Lewis's *Reformation Settlement*, pp. 139, 154 ; Ingram's *England and Rome*, p. 208. Mr. Lunn says, " The 2 documents in Bonner's Register immediately preceding Scory's rehabilitation, both describe Q. Mary as ' Supreme Head of the Church of England.' They are both licenses to preach ; the one issued by Bonner, the other by the Queen herself."

[2] Archbishop Parker's *Correspondence*, p. 66.

shews that Sandys himself approved the change. But all the Puritans were not of this way of thinking. Robert Beal, Clerk to the Privy Council, raised a question in the Commons as to "the validity as well of the Parliaments lately had, as this Parliament, lacking, in the writ of summons, 'Supremum Caput';" which shews that even in convoking this very Parliament Elizabeth had omitted to use the title, from a regard, no doubt, to the Marian repeal of the 26 Henry VIII., cap. i.[3] However, on February 9th, 1559, a bill was introduced, which on May 9th received the Royal assent, and became the celebrated Statute of the Royal Supremacy (1 Elizabeth, cap. i.). By this Act the title of SUPREME GOVERNOR was substituted for that of Supreme Head.

We learn from the *Spanish State Papers*, p. 37, that before March 19th, 1559, the Lord Treasurer, the Marquis of Winchester, "had promised" the Spanish Ambassador 'that the Queen would not take the title of Head of the Church"; and on April 11th the Count de Feria reported to Philip: "The Queen has already declared in Parliament that she will not be called Head of the Church, whereat the heretics are very dissatisfied. Cecil went yesterday to the Lower House, and told them from the Queen that she thanked them greatly for their good will in offering her the title of Supreme

---

[3] The Supremacy Act of Henry VIII. was repealed by 1 and 2 Philip and Mary, cap. viii., which repeal was *continued* by 1 Elizabeth, cap. i., sec. xiii. It is necessary to state this, because "authorities" so great as Hale, Coke, and Dyer have stated otherwise. But Elizabeth's Supremacy Act, 1 Elizabeth, cap. i., gave to the Crown, in addition to *all* the powers of Henry's Act, jurisdiction also in "schisms"; the *title* of the Monarch, with its vague indefinite claim of autocratic power, being the only subtraction.

Head of the Church, which, out of humility, she was unwilling to accept, and asked them to devise some other form with regard to the supremacy or primacy."[4]

So that the earliest Elizabethan reprint of Edward's Homilies, retaining, as it did, the old title, must have been printed before March 19th, 1559. Its text was based on the edition by Whitchurch of 1549. It seems a pity that the S. P. C. K. do not see their way to giving on p. 110 of their octavo edition, a footnote stating that the original words, "Supreme Head," were changed by Elizabeth in 1559. Convocation sanctioned a similar change in Article XXXVII., which, in King Edward's time, ran, "The King of England is Supreme Head, in earth, next under Christ, of the Church of England and Ireland"; but, in 1563, this was altered into the present form. "Supreme Head" has not been the legal title of any English Sovereign since the year 1554.

***

Date of the Second Book of Homilies.

A curious document, drawn up by some of the bishops, exists in two separate MSS. now preserved in the libraries of the Inner Temple, and of Corpus Christi, Cambridge. Among other provisions suggested in this draft, came this one:—

"Item, homilies to be made of those arguments which be shewed in the book of Homilies, *or others*[5] of some convenient

---

[4] *Spanish State Papers*, p. 52.
[5] The allusion is to the Advertisement appended (in July, 1547, by the Privy Council) to the First Book of Homilies as described above, p. 235. "Other arguments" were adopted, in the case of the Lord's Supper, from what it would have been lawful to publish in 1547, while the Six Articles Act remained in force.

arguments, as of the sacrifice of the Mass, of the common prayers to be in English, that every particular Realm may alter and change their public rites and ceremonies of the Church, keeping the substance of the faith inviolably, with such like. And that these be divided to be made by the bishops." [6]

The copy in the Inner Temple,[7] reads "Church," instead of "Realm," and adds at the end—"every bishop two, and the Bishop of London' [Grindal] 'to have four."

Strype has blended these two versions in his *Annals*, I.-i.-319, and has been followed by Cardwell. The date of this document can be approximately ascertained, because more than one of the "*items*" in it were adopted in the "Articles agreed upon" by the High Commissioners at Lambeth on April 12th, 1561.[8]

The Corpus Christi MS. contains, in addition, some "Resolutions and Orders" (printed by Strype, *Annals*, I.-i.-329), which also shew that the Homilies had not then been composed. The second of these Orders urges people to frequent Communions "in such form as is already prescribed in the book of Common Prayer, and as *shall be* further declared in an homily concerning the virtue and efficacy of the said Sacrament."[9]

Hence we learn that the compiling or selection of the Homilies to form the "Second Book" had not been effected much before April, 1561. On the other hand, they must have been completed before January 12th, 1563, when that Convocation assembled, in

---

[6] Parker MSS., Corpus Christi College Library, Cambridge, "P. 106."
[7] Petyt MS., Vol. XXXVIII.
[8] Cardwell's *Documentary Annals*, I.-264. Strype's *Parker*, I.-194.
[9] C. C. C. MS., "P. 106," p. 423.

which, on January 29th, the Thirty-nine Articles were subscribed by the bishops, containing an endorsement of the Second Book of Homilies, enumerating each by name except, of course, the "Homily against disobedience and wilful rebellion." This last was occasioned by a rising in the North, which commenced in November, 1569, and was subdued before Christmas. This latest of the Homilies was written early in 1570, and ran through five editions before being incorporated, in 1571, with the rest, in the revised edition of our thirty-fifth Article, which was then (for the first time) enacted by Parliament.

Authors of the Homilies—Second Book.

Mr. Griffiths has, with great acuteness, tried to discern the names of the separate writers. To Jewel he refers the lion's share. Those on "The right use of the Church," "Against peril of Idolatry," "For repairing of churches," "Of Prayer," "Of the place and time of Prayer," "Of Common Prayer and the Sacraments," "Of the worthy receiving of the Sacraments," "For Whit-Sunday," and "Against idleness" —are all due to him. Each of these gives the Scripture quotations from a free translation of the Vulgate, and the one on "Idolatry" was largely taken from a treatise by his friend Bullinger (*De origine erroris in Divorum et sacrorum cultu*) which had been published in 1528 and 1539. Grindal wrote the Homily on "Fasting" in its original form; though, as we shall see by-and-by, it was much altered subsequently. Pilkington probably wrote the one "Against Gluttony," a few sentences of it being taken from his exposition upon Haggai, published in 1560; and a large portion of it being a translation from Peter Martyr's *Commentary on the Book of Judges*. Pilkington, too, is probably responsible for that "Against excess of apparel." Several passages in the "Information for them that take offence at certain places of Holy Scripture," are taken from Erasmus. The two on the "Passion" and the "Resurrection" are taken from Taverner's *Postils*; but two instructive and important changes were then made which deserve especial and separate notice.

Easter Day being the time for "every parishioner to communicate," the Homily naturally referred to that subject; but the passage, "call to thy mind that therefore thou hast received into thy possession the everlasting verity, our Saviour Christ, IN FORM OF BREAD, to confirm thy conscience," was altered, in 1563, by *striking out the words in small capitals*. Canon Knox Little should make a note of that erasure, which is on p. 465 of the S. P. C. K. octavo edition, or p. 436 of Dr. Corrie's. On p. 467 (*Corrie*, p. 438), may be found another: "How dare we be so bold as to renounce the presence of the Father, the Son, and the Holy Ghost NOW RECEIVED IN THIS HOLY SACRAMENT?" Here again the words printed in small capitals have been carefully eliminated. Compare Cardwell's edition of *Taverner*, pp. 193, 195.[10]

The Homily for "Rogation" week is probably due to Archbishop Parker; while that on "Matrimony" is taken partly from a homily by Chrysostom, and partly translated from an address by Veit Dietricht, a Lutheran, of Nuremberg. Two-thirds of the first part

---

[10] "Penance and remission of sins" was altered into "pardon and remission of sins."

of that on "Repentance" are taken from Rodolph Gualter; and the authorship of the rest has not hitherto been traced. The Elizabethan Preface, which is still reprinted, was draughted by Bishop Cox.[10a]

Final Revision by Queen Elizabeth.

Though Elizabeth prudently declined the title of Supreme Head, she, in fact, acted as such. In hardly a single instance did she allow Convocation to have the "last word." According to her own notions, she succeeded to the powers formerly wielded by the Pope;[11] and in this spirit she altered the Statutory Book of Common Prayer—striking out the two rubrics as to Ornaments and the place for Morning Prayer, and substituting for them, *without any authority*, two brand-new inventions of her own. Other changes continued to be made throughout her reign, which it is difficult to trace, or even specify; for hardly any two editions of the Elizabethan Prayer Books agree together. In the same spirit she struck out the Twenty-ninth Article, after it had been enacted by Convocation in 1563, to say nothing of the famous introductory clause in Article XX., of which many deem her the sole author. The Canons of 1571 underwent her careful editorship, though they failed, after all, to obtain her final approval.[11a] Nor did the Homilies escape like changes. They had received formal sanction from Convocation on February 5th, 1563, but were detained in the custody of the Queen till the following July, though Archbishop Parker had

---

[10a] Strype's *Annals*, I.-i.-516. See Lansdowne MS. 982, fol. 6, dorso.
[11] Strype's *Life of Whitgift*, I.-495.
[11a] Cardwell's *Synodalia*, I.-113.

been urgent with Cecil, the Prime Minister, to get them out for his Visitation "after Midsummer."[12]

In the British Museum is the identical copy which Archbishop Parker had procured to be handsomely bound for presentation to her Majesty, and which shews the state in which the book left the hands of the prelates. The press-mark of this unique copy is " C. 25. h. 3." From this, the original text, Elizabeth, before sanctioning its publication, made the six changes following:—

I. "AN ADMONITION TO ALL MINISTERS ECCLESIASTICAL," was prefixed, which affected to give leave to the clergy to change the appointed lessons at their own discretion, although the new Kalendar had been issued under a *statutory* Order so recently as February 15th, 1561.[13]

II. In the Homily on "Idolatry" two significant changes were made by the Royal editor; an explanation of which will be found by comparison with the dates of the incidents mentioned, in my *Queen Elizabeth's Crucifix, its secret history and real meaning*,[14] as also with the Spanish State Papers, I.-105, 179. Her own vacillation in the matter of the crucifix led to the following changes of a passage in "Part I.," which may be found on p. 192 of the 8vo. edition. After quoting 2 Corinthians vi.-14-16, it runs on,

"Which place enforceth both that

[*Synodical Version*.]	[*Cæsar's Version*.]
neither the material church or temple ought to have any	we should not worship images, and that we should not have

---

[12] *Parker Correspondence*, p. 177. [13] *Ibid*, p. 135.
[14] Published by J. F. Shaw & Co. Price One Penny.

images in it (for of it is taken the ground of the argument), neither that any true Christian ought to have any ado with filthy and dead images, for that he

images in the temple, for fear and occasion of worshipping them, though they be of themselves things indifferent; for the Christian

is the holy temple and lively image of God, as the place will declare to such as will read and weigh it."

Still more clearly, at the opening of the "Third Part" of the same Homily, the writer had said "the word of God speaketh against not only idolatry and worshipping of images, but also against idols and images themselves." This was too much for the proprietor of the crucifix, so the Queen herself added "(I mean always thus herein, in that we be stirred and provoked by them to worship them, and not as though they were simply forbidden by the New Testament without such occasion and danger.)" To make this addition read smoothly, the next words (which had originally formed part of the first sentence) were altered by interpolating "ye" and beginning as a fresh sentence —"And ye have heard likewise," &c., p. 223 of the S.P.C.K. octavo edition.

III. The next emendation is of a different kind. It occurs in the Homily "of Fasting," in which the last paragraph in the "First Part" (beginning "Lord have mercy upon us," &c., at the foot of p. 300 of the octavo edition) and the next five pages of the "Second Part," up to "Now shall be shewed briefly what time is meet for fasting" were added. This very large interpolation was inserted more than a month after the Homilies had been in the hands of the Queen, having been occasioned by a Bill brought in on March 9th, which ultimately became the Statute 5 Elizabeth, cap. v.

The language of that Act deserves attention. It ran, "not for any superstition to be maintained in the choice of meats: be it enacted that whosoever shall by preaching, teaching, writing, or open speech, notify that the eating of fish and forbearing of flesh mentioned in this statute is of any necessity for the saving of the soul of man, or that it is the service of God, or otherwise than as other politic laws are and be, shall be punished as spreaders of false news are or ought to be." It is evident from Archbishop Parker's *Correspondence*, that his own views about fasting were in accordance with the statute.[15] This quaint statute was only repealed in 1868 by the 31 & 32 Victoria, cap. xlv., sec. 71.

IV. A more important addition, though less bulky, was an interpolation (on page 376 of the octavo edition) dealing with the theological definition of the word "Sacrament." Both versions read—"And as for the number of them, if they should be considered according to the exact signification—

[*Synodical definition.*]

as fully so expressed and commended by Christ in the New Testament, there be but two, viz. Baptism and the Supper of the Lord."

[*Cæsar's definition.*]

of a sacrament, viz. for visible signs expressly commanded in the New Testament, whereunto is annexed the promise of free forgiveness of our sin, and of our holiness and joining in Christ, there be but two, viz. Baptism and the Supper of the Lord. For, although Abso-

---

[15] See *Parker Correspondence*, pp. 216, 235.

lution hath the promise of forgiveness of sin, yet by the express word of the New Testament it hath not this promise annexed and tied to the visible sign, which is imposition of hands. For this visible sign, I mean laying on of hands, is not so expressly commanded in the New Testament to be used in Absolution, as the visible signs in Baptism and the Lord's Supper are; and therefore Absolution is no such sacrament as Baptism and the Communion are. And, though the Ordering of Ministers hath his visible sign and promise, yet it lacks the promise of remission of sin, as all other sacraments besides do. Therefore neither[16] it nor any other sacraments else be such sacraments as Baptism and the Communion are."

This interpolation is quoted with much unction by Ritualistic writers, as by Canon Little in his reply to Archdeacon Farrar, p. 26, where he employs it to overrule the plain teaching of Article XXV. What must be his feelings on discovering that he was actually

---

[16] It was on this ground that Bishop Geste at one time attacked our Twenty-fifth Article, among others, as being "not true." He urged "that it cannot be well denied but that ordering is a sacrament of the gospel; but yet not such one as baptisme and ye Lord's Supper be bycause by orderynge to the person whiche is ordered no forgynes of synes is offered, nor his faith herein is confirmed."—*State Papers, Domestic*, Elizabeth, Vol. LXXVIII. No. 37.

preferring the theories of the daughter of Anne Boleyn, to language which had been sanctioned by the "sacred Synod" of Canterbury!

V. Elizabeth's next excursus into theology was more happy. In the "Sermon on the Nativity" (p. 432 of the octavo edition) a sentence runs—"We are evidently taught in [the] Scripture, that our Lord and Saviour Christ consisteth of two several natures:

[*Synodical dogma.*]	[*Royal dogma.*]
as touching his outward flesh, perfect man, as touching his inward spirit	of his manhood, being thereby perfect man; and of his Godhead being thereby perfect God."

Here the Queen has been more accurate than her prelates in recognising that the "inward spirit" might belong to the humanity of Christ, so that her language was less ambiguous than that of the Synod.

VI. A very important tampering with the original is seen at p. 478 of the octavo edition, where, in the last paragraph, after the first two sentences, in the original edition came a sentence which Elizabeth *struck out*. It will be remembered that she also struck out the Twenty-ninth Article at the same time, and doubtless for the same reason, viz. to conciliate the Lutheran as well as Romanist believers in a "real," *i.e.* local presence. Hence, in despite of Convocation, she got rid of the following—

"WHEREFORE THUS SAITH ST. AUGUSTINE: 'HE WHICH IS AT DISCORD WITH CHRIST DOTH NEITHER EAT HIS FLESH NOR DRINK HIS BLOOD, ALTHOUGH HE RECEIVE, TO THE JUDGMENT OF HIS DESTRUCTION, DAILY THE OUTWARD SACRAMENT OF SO GREAT A

THING.'" In the margin had been written a reference to "Lib. de Trinitate," which, of course, was also erased by "great Eliza," as part of her State policy, if not also to accord with her own private belief.

Elizabeth's revised version was at length[17] allowed to appear before the end of July, 1563, for Grindal on August 1st speaks of the "second tome of homilies, now lately set forth by the Queen's majesty's authority," and orders churchwardens to procure copies with all speed "at the charges of the parish."[18]

**

One more alteration by Royal hands the homilies underwent in 1623, when the "English Solomon" enriched the Homily "Of the right use of the Church," Part II., with a couple of footnotes, indicative of that "statecraft" of which he was so proud to think himself a master. They were appended to the sentence (on p. 176 of the octavo edition) relating to the censure on the Emperor Theodosius, and his excommunication by a bishop. James gravely notes—"The people's fault was most grievous: the sentence executed otherwise and more cruel than it should." Again, "He was only dehorted from receiving the sacrament, until by repentance he might be better prepared." These marginal notes, which are amusing enough in the light of contemporary history, have been very properly removed. But have the far greater ones made by Elizabeth one whit more of "Church authority" than his?

---

[17] Dr. Cardwell thinks that Archbishop Parker designed to have added another of Taverner's *Postils* relating to the authority of the Pope, and adds, "it is not improbable that he was prevented by the Queen."—*Preface to Taverner*, p. xvi.

[18] Grindal's *Remains*, pp. 81, 94.

Moral.

At any rate these curious facts add another illustration of the fact that every one of the passages in our Formularies upon which the Priest-party most rely is due to the arbitrary and unconstitutional interference of "Cæsar," *i.e.* the personal Sovereign. The Ornaments Rubric of Elizabeth, that on the "accustomed place," the second half of the Catechism relating to the sacraments, probably the two alterations above mentioned in the Thirty-nine Articles, and certainly the changes in the Homilies in favour of images, and the "real" presence (*i.e.* local residence) of the body of Christ within the consecrated materials of the Supper,—each and all of these "high" adulterations was effected, *not* by "successors of the Apostles," nor by any "Sacred Synod," but by the "Erastian" authority or intervention of the individual layman or woman who for the moment occupied the throne. Mr. Gladstone has stated the humble origin of these "improvements" as coarsely and nakedly as anybody. He says:—

"To modify the articles of her own mere motion by insertion and exclusion, to sequester and virtually depose at her will an Archbishop of Canterbury, were lawless acts . . . by no means isolated or impulsive, but were parts of a scheme or system. . . The essence of this scheme or system, undertaken in concurrence with an arbitrary civil government, it may be in a larger or smaller degree for the sake of it, was to build up the Church, beneath the shadow of the prerogative. . . The point in which Elizabeth stands alone, as far as I know, is this, that she pursued her work, from first to last, mainly IN OPPOSITION TO THE CHURCH'S RULERS."[19]

---

[19] *Nineteenth Century*, November, 1888, pp. 783-4.

XI

The Declaration on Kneeling

AT the end of our Communion Service, in a different type from the final Rubrics, is a long Declaration directed expressly against the worship of the Host prescribed by the Council of Trent. Among the canons passed in the thirteenth session of that Council, on October 11th, 1551, were the following :—

Canon IV. " If any one shall say, that, after consecration, in the admirable sacrament of the Eucharist, there is not the body and blood of our Lord Jesus Christ, but *only in the use* (' sed tantum in usu '), while it is being taken, but not before nor after; and that in the hosts or consecrated particles which are reserved or remain after communion, there does not remain the true body of the Lord; let him be accursed."

Canon VI. " If any one saith that in the Holy Sacrament of the Eucharist, Christ the only begotten Son of God is not to be adored with the worship, even external, of *latria;* and is therefore neither to be venerated with a special festive solemnity, nor to be solemnly borne in processions, according to the laudable and universal rite and custom of Holy Church, or is not to be exhibited publicly to the people to be adored, and that the worshippers thereof are idolaters; let him be accursed."

These cursory observations did not escape the notice of Cranmer, who wrote (March 20th, 1552) to Calvin, saying: "Our adversaries are now holding their councils at Trent for the establishment of their errors.... They are, as I am informed, making decrees respecting the worship of the bread ($\pi\epsilon\rho\grave{\iota}$ $\tau\hat{\eta}s$ $\mathring{a}\rho\tau o\lambda a\tau\rho\epsilon\acute{\iota}as$); therefore we ought to leave no stone unturned, not only that we may guard others against this idolatry, but also that we may ourselves come to an agreement upon the doctrine of this sacrament."[1] He had previously written similar letters to Melancthon and to Bullinger.

In September he sent a copy of the "Articles of Religion" which he had been compiling to two distinguished laymen, Sir William Cecil and Sir John Cheke; and on October 21st the six Royal Chaplains —one of whom was the afterwards celebrated John Knox—were also invited to "report" upon the draft Articles. Their signatures to the document are still preserved.[2]

At the beginning of the month of October, 1552, Knox preached at Court before the King, "inveighing with great freedom against kneeling at the Lord's Supper."[3] This caused "some disputes among the Bishops." Hooper, no doubt, sided with Knox.[4]

Such dissensions were singularly ill-timed, because the newly-revised Prayer Book, containing a rubric requiring all communicants to kneel, was already in print—two of Grafton's editions being dated "August,

---

[1] Cranmer's *Miscellaneous Writings*, Parker Society, p. 432.
[2] Hardwick's *History of the Thirty-nine Articles*, p. 80, p. 75 second edition.
[3] *Original Letters*, p. 591.   [4] *Early Writings of Hooper*, p. 536.

1552 "⁵—and the book was to come into compulsory use on November 1st. Evidently no time was to be lost if a peaceable reception of the new book was to be ensured. Accordingly, on the 7th of October Cranmer wrote as follows to the Privy Council :—

DOMESTIC STATE PAPERS, ED. VI. VOL. XV. No. 15.

"After my right humble commendations unto your good Lordships.

"Where I understand by your Lordships' letters that the King's Majesty his pleasure is that the book of common service should be diligently perused, and therein the printer's errors to be amended. I shall travail therein to the uttermost of my power, albeit I had need first to have had the book written which was past by Act of Parliament, and sealed with the Great Seal, which remaineth in the hands of Mr. Spilman, Clerk of the Parliament, who is not in London, nor I cannot learn where he is. Nevertheless, I have gotten the copy which Mr. Spilman delivered to the printers to print by, which I think shall serve well enough. And where I understand further by your Lordships' letters that some be offended with kneeling at the time of the receiving of the Sacrament, and would that I (calling to me the Bishop of London [Ridley] and some other learned men, as Mr. Peter Martyr or such like) should with them expend and weigh the said prescription of kneeling, whether it be fit to remain as a commandment, or to be left out of the book. I shall accomplish the King's Majesty his commandment, albeit I trust that we with just balance weighed this at the making of the book, and not only we, but a great many Bishops and others of the best learned within this realm and appointed for that purpose. And now the book being read and approved by the whole State of the realm, in the High Court of Parliament, with the King's Majesty his royal assent—that this should be now altered again without Parliament—of what importance this matter is, I refer to your Lordships' wisdom to consider. I

---

⁵ Whitchurch had one or two editions still earlier. See Cardwell's *Two Prayer Books of Edward*, p. xli. ; and *History of Conferences*, p. 34. n.

know your Lordships' wisdom to be such, that I trust ye will not be moved with these glorious and unquiet spirits which can like nothing but that is after their own fancy, and cease not to make trouble and disquietness when things be most quiet and in good order. *If such men should be heard, although the book were made every year anew, yet it should not lack faults in their opinion.* 'But,' say they, 'it is not commanded in the Scripture to kneel, and whatsoever is not commanded in the Scripture is against the Scripture, and utterly unlawful and ungodly.' But this saying is the chief foundation of the error of the Anabaptists, and of divers other sects. This saying is a subversion of all order as well in religion as in common policy. If this saying be true, take away the whole book of service. For what should men travail to set an order in the form of service, if no order can be set but that is already prescribed by the Scripture? And because I will not trouble your Lordships with reciting of many Scriptures or proofs in this matter, whosoever teacheth any such doctrine (if your Lordships will give me leave), I will set my foot by his, to be tried by fire, that his doctrine is untrue, and not only untrue, but also seditious and perilous to be heard of any subjects, as a thing breaking the bridle of obedience, and loosing them from the bond of all princes' laws.

"My good Lords, I pray you to consider that there be two prayers which go *before* the receiving of the Sacrament, and two immediately follow—all which time, the people praying and giving thanks, do kneel; and what inconvenience there is that it may not be thus ordered I know not. If the kneeling of the people should be discontinued for the time of the receiving of the Sacrament, so that at the receipt thereof they should rise up and stand or sit, and then immediately kneel down again—*it should rather import a contemptuous than a reverent receiving of the Sacrament.*[6] 'But it is not expressly contained in the Scripture' (say they) 'that Christ ministered the Sacrament to his Apostles kneeling.' Nor they find it not

---

[6] Hence the second reason assigned in the "Black Rubric," viz. "For the avoiding of such profanation and disorder in the Holy Communion as might otherwise ensue."

expressly in Scripture that he ministered it standing or sitting. But if we will follow the plain words of the Scripture, we shall rather receive it lying down on the ground, as the custom of the world at that time almost every where, and as the Tartars and Turks use yet at this day to eat their meat lying upon the ground. And the words of the Evangelist import the same, which be ἀνακεῖμαι and ἀναπίπτω, which signify properly, to lie down upon the floor or ground, and not to sit upon a form or stool. And the same speech use the Evangelists where they show that Christ fed five thousand with five loaves, where it is plainly expressed that they sat down upon the ground and not upon stools.

" I beseech your Lordships to take in good part this my long babbling, which I write as of myself only, because the Bishop of London is not yet come, and your Lordships required answer with speed, and therefore am I constrained to make some answer to your Lordships afore his coming. And thus I pray God long to preserve your Lordships and to increase the same in all prosperity and godliness.

" At Lambeth, this 7th of October, 1552.

" Your Lordships to command,

"T. CANTR."

(Indorsed) "To my very Good Lords of the King's most honourable Council."

The result was that the danger was averted by an Order of Council, dated October 27th, 1552 (*i.e.* only four days before the Feast of All Saints, when the book was to come into use), directing the Lord Chancellor (Bishop Goodrich) " to cause to be joined unto the Book of Common Prayer lately set forth, a certain Declaration signed by the King's Majesty, and sent unto his Lordship, touching the kneeling at the receiving of the Communion."[7] Although the time was short,

---

[7] MS. Council Book, A.D. 1500-1553, fol. 630. This Declaration is enrolled upon the Close Roll as a Royal Proclamation, 6 Edward VI., pars. 8. Gasquet, p. 297.

this was done with so much care that few copies are known to exist which do not contain it. On the other hand, only one edition by Grafton is known in which it formed part of the book as originally printed.[8]

Its language should be compared with that of the Twenty-ninth Article of 1552-3 (to which Knox[9] subscribed):—

ARTICLE XXIX. OF 1552-3.	POST COMMUNION DECLARATION OF 1552.
"Forasmuch as the truth of man's nature requireth	"Although no order can be so perfectly devised but it may be of some, either for their ignorance and infirmity, or else of malice and obstinacy, misconstrued,

---

[8] In the quarto edition by Whitchurch, 1552, of which there are two copies in the British Museum (C. 23. b. 26 and C. 25. h. 5), the declaration forms part of the book. " In one by Oswen (Bodleian) it is printed on a separate leaf. In four books by Grafton (three of which are in the Bodleian and one in the possession of Dr. Routh) and in one by Whitchurch (St. John's) it stands No. 4 amongst the other Rubrics, but in each of these it seems, from the paging and other marks, clearly to be no part of the original impression. In one other, however, by Grafton (Bodleian) in which it also stands No. 4, it is to all appearance not an after insertion. A learned writer in the *Irish Ecclesiastical Journal*, No. 3, states that in five copies by Whitchurch he found it inserted on a separate leaf, which in one book is placed after the Commination; that in four others by Whitchurch it stands on the face of a leaf, and is placed after the fourth Rubric."—Bulley's *Tabular View*, p. 80; compare Cardwell's *History of Conferences*, p. 34, and Ketley's *Liturgy of Edward VI.*, p. 283.

[9] One change in the wording of Article XXXVI. (which stood in the original draft as Article XXXVIII.) seems due to Knox and one of his brother chaplains who wrote, " Besides our judgment on the Articles, . . . we offer you our confession on the Thirty-eighth Article." After repeating their objections against kneeling, they conclude " And though some withstand us out of zeal, we suppose, for the truth, yet these, on considering how necessary it is that kneeling be avoided, will doubtless persuade you not to bring that thing under a law whereof ye have no commandment nor example in Christ and His Apostles."—Lorimer's *Knox in England*, p. 126. The change in the wording of the Article mentioned below, p. 279, note, was the result.

that the body of one and the self-same man cannot be at one time in diverse places, but must needs be in some one certain place: therefore the body of Christ cannot be present at one time in many and diverse places. And because (as Holy Scripture doth teach) Christ was taken up into heaven, and there shall continue unto the end of the world, a faithful man ought not either to believe or openly to confess the real and bodily [realem et CORPORALEM] presence (as they term it) of Christ's flesh and blood, in the sacrament of the Lord's Supper."

depraved, and interpreted in a wrong part. And yet because brotherly charity willeth, that so much as conveniently may be, offences should be taken away: therefore We willing to do the same.

Whereas, it is ordained in *the Book of Common Prayer*,* *in* the administration of the Lord's Supper, that the Communicants *kneeling should receive the Holy Communion:* which *thing being* well meant for a signification of *the* humble and grateful acknowledg*ing* of the benefits of Christ, given unto *the* worthy receiver, and *to* avoid the profanation and disorder, *which about* the Holy Communion might else ensue; *lest yet* the same kneeling *might be thought or taken otherwise,* WE *do* declare that *it is not meant* thereby that ANY adoration is done, *or ought to be* done, either unto the sacramental bread and wine there bodily received, or unto any *real and essential* presence *there being* of Christ's natural flesh and blood. For *as concerning* the sacramental bread and wine, *they* remain still in their very natural substances, and therefore may not be adored (for that were idolatry to be abhorred of all faithful Christians). And *as concerning* the natural body and blood of our Saviour Christ, *they* are in heaven and not here. For it is against the truth of Christ's *true* natural body to be in more places than *in* one at one time."

---

* The italics indicate verbal differences from the present form, which dates from 1662.

The Declaration was signed by the King,[10] but being merely a Royal Proclamation, and forming thus no part of the statutory Prayer Book, it was not re-enacted in 1559, when the "Second Prayer Book of Edward" *alone* was restored by the Elizabethan Act of Uniformity, 1 Elizabeth, cap. ii. This, however, mattered little until the rise of Laudianism, when we find the Lords' sub-committee of Divines in 1641 entertaining a suggestion that it was "fit to insert a Rubric, touching kneeling at the Communion, that [it] is, to comply in all humility with the *prayer* which the minister makes when he delivers the elements."[11] At the Savoy Conference, 1661, the restoration of Edward's Declaration was strongly urged,[12] but no concession whatever was made by the Bishops, who held that "the sense of it is sufficiently declared in the XXVIIIth Article."[13] Neither "Cosin's Book," now at Durham, nor "Sancroft's Book," now in the Bodleian, nor the Debates in Convocation, nor the "Annexed MS." now attached to the Act of Uniformity, *in its original text*, contained anything corresponding to this Declaration. The list of "alterations and additions" prefixed to the photo-zincographed reprint of the book of 1636, as published by Government for the Royal Commission on Ritual in 1870, p. 3, was drawn up by Dr. Pearson (better known as Bishop Pearson *On the Creed*), December 16th, 1661, and contains no allusion whatever to this important change. It is clear, therefore, that we are not indebted to the "sacred synods" for this valuable restoration.

Its history is given by Bishop Burnet, who, as a

---

[10] Strype's *Cranmer*, B. II., c. 33.
[11] Cardwell's *Conferences*, 275.   [12] *Ibid.*, p. 322.   [13] *Ibid.*, p. 354.

near contemporary, must be accounted a competent witness.

"There were some small alterations made in the Book of Common Prayer, together with some additions, the most important [of which] was that concerning kneeling in the sacrament, which had been put in the second Book of Common Prayer set out by Edward VI., but was left out by Queen Elizabeth, and was now by Bishop Gauden's means put in at the end of the office of the Communion. Sheldon opposed it, but Gauden was seconded by Southampton and Morley.[14] The Duke complained of this much to me as a Puritanical thing, and spake severely of Gauden, as a popular man, for his procuring it to be added."[15] When we remember that "the Duke" of York was a zealous Papist, afterwards James II., and that Gauden (though *not* on the Committee of Convocation) was in high favour with Charles, and, as his chaplain, might be present at the Council Board, at which the Earl of Southampton (though *not* on the Committee of the House of Lords) yet as Lord High Treasurer and a tried friend of Charles, would be an influential[16] Privy Councillor—

[14] Bishop Morley accounted among the "absurd and blasphemous consequences" of Transubstantiation, "*especially* the idolatrous adoration of the consecrated elements." See Goode's *Tract XC. Historically Refuted*, p. 183.

[15] Harleian MSS. 6584, p. 158. Burnet adds: "Thus was the Act of Uniformity prepared for the Parliament." Compare Burnet's *History of his Own Times*, I.-315, ed. 1823.

[16] Burnet says (*ibid.*, p. 147): "Southampton was for healing the Church by concessions on both hands, but when he saw that all the affair was put into Sheldon's hands, he withdrew from the meetings that were held about it, and declared against their methods." Burnet had previously said of Southampton (p. 146), "His great parts together with his great merits made him to be considered as one of the first men of England. He was made Treasurer, and Clarendon was proud of his friendship and valued himself upon it." Lord Macaulay,

we can well believe that Mr. Milton and Canon Swainson are right in supposing that this alteration (with certain others) was made in the Prayer Book *after it left Convocation*, but before it was submitted to Parliament. Both Gauden and Morley had been present at the Savoy Conference, and were acquainted therefore with the strong feeling which existed in favour of the Declaration. The Prayer Book had received the final signatures of the Convocations on December 20th, 1661, and the book had been forwarded in due course to the King, but it was not until February, 1662, that it was brought forward formally in the Council. The following extracts from the Council Book are given by Bishop White Kennet in his Register, pp. 631-2.

"February 19, 1661-2. Ordered by His Majesty present in Council that the Book of Common Prayer lately presented to His Majesty from the Convocation be brought to the Board on Friday next."

"February 21, 1661-2. Ordered that the Council meet on Monday next, at three in the afternoon, to *continue the debate* upon the amendments of the Book of Common Prayer, and that the Right Revs. the Lords Bishops do make choice of four of their body to attend the Board at that time, whereof the Right Rev. Father in God, the Lord Bishop of London, to be one."

"February 24, Whitehall Council. This day, according to an order of the 21st of this instant February, appeared at the Board the Right Rev. Fathers in God the Lord Bishop of London, the Lord Bishop of Durham, the Lord Bishop of Salisbury, the Lord Bishop of Worcester [Morley], and the Lord Bishop of Chester, at which time the Book of Common Prayer, with the amendments and additions as it was presented by the Lords Bishops, was read, and approved, and ordered to be transmitted to the House of Peers," &c.

---

referring to this MS. of Burnet's (written ten years before his published history of William's Reign), says: "I must own that I generally like his first thoughts best." *History of England*, III.-19.

The Declaration, in the form in which we now have it, was added by Sancroft in a handwriting quite different from that of the rest of the MS., and separated from it by a broad red line. Sancroft (though *not* a member of Convocation) acted as secretary at *every* stage of the revision of 1661-2.

⁎

We have seen that the Declaration was essentially Protestant, both in its source and motive. It was aimed directly at the Tridentine wafer-worship, and any one who compares it in its present form, as adopted in 1662, will see that the alterations (to which attention was called by the use of *italics*, p. 260) are merely verbal.

"The only question then is, Why did the revisers of 1662 substitute the word 'corporal' for the words 'real and essential,' seeing that they left the meaning of the clause the same as they found it? The reason clearly was, that men were no longer familiar with the language of the schools, and therefore the denial of any 'real and essential presence' might be considered a denial of any true presence whatever, which was very far from the meaning of those who had employed that phrase."[17] The Realistic philosophy of Aquinas, which made "essence" equivalent to "substance," had, in the seventeenth century, lost its hold on men's minds; but in 1552 the scholastic terms "real and essential," when used of a "body" (*corpus*), would be universally understood as equivalent to "corporal,"

---

[17] Scudamore's *Notitia Eucharistica*, p. 955; Dr. Stephens' *Notes on Common Prayer*, p. 1244; and Perry, *On Kneeling*, p. 368, like Archdeacon Freeman's *Principles of Divine Service*, II.-i., p. 127, admit that *no change* of meaning was intended by the verbal alterations of 1662.

and were in fact expressed by that word in the Twenty-ninth Article, published at the same time by the authors of this very Declaration.[18]

The pivot sentence upon which the whole Declaration hung remains unchanged, viz. that the body of Christ, which "*is*" in heaven, is "*not* HERE." That was, and is, absolutely fatal to *any* theory of "presence" in the sense of residence within the elements. It was not merely a corporal *manner* of presence (which no Romanist ever affirmed), but "ANY corporal presence" at all which is expressly rejected.

It deserves notice, moreover, that the reason assigned for kneeling, viz. "signification of our humble and grateful acknowledgments of the benefits of Christ therein given," is precisely the same as for kneeling at the absolution before consecration, or at the benediction after. And this was pointed out by the "very authors of the kneeling, most holy men and constant martyrs of Jesus Christ," as Bishops Grindal and Horn termed them.[19] Their letter was written A.D. 1567, and it is interesting to note that these two leading "revisers of the Prayer Book" in 1558-9 say that the Declaration was "most diligently declared, published, and impressed upon the people," long after its disappearance from the printed Prayer Books.

[18] Archbishop Parker's draft of the Twenty-eighth Article of 1562, given in Lamb's *History of the Thirty-nine Articles*, p. 12, is as follows:—

"Christus in coelum ascendens, corpori suo immortalitatem dedit, naturam non abstulit, humanæ enim naturæ veritatem (juxta scripturas) perpetuo retinet, quam uno et definito loco esse, et non in multa, vel omnia simul loca diffundi opertet. Quum igitur Christus in coelum sublatus, ibi usque ad finem seculi sit permansurus, atque inde, non aliunde (ut loquitur Augustinus) venturus sit, ad judicandum vivos et mortuos, non debet quisquam fidelium, carnis ejus et sanguinis, realem, et corporalem (ut loquuntur) presentiam in Eucharistia vel credere vel profiteri."

[19] *Zurich Letters*, I.-180.

Cranmer, as we saw, expressly assigns the same reason. Bishop Ferrar, who was put to death, under Mary, for saying that the sacrament of the altar "is not to be ministered at an altar, lifted up, or in any wise adored," had nevertheless been accused of "superstition" by certain false brethren, to whom he replied, that "he kneeleth in the choir bareheaded, as well at Matins *before* the Communion, as at Evensong *after*, without any superstition: he thinketh it not necessary for the Communion's sake to *leave* kneeling to Christ. But he diligently taught the people not to kneel or knock to the visible show or external show of the Sacrament."[20]

In Aless' version, before the words of distribution addressed *to* the Communicant in the *Order of Communion*, 1548, the rubric "Shall say these words" was rendered "utantur hâc formâ orationis": and similarly "shall say," before giving the cup, is rendered "sic orabit."

The Royal Advertisements of 1566 rested kneeling at reception upon the Injunctions of 1559, which merely specify "That in the time of Litany, and all other collects and common supplications to Almighty God, all manner of people shall devoutly kneel."[21] Archbishop Whitgift defended the practice on the same ground: "It is the meetest manner of receiving this sacrament in mine opinion, being commonly used in praying and giving of thanks, both of which are annexed to this sacrament and are to be required in communicants." "There is no such peril in kneeling at the communion as you surmise: for the gospeller is better instructed than so grossly to err. And as for the learned papist

---

[20] Foxe's *Acts and Monuments*, VII., pp. 12 and 25, note.
[21] Cardwell's *Documentary Annals*, I.-199. The side-heading in the Elizabethan copies was "Reverence at Prayers."

he is so far from worshipping that he disdaineth that Holy Communion, jesteth at it, and either abstaineth from coming unto it, or else cometh only for fear of punishment, or *pro forma tantum* for fashion's sake: and the most ignorant and simple papist that is knoweth that the communion is not the mass: neither do they see it lifted up over the priest's head with such great solemnity as they did *when they took it to be their God*. No truly, the contempt of that mystery is more to be feared in them than worshipping: and to be short, if they be disposed to worship, they will as well worship sitting as kneeling." [22]

Bishop Andrewes in his Notes on the "prayer of the priest" urges—"Et quamquam schismatici cavillantur debitum genuflexionis ritum, orantibus quis alius gestus usurpandus nisi supplicatorius?" [23]

The anonymous writer who poses under the name of "Bishop Cosin" urged the introduction of the words, "the people still kneeling," into the Rubric before the absolution at Morning prayer on this ground:—

"Else there will be no excuse for us, nor no reason left us to render to the Puritans, why our Church should more punish them, or hinder them from the benefit of the Sacrament for not kneeling then, than it doth to punish other men, or hinder them of the benefit of absolution, for not kneeling in time of confession. *It is a like case.*" [24]

Bishop Wren also—at whose house the committee for revising the Prayer Book met—urged that the "benediction," as the Scotch Liturgy calls the words of distribution, "is a proper *prayer*, and of blessing: whereby it is a sufficient reason why every one

---

[22] Whitgift's *Works*, Parker Society edition, III.-90, 95.
[23] Cosin's *Works*, Anglo-Catholic Library, V.-113.
[24] Nicholls' *Appendix*, p. 18.

should kneel when they receive."[25] "Now to stand at Communion, when we kneel at prayers, were not decent," was the strongest argument of the Bishops at Savoy.[26] Thus, the reasons uniformly assigned by authority for the posture of kneeling at reception exclude all conception of worship such as Bishop Cosin himself declared "neither is nor ought to be directed to any sensible object, such as are the blessed elements."[27]

Edward Reeve, B.D., vicar of Hayes, Middlesex (a Laudian controversialist attacked by Prynne in his *Quench Coal*), wrote *The Christian Divinity*, published in 1631,[28] at p. 168 of which he defends kneeling at reception on the ground that the words of administration are a prayer. "Is it seemly, decent, or orderly, that people both before and after the receiving of the sacrament should continue kneeling, and in the very act of receiving should stand or sit, especially whereas it is now taken with and in prayer."

The author of the Declaration on Kneeling is supported by every school of Anglican Divines (till Newman)[29] in his teaching that "our Saviour Christ . . . hath given us warning . . . that we should not give credit to such teachers as would persuade us to worship a piece of bread, *to kneel to it* . . . to follow it in procession, to lift up our hands to it, to light candles to it, to shut it up in a chest or box . . . having always this pretence or excuse for our idolatry, 'Behold, here is Christ!'"[30]

---

[25] Jacobson's *Fragmentary Illustrations*, p. 82.
[26] Cardwell's *Conferences*, p. 350.
[27] Cosin's *Notes on Common Prayer*, Works V.-345.
[28] British Museum, 472. A. 17; 4to.
[29] Pusey and Keble hesitated long before adopting the Romish novelty of "adoration." See Liddon's *Life of Pusey*, Vol. III., p. 461.
[30] Cranmer's *Works*, I.-238.

XII
The Ordinal and Article XXXVI

IN the Prayer Books which one can purchase nowadays in the shops, the Psalter, Ordinal, and Thirty-nine Articles, together with any hymns which a bookseller may choose to add, are commonly bound up in the same volume. But, until the last Revision of the Prayer Book in 1662, none of these formed any part of the "Prayer Book" properly so called. The title-page then contained only the words "The Book of Common Prayer, and Administration of the Sacraments, and other Rites and Ceremonies of the Church of England;" and the table of "Contents" then ended with the Commination Service. A partial exception is found only in the "Second" Prayer Book of Edward, which enumerated as one of the "Contents," "The Form and Manner of Making and Consecrating of Bishops, Priests, and Deacons": the Ordinal being bound up with these later Edwardine books, though with a separate title-page and a separate imprint.

Although this may seem at first sight a very trivial matter, it gave rise at one time to serious difficulties, which could only be met by passing a special Act of

Parliament, and by a material alteration of the Thirty-sixth "Article of Religion." Yet the circumstances are so little known that various writers have sought to construct an "argument" in favour of Ritualism out of the language of Article XXXVI.!

The words of that Article (as drawn up in 1562) are these :—

"The Booke of Consecration of Archbyshops and Byshops, and Orderyng of Priestes [Praesbyterorum] and Deacons, lately set foorth in the tyme of Edwarde the Syxte, and confyrmed at the same tyme [illis ipsis temporibus] by aucthoritie of Parliament, doth conteyne all thynges necessary to suche consecration and orderyng: neyther hath it any thyng, that *of itselfe* [ex se] is Superstitious or ungodly. And therefore, whosoever are consecrate or ordered accordyng to the Rites of that Booke, sence the seconde yere of the aforenamed King Edwarde unto this time, or hereafter shalbe consecrated or ordered according to the same Rites, we decree all such to be ryghtly, orderly, and lawfully consecrated and ordered."

"See!" says the Ritualist, "Your Protestant parsons in subscribing this Article have to declare that there was 'nothing superstitious' in an Ordinal which 'since the second year of Ed. VI.' included a celebration of Holy Communion according to the 'First Prayer Book of Ed. VI.', which, at that time, involved the use of the 'High Altar' and of the sacrificial vestments."

But will this "argument" bear investigation ?

The Ordinal did not exist at all in the "First" Prayer Book of Edward, nor did it come into being till long after the close of the *third* year of Edward VI. On January 31st, 1550, *i.e.* in the beginning of the *fourth* year of Edward VI., was the Act (3 and 4 Edward VI., cap. xii.) passed in despite of the protests of five of the bishops, to authorize the appointment of twelve Royal Commissioners to draw up an Ordination Service. The text of the Act may be seen in Collier's *History*, V.-375. In the minutes of the Privy Council (February 2nd, 1550)[1] these Commissioners are described as "*Appointed by the Lords* to devise orders for the creation of bishops and priests." The draft form had been previously prepared by Cranmer and Ridley,[2] so that the signatures of the Commissioners were ready by February 28th; Heath, Bishop of Worcester, alone refusing to sign. The book was printed in March,[3] 1550, and was used for the first time[4] June 29th, 1550, at the consecration of Bishop Ponet. The office for the celebration of Holy Communion formed no part of this "Book," nor did that office constitute any part of the ordination proper: though (as in the case of newly-married persons) it was directed that *after* the Ordination "then shall the bishop *proceed to* the Communion, and all that *be ordered* shall tarry and receive the Communion the *same* day." Or, as it was expressed in the "Ordering of Bishops," "then shall the Archbishop *proceed to* the Communion, with whom the new consecrat*ed* bishop shall also communicate."

---

[1] Dasent's *Acts of the Privy Council*, II.-379. Convocation stood prorogued from Monday, February 3rd, to April 22nd. (Wilkins, IV.-60, apud Lewis' *Reformation Settlement*, p. 91.)

[2] Estcourt's *Anglican Ordinations*, p. 25. Clay's *Book of Common Prayer Illustrated*, p. 194, note.

[3] Before March 27th, *Original Letters*, Parker Society, p. 81, and being dated "1549," must have been prior to March 25th, 1550, New Style.

[4] Foxe, however, says that in the third year of Edward VI. Robert Drakes was "admitted minister of God's holy word and sacraments, not after the order then in force, but after such order as was afterwards established." (*Acts and Monuments*, VIII.-107.) The "third year" of Edward expired January 27th, 1550.

The terms of Article XXXVI. bind every subscriber to the doctrine that to "proceed to Holy Communion" and to "communicate the same day" is neither a "superstitious nor ungodly" requirement from newly-ordained persons. But the "book" itself (*i.e.* the Ordinal of 1550) neither names nor specifies the Communion *Office* of the First Prayer Book, the requirements of which were, in fact, abolished by the very same Royal Commission which put forth the Ordinal of 1550—a "book" which derived its sanction solely from a *Royal* Commission based upon a previous "Act" of *Parliament*. To this "Erastian" book, then, Ritualists profess to feel bound by Article XXXVI., although the Litany (which, unlike the Communion office, did form *part of* the Ordination Service proper) then prayed for deliverance "from the tyranny of the Bishop of Rome and all his detestable enormities"!

The official sweeping away of "altars" preceded in every instance the use of the new Ordinal. Cranmer's action in 1549 will be seen from the "Memorandum" which is reproduced verbatim on p. 282. Ridley, one of the draughtsmen of the "book," assisted Archbishop Cranmer at the first consecration held under the "book" on June 29th, 1550, at which, we are told by Strype,[5] that, *after* the ordination "the Lord's Supper was celebrated *upon a table*, covered with a white linen cloth." We know that this was subsequent to the issue of Ridley's celebrated injunction substituting tables for altars, because King Edward's journal mentions that Sir John Yates, the Sheriff, had gone down to Essex the week before Ponet's consecration,

---

[5] *Life of Cranmer*, Book II., cap. xxiv. See Trevor *On the Disputed Rubrics*, p. 15 note.

viz. June 23rd, "to see the Bishop of London's injunctions performed, which touched upon the plucking down of superaltaries, altars, and such like ceremonies and abuses."[6] On November 19th in the same year (1550), the King's journal adds: "There were letters sent to *every* bishop to pluck down the altars." These "letters" mention that even at that date "the altars within the more part of the churches of the realm upon good and godly considerations *are* taken down," and then ordered the remaining altars to be similarly "taken down, and *instead of them* a table to be set up in some convenient part of the chancel."[7] It was not until this order had been executed that the remaining consecrations under the Ordinal of 1550 took place. Ritualists will decide for themselves whether "all such *were* rightly, orderly, and lawfully consecrated" or not. The oath in the unrevised Ordinal of 1550, "So help me God, all saints, and the holy evangelist," was struck out by King Edward himself, *before* the Ordinal was used, upon the application of the martyr-bishop Hooper. Professor Jelf in his Lectures on the Thirty-nine Articles,[8] observes, "As the delivery of the chalice with the bread was omitted in the Revised Prayer Book of 1552, which was published *before even the first edition* of the Articles, it is clear that the present article is in no way concerned with it. It was a very natural ceremony to introduce into such a rite, but was apparently discontinued as not having been contained in the most ancient rituals, and perhaps in part as having been connected in the Roman church

---

[6] Burnet's *History of the Reformation*, II.-ii.-24.
[7] Cardwell's *Documentary Annals*, No. XXIV.   [8] p. 386.

with the commission to offer sacrifice." The Second Prayer Book was enacted April 14th, 1552: the Thirty-nine Articles were not ready till November 23rd, 1552, and were not published till May 20th, 1553.[9] The only remaining bits of "Ritualism" left in the Ordinal of 1550 were that *lay candidates* for deacon's orders were to wear a "plain albe," while the one who read the Gospel was to "put on a tunicle"; each of the bishops at the consecration of a new bishop wearing, *not* the sacrificial "vestment," but "a surplice and cope,"[10] the pastoral staff being also then used.

Now, it is to be observed that the Thirty-sixth Article gives no sort of commendation or approval even to this diluted Ritualism. It only maintains that the validity of the Edwardian ordinations was not destroyed by any such imperfection in the temporary "book" of 1550 as "of itself" (*ex se*) could be considered intrinsically "superstitious and ungodly." And this contention is most reasonable. For the symbolism of ritual depends solely upon association of ideas; and the abolished "altar," the abrogated stole, chasuble, and mitre (like the expunging from the old Pontifical of unction, exorcism, crossings, and of the pretended conveyance of "power to offer sacrifice"), all alike witnessed to a fundamental change in doctrine from

---

[9] Cardwell's *Synodalia*, I.-3, note.

[10] "It is noticeable that these two vestments are the only two which in the Catholic rites are given no significance by a form of investiture. Moreover, though the alb is now strictly a sacerdotal dress, yet both it and the cope had been commonly worn by *lay* assistants in the ancient worship." (Hutton's *Anglican Ministry*, p. 99, note.) He adds, p. 192: "*It is certain that in England Mass was never said in a cope.*" The testimony of this Priest of the Oratory of St. Philip Neri (who writes with the express sanction of Cardinal Newman) is corroborated by Mr. Scudamore in the second edition of his *Notitia Eucharistica*, p. 67, note. See above pp. 117, 119, for detailed proofs.

the Popish Mass-sacrifice to the Evangelical Sacrament of the Lord's Supper.

To prove that the Thirty-sixth Article gives no direct commendation to the Ordinal of 1550 but only maintains its sufficiency, it needs but to contrast its cold, guarded, and purely negative language with the warm and cordial positive approval bestowed upon the *Second* Prayer Book and upon the *revised* Ordinal of 1552, by the Thirty-fifth of the " Forty-two Articles " drafted by Cranmer, and published in May, 1553. It was intitled "Of the Booke of Praiers, and Ceremonies of the Churche of Englande," and said—

" The booke whiche of very late time (*nuperrimè*) was geuen to the Churche of Englande by the Kinges aucthoritie, and the Parlamente, conteining the maner and fourme of praiying and ministring the Sacramentes in the Churche of Englande, *likewise also* the booke of ordring ministers of the Churche (*similiter et libellus eàdem authoritate editus*) set foorth by the forsaied aucthoritie, are godlie, and in no poincte repugnant to the holsome doctrine of the Gospel but agreable thereunto, ferthering and beautifiyng the same not a litle, and therfore of al faithful membres of the Churche of Englande, and chieflie of the ministers of the Worde, thei ought to be receiued, and allowed with all readinesse of minde and thankes geuing, and to be commended to the people of God."[11]

It may seem strange that the thoroughgoing approbation of the Second Prayer Book and of the Ordinal as revised in 1552 thus given by the Synod of London (under the guidance of Cranmer, Ridley and the rest of the compilers of the " First " Book, and of the unrevised Ordinal of 1550, both of which books

---

[11] Hardwick, *History of the Thirty-nine Articles*, p. 312, or 322, second edition.

they themselves had deliberately superseded), should have been withdrawn in 1562 in order to substitute in its stead a frigid affirmation of the bare validity of all ordinations effected "since the second year of Ed. VI."

Most assuredly this was not due to any preference felt in 1562 for the Ordinal of 1550; for at the consecration of Archbishop Parker, and at each of the subsequent consecrations during the reign of Elizabeth, the revised Ordinal of 1552 was exclusively followed. No pastoral staff, alb or tunicle was used at any ordination after the accession of Queen Elizabeth. Copes were used at the administration of the Lord's Supper which *followed* Parker's consecration; but even this was not in accordance with the Prayer Book of 1549, for the priests who read the Epistle and Gospel also wore surplices and copes *instead of* " albs with tunacles," thereby destroying the " *distinctive* " dress of the celebrant.

The explanation of the change is found in a very curious legal and historical episode. The Prayer Book of 1549 (" First " Prayer Book of Edward) and the Ordinal of 1550 were compiled at different dates and enacted by two separate statutes—viz. 2 and 3 Edward VI., cap. i.; and 3 and 4 Edward VI., cap. xii. By the second Act of Uniformity, however (1552), *i.e.* 5 and 6 Edward VI., cap. i., *both* the revised books were "annexed" to the statute which, after enacting the "Second" Prayer Book, went on, " adding *also* a forme and manner of making and consecrating of archbishops, bishops, priests, and deacons to be of *like* force, auctoritie, and value, as the same like foresaid book entitled *The Boke of Common Prayer*, was before " ; the penalties of the former Act, 2 and 3 Edward VI., cap. i., being made applicable to—"*also* the said form of making archbishops, &c., thereunto annexed." It will be remembered that the Thirty-fifth Article of 1552 cited above, similarly discriminates the "*libellus de ordinatione*" from the Prayer Book as being "*similiter . . . eâdem authoritate editus.*" Under Mary, the statute Mary 1, Session 2, cap. ii., repealed *separately* the Ordinal and the Prayer Book of Edward. Yet, under Elizabeth, the Act of Uniformity, 1 Elizabeth, cap. ii., enacted that, "the said statute of repeal, and every thing therein contained *only*[12] *concerning the said book*," *i.e.* the Prayer Book, "shall be void and of none effect." It was probably owing merely to the carelessness of the lawyers in drafting the Bill that the need of a *separate* mention of the Ordinal had been overlooked; though curiously enough, the mention of it was also omitted from the Table of "Contents" in Elizabeth's inaccurate reprint of Edward's Second Book.[13]

---

[12] Several other statutes of Edward repealed by 1 Mary, session 2, cap. ii., were left untouched by the Elizabethan Act of Uniformity.

[13] *Elizabethan Liturgies*, Parker Society, p. 26. It would be too harsh a conjecture to suppose that Elizabeth designed to keep the Bishops dependent upon her future statecraft by leaving their legal position open to cavil; but, as Canon Estcourt remarks (*Anglican Ordinations*, p. 100), "it seems strange that nothing had been done in the Parliament of 1559 to obviate these legal difficulties. The attempt, however, was made, for a Bill was passed through the Lower House 'for Collating of Bishops by the Queen's Highness, and with what rites and ceremonies' (*Commons' Journals*, Vol. I., p. 58). In the House of Lords it was also read a first time on the 22nd of March (*Lords' Journals*, Vol. I., p. 568), and described as a Bill 'for the Admitting and Consecrating of Archbishops and Bishops'; but there is no other notice of it in the Journals, though D'Ewes states that it was read a second and third time." (D'Ewes' *Journal*, p. 26, edition 1682.)

Elizabeth's Act of Uniformity had received the royal assent on May 8th, 1559; but when, in December of the same year, it became necessary to consecrate Archbishop Parker, it was found that the *legal* authority of the Ordinal of 1552 was then disputable. Canon Estcourt has reproduced in facsimile a State paper detailing the steps intended to be taken in Parker's consecration, with side-notes in the handwriting of Cecil and of the Archbishop elect. The last of the memoranda was in these words: "The order of King Edward's book is to be observed, for that there is none other special made in this last session of Parliament"; upon which Secretary Cecil minutes: "This book is not established by Parliament."[14]

However, as the Ordinal of 1552 was in fact used, the Romish controversialists naturally seized upon this technical weakness in the Anglican position, and (as the Act of 8 Elizabeth witnesses) their cavils greatly disturbed the minds of "the common sort of people." It became necessary therefore to exact from all would-be clergymen a profession of their acquiescence in the validity of every ordination "since the second year of Edward VI.", when the old Pontifical ceased to be used, inasmuch as it was essential to include the five (or six) episcopal consecrations which had been celebrated in accordance with the unrevised Ordinal of 1550, because (the strength of a chain depends upon its weakest part, and) two of Parker's consecrators, viz. Scory and Coverdale, had themselves been consecrated under the unrevised Ordinal of 1550. Hence, Puritan candidates

---

[14] Strype's *Life of Archbishop Parker*, I.-81, edition 1821. Cf. Palmer, *Origines Liturgicæ*, II.-286.

for ordination were required to profess that there was nothing "superstitious"[15]; while Romishly inclined persons had to admit that there was nothing "ungodly" in the rites actually used which could "of itself" have been so essential as to invalidate the Anglican succession.

Matters were brought to a crisis by Bonner's refusal to take the Oath of Supremacy before Bishop Horn, his diocesan, on the ground that the latter was not legally a Bishop at all, since the statute of Mary repealing the Ordinal of Edward had never been legally set aside.[16] The objection puzzled the judges, and to obviate its force the statute 8 Elizabeth, cap. i., was passed, declaring all past as well as future consecrations under the Ordinal of 1552 to be in good law. Hence it is that the present Act of Uniformity, 14 Charles II., cap. iv., rested the authorisation of the then existing Prayer Book upon 1 Elizabeth, cap. ii., and that of the Ordinal upon 8 Elizabeth, cap. i., "respectively."

The Act 8 Elizabeth, cap. i., section 2, similarly described how Edward caused a book "intituled" the Prayer Book to be enacted, "but *also* did add and put to the same book a very godly" form of ordination which, the 1 Elizabeth, cap. ii. being passed, the Queen had ordered all consecrations to be thenceforth "accord-

---

[15] The original draft of the Article in 1552 had contained the words "quoad ceremoniarum rationem salutari Evangelii libertati, si *ex sui naturâ* ceremoniæ illæ æstimantur, in nullo repugnant"; but Knox and his friends having protested against kneeling at the Supper as "seeming to allow idolatry to triumph" the wording was altered by leaving out all mention of "ceremonies" and retaining only the "quoad *doctrinæ* veritatem pii sunt." Dr. Lorimer's *Knox in England*, p. 126. Hardwick's *History of the Thirty-nine Articles*, p. 322. Appendix iii.

[16] Strype's *Life of Archbishop Parker*, I.-122.

ing to such .. orders *annexed to* the said book of Common Prayer." The third section confirmed the re-enacted Prayer Book of 1552, *and* "such order .. as set forth .. *and added to* the said book of Common Prayer .. in 5 and 6 Ed. VI."[17] The Canons of 1571 still continued to treat the Ordinal as a separate "liber."[18]

Canon Swainson in his *History of the Act of Uniformity* shews that many interlineations and amendments had to be adopted in the draft bill of 1662, to prevent a recurrence of a similar objection in the future; and the thirty-first section of the existing Act of Uniformity expressly provides "that all subscription shall be applied *for and touching the said six-and-thirtieth Article* unto the booke containing the form and manner of making, ordaining, and consecrating of bishops, &c., in *this* Act mentioned," *i.e.* to the *present* Ordinal, "anything in the said Article to the contrary in any wise notwithstanding."

To sum up then the foregoing evidence, the Thirty-sixth Article *could not* have been designed to express any approbation whatever of the thrice-discarded Communion Office of Edward's "First" Prayer Book (A.D. 1549) for the following reasons:—

First.—That office had been rejected by the framers of the Thirty-sixth Article in favour of the Revised Book of 1552, from which, as Archbishop Whitgift points out, even the ornaments of the Ordinal of 1550 had been excluded. He said, "In the book now allowed of making deacons and ministers, and consecrating of bishops, there is neither required alb,

---

[17] See Stephens' *Ecclesiastical Statutes*, I.-417, and 418, 419.
[18] Cardwell's *Synodalia*, p. 127.

surplice, vestment, nor pastoral staff: read the book from the beginning to the ending. And therefore this is a false and untrue report."[19] It was not until 1662 that "habits" were enjoined by the ordinal. No single member of the Convocation of 1562 (which originated the Article) officiated at an "altar," wore a sacrificial "vestment," or made any use either of the Ordinal of 1550 or of the "First" Prayer Book of Edward.

Second.—The Article was aimed at a notorious public denial of the validity of Anglican orders; a denial based in no wise upon the mode of celebrating the Lord's Supper, but upon the (then recent) omission from 1 Elizabeth, cap. ii., of all *separate* mention of the Ordinal of 1552, and upon the alleged insufficiency of the "rites" which had been *actually* used.

Third.—The Ordinal of 1550 was never contained in the same "book" with the Communion Office, which Office at *no* time formed any part of the "book" referred to in the Thirty-sixth Article. Indeed, the Communion Office of the "First" Book of Edward was so temporary a makeshift that it was not reprinted after 1549 (the date of its issue), at which date the Ordinal did not exist. The framers of the Ordinal of 1550 were the very men who (at the same session of the Royal Commission), swept away the ornaments of the "second year of Edward VI." Ordination did not in any way consist of a celebration of the Lord's Supper which "according to the rites of that book," could not take place until the "right, orderly, and lawful ordering" had been completed. Therefore, the exemp-

---

[19] Whitgift's *Works*, I.-488, III.-472.

tion from censure (for it amounts to no more than that) of the Ordinal, did not "of itself" include the supplemental Communion Office (*not* contained in that "book") which must stand or fall by its own merit. Those who "were ordered according to the rites of that book," did not, *in fact*, officiate at an "altar," nor wear the sacrificial vestments. And it must be obvious that inasmuch as all the successive generations who had to subscribe the Thirty-sixth Article were themselves ordained by the Ordinal of 1552, this latter is "the book" which, having been specially assailed in 1561, was *directly* referred to in the Thirty-sixth Article composed on that very occasion.

Fourth.—Even though the Thirty-sixth Article were (for the sake of argument) supposed to refer exclusively and directly to the Ordinal of 1550, or even to any and every supplemental or collateral service mentioned or implied therein, the present Act of Uniformity, 14 Charles II., has nevertheless completely transferred all such reference to the Ordinal of 1662:—"*Anything in the said Article to the contrary, notwithstanding.*"

MEMORANDUM.

Extract copied from Administration Book of the Consistory Court of Norwich, 1549-1555, now in the Probate Registry at Norwich.

"M^d Quod die Dnīca septimo die mensis Decembris Anno Dñi mill^{mo} quingentesimo quinquagesimo Regni vero Illustriss. ac potestiss. in Christo principis et Dñi nostri Dñi Edwardi sexti Dei gra. Angliæ Franciæ et Hiberniæ Regis fid. def. and in terra Ecctie Anglicane & Hiberniæ Capitis Supremi Anno quarto. Reverendus pater Thomas permissione divina Norwicens. Epūs in domo Capitulari infra Ecctiam Cathedr. Sancti Trinitatis Norwicen. (post quamdiu concionem iɓm factam) pr^re declaravit clero et poplo quod deus Illustriss' Dns noster Rex quasdem lras sibi scripsit honorabilissimis et quendam librum impressum cum quibusd^m rationibus declar.

"After moost hertie comendacon wheras I have the second day of this instant Decembre received the King his moost honorable lres undre his Highness signet and signed with his moost gracious hande concerning the taking down of aulters w^thin my diocesse and in leu of them a decent table to be sett up in some convenient place of every chaunsell and also a little boke imprinted shewing certeyn reasons why the Lord's boarde shuld rather be after the foorme of a table then of an altar the copye of which said lres & boke I send unto you herin enclosed and knowing that the moste parte of all altars within this my diocesse be all redye taken downe by comandment of my Lorde of Canterbury his Grace's visitors in his late visitacon this diocesse then being voyed yet myndyng moost humblie to obey the said lres and to do my dutie in accomplishing the same as apperteyneth Thes shalbe to require you and in the Kings majestys behalf to comand you that ymediatlie upon the receipt hereof with all diligence and celerity takyng with you such grave precher as shalbe nere unto you you do repayre to such markett townes and gret townes w^tin your archdeconry where calling before you the curats and churchwardens of the parishes about the same I charge you to sett fourth the Kings plesur and procedings in the premises according to the trewe purpote effecte and meaning of the said most honorable letter w^t such further reasons apte for the same as shalbe theught most convenient and agreable by you and the said precher as you woll answer at your parrell Thus fare you well—at Norwich this thred daie of Decembre 1550."

XIII
Article Thirty=one

THE stern and uncompromising language of our Thirty-first Article has always been a thorn in the side of Romanisers. They teach (as the Church of Rome teaches) that in the sacrifice of the Mass "the priest doth offer Christ for the quick and the dead, to have remission of pain or guilt."

It is in this belief that "frequent celebrations" are multiplied, and that non-communicating attendance (*i.e.* what Romanists call "hearing Mass") is encouraged: for this also it is that two, three, or more stone "altars" are again set up, and the sacrificial vestments and "Eastward" (*i.e.* mediatorial) position are re-introduced.

Yet, in the midst of solemn functions and gorgeous pageantry, they seem never able to quite shake off the consciousness that the Church to which their allegiance has been pledged, has pronounced the whole thing a "blasphemous fable and a dangerous deceit."

Dr. Newman, in his celebrated *Tract XC.*, invented a theory that authorised Roman doctrine could not be denounced in the Thirty-first Article for two reasons.

First, that "the sacrifices of Masses" were spoken of in the plural number, not the sacrifice of the Mass; and secondly, that the decrees of Trent relative to the Mass-sacrifice had not been drawn up when this Article was drafted.

How such a "non-natural interpretation" could have satisfied any candid mind passes comprehension. But Dr. Newman has since "remarked" that "although the ninetieth *Tract for the Times* did not even go so far as to advocate the *Sacerdotium* in the Catholic sense, but only the possibility of interpreting the Thirty-first Article in a sense *short of its denial*, Dr. Routh' [the Venerable President of Magdalen College] 'told the Bishop of Oxford, who consulted him on the point, that such interpretations generally as those advocated in the *Tract* were a simple novelty in Anglican history; and secondly, that though in that *Tract* the liberty to hold it, consistently with the wording of the Thirty-first Article, was undoubtedly maintained, still, as far as my memory goes, neither the writer of the *Tract*, nor his friends, *distinctly* held the Catholic doctrine themselves." "I had begun the movement with vague incomplete views, which *cleared as I went on*, but were not definite and consistent till I joined the' [Roman] 'Catholic Church."[1]

Having thus got himself out of the fog so far as to understand his own "completed" views, Dr. Newman frankly owns in his *Via Media* (reprint of *Tract XC.*, with notes), II.-316, that the excuse which he had put

---

[1] Preface to Hutton's *Anglican Ministry*, p. xvi. Mr. Hunt, in his *History of Modern Religious Thought*, I.-165 n., shews that the Caroline High Church divines never dreamed of Dr. Pusey's method of eviscerating the Thirty-first Article.

forth in the first edition of the *Tract* will not hold water. He says, " Masses for the quick and dead are not an abuse, but a distinct ordinance of the Church herself. . . . I do not see how it can be denied that this Article calls *the sacrifice of the Mass itself*, in all its private and solitary celebrations—to speak of no other— that is, in all its daily celebrations from year's end to year's end, *toto orbe terrarum*, a blasphemous fable."

In this view Cardinal Newman is supported by every theologian of his own Church. Canon Oakley adopts as his own the language of another distinguished pervert, Canon Estcourt, who says that Article XXXI. is both "false and impious, nor can it be defended on the ground of the phrase 'sacrifices of Masses' being in the plural number, because the term '*sacrificia missarum*' is equally correct, and has the same meaning with '*sacrificium missæ*.' Thus in the *Missa pro defunctis*, ' anima famuli tui his sacrificiis purgata, et a peccatis expedita.' This Article is therefore nothing else than a charge of blasphemy and imposture on the most holy Sacrifice of the Eucharist."[2] Dr. Lingard, in his *History*,[3] also says, "the Mass is pronounced a blasphemous forgery by the Article."

Though no one would go to Roman Catholic writers for the interpretation of Protestant Articles, they may fairly be quoted in disproof of the notion that Anglican formularies are patient of any such meaning as Papists could admit to be " Catholic."

Before the Reformation every one of the English Pontificals agreed in using the following words at the Ordination of priests :—" Receive power to offer sacrifice to God, and to celebrate Masses [*plural*] as well for

---

[2] *Letter to Manning*, 1866, p. 73.   [3] VI.-677.

the living as the dead." The Sarum, Exeter, Bangor, and Winchester Pontificals agreed in this, which was therefore "commonly said."[4] The Winchester Pontifical had also a blessing upon the hands of the priests "to the consecrating sacrifices [*hostias*] which are offered for the faults and negligences of the people."[5]

Long before the Council of Trent this had been "commonly said" in England. Canon Estcourt says, "the use of the plural number in the Article raises no distinction whatever. There is no difference between 'the sacrifice of the Mass' and 'the sacrifices of Masses.' It is not merely 'commonly said'; it is a theological truth; it is a matter of faith, that 'in the sacrifices of Masses the priest does offer Christ for the quick and dead, to have remission of pain and guilt.'"[6] "These,' says Bishop Ullathorne, 'are the very words that the Church has used at various times to profess the Catholic faith upon the subject of the holy sacrifice. In the Confession of Faith proposed to the Emperor Michael Palæologus by Pope Clement IV. in the year 1267, and again by Gregory X. in 1272, and accepted and presented by the Emperor to the Pope at the Council of Lyons, there are these very words. The Greek terms for 'the sacrifices of Masses' are λειτουργιῶν ἱεροτελεστίαι [*plural*]. Afterwards, in the Council of Florence, in 1439, the terms of the Confession of Faith just mentioned were embodied in the definition of faith then decreed."[7]

The language of the Council of Florence was, that "if any true penitents shall depart this life in the love

---
[4] Estcourt's *Anglican Ordinations*, p. 269.
[5] Maskell, *Mon. Rit.*, III.-210, *cf.* I.-144.
[6] Estcourt's *Anglican Ordinations*, p. 270.
[7] *Anglican Theory of Union*, pp. 50-2.

of God, before they have made satisfaction by worthy fruits of penance for faults of commission and omission, their souls are purified after death by the pains of purgatory; and that for their relief from these pains, the suffrages of the faithful who are alive are profitable; to wit, the sacrifices of Masses" [*plural*], &c.⁸

This, then, was the received and authorised belief of the Anglo-Roman Church; whereas the Reformed Church of England, as Cranmer expressed it,⁹ " meant in nowise that it is a very true sacrifice for sin, and applicable by the priest to the quick and dead."

When, therefore, Archbishop Cranmer drafted, in 1552, the original form of our Thirty-first Article, he fitly described the Romish belief as being that which was "commonly said," just as in Article XXV. the Romish sacraments are said to be " commonly called sacraments": the birthday of Christ was "commonly called Christmas"; the Athanasian Creed was " commonly called the Creed of St. Athanasius," and the Prayer Book itself the Book of "Common" Prayer. "Vulgo dicebatur" does not mean that it was said by the vulgar, any more than "the vulgar tongue" in the Baptismal Office means the language of illiterate persons.

Such being the circumstances under which the Article was drawn up, it would matter little whether the decrees of Trent were specifically aimed at, since no change¹⁰ in the "vulgar" doctrine of "sacrifice"

---

⁸ Session xxv.   ⁹ *Works*, I.-353. Parker Society.

¹⁰ Canon Faussett, Margaret Professor of Divinity, pointed this out in 1841. "What beyond the merest shadow of pretence is there for insinuating or assuming any essential distinction between the well-understood doctrines of the Church of Rome before the Council of Trent and those established by the more formal decrees of that Council?"—*Lecture before the University of Oxford*, p. 22.

was made at that Council. Nevertheless, as a fact, the language of this Article was altered into its present form with the view of giving an express contradiction to the Tridentine decrees.

Thus, the title was altered from "*Of the perfect oblation of Christ made upon the cross*" to "*Of the one* (*unicâ*, i.e. *unique*) *oblation of Christ* FINISHED *upon the cross*," and the words "forged fables" were altered into "blasphemous fables" in order[11] to meet exactly the requirements of the Fourth Canon of the Twenty-second Session of Trent, which, on September 17th, 1562, had laid it down that "if any one shall say that by the sacrifice of the Mass, a *blasphemy* is cast upon the most holy sacrifice of Christ, accomplished on the cross, or that it is thereby derogated from, let him be accursed." At a later Session the same Council in its decree concerning purgatory (which *followed* the publication of the English Thirty-nine Articles) adopted the exact phrase "the sacrifices of Masses" as the equivalent of "the acceptable sacrifice of the altar."[12]

Another indication is pointed out by Mr. Dimock.

"And, still further, it should be well observed that the Articles as issued in 1553, instead of the word 'propitiation' in the English version, had the expression 'the pacifying of God's displeasure,' which was to be attributed to the one Sacrifice of Christ once offered; and that the Council of Trent attributes just this 'pacifying of God's displeasure' to the Sacrifice of the Mass, in the words ' Hujus quippe oblatione placatus Dominus ' —words which again are taken up by the Catechism of Nowel, when it said of the Sacrifice of the Cross, ' Quo *solo* placatus nobis Deus efficitur.' " (*Dangerous Deceits*, p. 20.)

---

[11] So in the Twenty-second Article, "The doctrine of School-authors" (Scholasticorum) was altered into "The doctrine of Romanists" (Romanensium). Hardwick, p. 89. Oakley's *Letter to Manning*, p. 64. [12] Session xxv.

The dates of these theological rejoinders should be noted. The Articles of 1563 (commonly called 1562, *i.e.* Old Style) were not presented by Convocation to the Queen till February, 1563, nor published till some months afterwards. The Trent Canons on the Mass-sacrifice had been emitted on September 17th, 1562. Our present English version of the Articles (translated by Bishop Jewel) was published, with the alterations above named, in 1571. Subscription to the Thirty-nine Articles was then, for the first time, enforced by Parliament in the Statute, 13 Elizabeth, chapter xii.

Cranmer wrote, March 20th, 1552: "Our adversaries are now holding their councils at Trent for the establishment of their errors .. they are making decrees respecting the worship of the Host: wherefore we ought to leave no stone unturned that we may guard others against this idolatry."[13] On the same day he wrote to Bullinger that a synod was to be held "especially for an agreement on the Sacramentarian Controversy."[14]

On the other hand, as the Court of the General Synod of the Church of Ireland laid down in their Judgment (depriving Mr. Hunt for Romish heresy) on February 20th, 1895: "The history, and the very terms, of these Tridentine Canons would suggest that they were directed against the language of Article XXXI., which had been previously used by the English Reformers," viz. in the Thirtieth Article of 1553.

On Elizabeth's accession the Lower House of Convocation affirmed, January 24th, 1559, "that in the Mass is offered the true body of Christ, and his

---

[13] *Original Letters*, I.-23.   [14] *Ibid.*, p. 24.

true blood, a propitiatory sacrifice for the living and dead."¹⁵ As a natural result, in framing the Act for Establishing the Book of Common Prayer, that Convocation was utterly ignored. But after the Romish bishops had been dispossessed, after the Prayer Book had been enforced in every parish by Royal Visitors who scoured the length and breadth of the land for that purpose, and so soon as the Archiepiscopal See of York had been filled (on February 20th, 1561, by the appointment of Thomas Young), the whole of the bishops, acting under a Royal Commission, drew up at Lambeth eleven Articles in the form of a " Declaration " to be publicly made by every clergyman.

These eleven Articles were compiled as a " test of doctrine," says Hardwick, " under the eye of Archbishop Parker with the sanction of the other Metropolitan, and the rest of the English prelates, and the clergy were required to make a public profession of it, not only upon admission to their benefices, but twice also in every year, immediately after the Gospel for the day."¹⁶

The ninth of these Articles, all of which are reprinted from Strype by Burnet, Wilkins, Hardwick, and Cardwell (though Collier " passes them mostly over "), was as follows:—

" Moreover, I do not only acknowledge that private Masses were never used amongst the Fathers of the Primitive Church. I mean public ministration and receiving of the sacrament by the priest alone, without a just number of communicants, according to Christ's saying, 'Take ye and eat ye,' &c.; but ALSO, that the doctrine, that maintaineth *the Mass* to be a

---

¹⁵ Cardwell's *Conferences*, p. 23.
¹⁶ *History of the Thirty-nine Articles*, p. 118; or p. 120, Ed. 1859.

propitiatory sacrifice for the quick and dead, and a mean to deliver souls out of purgatory, is neither agreeable to Christ's ordinance, nor grounded upon doctrine apostolic, but contrary-wise, most ungodly and most injurious to the precious redemption of our Saviour Christ, and His *only* sufficient sacrifice *offered once for ever* upon the altar of the cross." [17]

It seems probable that this very document may have been intended to be denounced at Trent by Canon iv. before quoted, as well as by Canon iii. which says :—

" If any shall say, that the sacrifice of the Mass is only one of praise and thanksgiving, or a bare commemoration of the sacrifice which was made upon the cross, but not propitiatory ; or that it only profits him who receives it, and ought not to be offered for the living and the dead, for sins, pains, satisfactions, and other necessities, let him be accursed." [18]

One object of these Articles was, no doubt, to weed out from the Convocation which met subsequently on January 12th, 1563, all supporters of the Mass; with the result that Canterbury Convocation, which had affirmed in 1559 what was "commonly said" about the Mass, rejected that same "vulgar" doctrine in 1563.

"Such," says Strype,[19] "was the pastoral care of Archbishop Parker, by whom, I believe, this Declaration was chiefly framed, that so all that came into livings and served the Church, might be purged of Popish doctrines and superstitions." [20]

---

[17] In addition to this "Declaration" another form in Latin was drawn up for subscription (in writing) by the ministers, viz. " missa, quæ consuevit a sacerdotibus dici, non erat a Christo instituta, sed a multis Romanis pontificibus consarcinata. Nec est sacrificium propitiatorium pro vivis et defunctis." MS. Petyt. Vol. 538, Vol. 38. On the next page follows the "Injunctions for Readers," which Strype, *Annals*, I.-225, has chosen to print separately, as though belonging to a different year. But evidence is lacking that this latter form was ever published or enforced. [18] Session xxii.
[19] *Annals*, I.-1-329. [20] Compare Strype's *Life of Parker*, I.-181-2.

The identity in doctrine between these "Eleven" provisional Articles and the "Thirty-nine" is shewn by the fact that the former were, even so late as 1566, still prescribed to Irish clergymen "by order and authority as well of the Right Honourable Sir Henry Sidney, General Deputy, as by the archbishops and bishops, and other Her Majesty's High Commissioners for Causes Ecclesiastical in the same realm."[21]

In 1615 the Irish Church drew up its own Articles, the Ninety-ninth of which said:—

"The Sacrifice of the Mass (*sing.*), wherein the priest is said to offer up Christ for obtaining the remission of pain or guilt for the quick and the dead, is neither agreeable to Christ's ordinance nor grounded upon doctrine Apostolic; but contrariwise most ungodly and most injurious to that all-sufficient sacrifice of our Saviour Christ, offered once for ever upon the cross, which is the only propitiation and satisfaction for all our sins."[22]

Evidently the Irish Convocation had never heard of any difference between the Sacrific*es* of Mass*es* and the Sacrifice of the Mass—a distinction which was absolutely unknown till its invention by casuists to excuse the violation of the subscription by which they had obtained admission to benefices within the Established Church. Dr. Bennet, in his *Essay on the Thirty-nine Articles*, A.D. 1715, says,[23] that in the original MS. of 1562, the English Article had "the Sacrifice (*sing.*) of Masses." And we are able to cite a witness of "infallible" authority, viz. Pope Pius the Fifth, who, in his celebrated Bull excommunicating Elizabeth in

---

[21] Hardwick's *History of the Thirty-nine Articles*, p. 121.
[22] Stephens' *Irish Prayer Book*, Preface, p. lxvii.
[23] p. 117.

A.D. 1569, said:—"She hath abolished the Sacrifice of the Mass and the Catholic rites."[24]

The Supreme Pontiff may at least be credited with knowing what "the Sacrifice of the Mass" meant.

Professor Jones, S.J., in his *Reply to Dr. Littledale* (Hodges) says:—

"In the *Profession of Faith*, published by Pius IV. in 1564, we have the doctrine of the Council summarised in the following article:—'I equally profess that in the Sacrifice of the Mass there is offered to God a true, proper, and propitiatory sacrifice for the quick and dead.' Each Article—that of Trent and the Anglican Church—was the outcome of prolonged and notorious controversy. It was a question, among all others, of central and conspicuous importance, for on it depended the true notion of the priesthood, the Episcopacy, and of the hieratic character of the Church. What each proposition meant in the mouths of its supporters *no man in Christendom has ever sincerely doubted.*"

**

Within the last few years, however, an anonymous writer in the *Church Times* invented a theory by which all reference to Roman doctrine might be evaded. It seems odd, of course, that this "happy thought" never occurred to anybody during the centuries when the Articles were most recent, and when the controversy with Rome was uppermost in men's minds. Yet it is now gravely contended that before the Reformation there was a general belief ("it was commonly said") that the Mass constitutes "a fresh propitiation for sin, distinct from that made upon the Cross of Calvary."[25] Also that the atonement wrought on Calvary related only to original sin and to

---

[24] "Missæ sacrificium, preces, jejunia, ciborum delectum, cœlibatum ritusque catholicos abolevit."—Burnet's *History of the Reformation,* II.-ii.-532.

[25] Green, *On the Thirty-nine Articles,* p. 254.

sins committed before baptism, whereas the Mass-offering was a propitiation for all sins committed *after* baptism. This outrageous fancy having been mistakenly imputed to Thomas Aquinas was mentioned in the Augsburg Confession,[26] and was, therefore, noticed in the *Apology of Melancthon*,[27] as well as in the representations made by the Lutheran ambassadors sent to negotiate with Henry VIII.[28] In this way it doubtless became known to some of the English Reformers.[29] And it is not improbable, therefore, that the *separate* mention of "original" and of "actual" sins in our Second and Thirty-first Articles *may* have been due to this apocryphal heresy. But that such an extreme and preposterous notion ever obtained any large circle of adherents there is not the slightest reason to believe. It is certain that in England it never formed (to say the least) a conspicuous feature in the controversy. For we have, on the one hand, the Protestant objections stated with great fulness of detail by Cranmer, Jewel, Hooper, and others, not one of whom singles out *this* particular form of misbelief as an object of special censure. On the other hand, we have such representative names as Tonstal, Gardiner, Joliffe, and Harding, not one of whom lends the least sanction or even recognition to any such notion.

Nay, more, when the Six Articles Act was in full force, and Bishop Shaxton was compelled to recant in order to avoid being burnt, the statement put into his mouth by the "Catholic" leaders, was that "the oblation and action of the priest is also a sacrifice of

---

[26] Francke's *Libri Symbolici*. Ed. 1847, p. 30.   [27] *Ibid.*, p. 267.
[28] Burnet's *History of the Reformation*, I.-ii.-505. Ed. 1829.
[29] Becon's *Works*, iii.-368, 377.

praise and thanksgiving unto God for His benefits, and NOT THE SATISFACTION FOR THE SINS OF THE WORLD, for that is *only to be attributed* to Christ's passion."[30] This was in 1546, ten years after Taverner had published in London his translation of the Augsburg Confession "at the commandment of his Master the right honourable Mayster Thomas Cromwell Chief Secretarie to the Kings Grace."[31]

Bishop John Wordsworth has constituted himself the patron of the new interpretation, but all his research (with the aid of the two members of the " Confraternity of the Blessed Sacrament" whose *De Hierarchiâ Anglicanâ*, intended for the Pope's own eye, he has graced with a preface), has been unable to furnish more than *two* writers on the Roman side (neither of them Englishmen, and one of these, as he admits,[32] unknown to the framers of the Thirty-first Article) whose words might *appear*[33] to sanction such an extravagant form of anti-Christian error. Indeed, the Romanists promptly and *publicly* repudiated the charge as being a gross exaggeration and a wanton misrepresentation on the part of their opponents. Their official reply given at the time was: " It was never heard of among Catholics, and very many whom

---

[30] Foxe's *Acts and Monuments*, Vol. V., App. No. xvii. Burnet's *History of the Reformation*, I.-ii.-400.
[31] *British Museum*, " c. 37, c. 9." [32] *Responsio ad Batavos*, p. 23.
[33] Professor Austin Richardson, in the *Dublin Review*, 3rd Series, Vol. XLV., p. 85, points out that Albertus Magnus, whose words had been attributed to Aquinas by mistake, merely meant that the merits of Christ's Death were applied to the baptized by the Mass, just as they had been applied to the unbaptized by Baptism. That explains (what might otherwise seem inexplicable) why the dividing line should have been fixed at "original sin." The universal prevalence of Infant baptism when Albertus wrote, would make such a division seem to Romanists to be both scientific and natural.

we have asked deny most constantly that it is so taught by them."³¹ "To us it is assuredly untrue that that was the opinion of any Catholic doctor, so far is it from being *a common opinion* among us" (tantum abest, ut apud nos vulgata sit ea opinio).³⁵

Mr. Dimock has exhaustively examined the writings of the Reformation period relating to this question, in two valuable works published by Elliot Stock, entitled *Dangerous Deceits* and *Missarum Sacrificia*, and as the result of his inquiry he throws out this challenge:—

"I will make bold then, to ask those who would now have us read this anti-Catharine sense into the Article, whether they can produce any *one* saying from any *one* of the writings of any one among the divines of any authority on either side of the controversy, which can fairly be said to give any solid support to their view, or bear witness to the fact of such a restraint of the sense of the Article having been regarded as admissible *in the century to which the language of the Article belongs?*"

Even the few eccentric writers who have been claimed as sanctioning the alleged heresy about "original sin" or an "independent" sacrifice in the Mass are shewn by Mr. Dimock to have been misunderstood. Hooker himself repudiated beforehand Bishop Wordsworth's charges. He said, "Whom [*i.e.* Christ] to have merited the taking away of no sin but original *is not their opinion*, which himself will find, when he hath well examined his witnesses, Catharinus and Thomas."³⁶

Pighi, to whom Jewel more than once refers as a leader among his opponents, after quoting the statement of the Augsburg Confession referred to above, says he had never heard of such a notion even in the

---

³¹ Responsio ad Conf. Augustanam Pontificia, in Francke's *Libri Symbolici*. Appendix, p. 60. Ed. 1847.
³⁵ Quoted by Mr. Dimock, *Dangerous Deceits*, p. 28.
³⁶ Hooker's *Answer to Travers*. Works, edited by Keble, III.-584.

disputes of the schools where the utmost latitude was always permitted.

"Nor do I think that they will be able to produce anyone, whether a schoolman or other, who puts forth an opinion of this kind: and even if they did, they are not acting candidly in attaching to us all the stupidity of one man, seeing that no such thing have we either read or heard of among ourselves: and by monstrosities of this kind they asperse our doctrine, blot and traduce it among the credulous populace who are ignorant of such matters."[37]

Bellarmine denounces it as an "impudent lie."[38]

Bossuet is no less emphatic. In his *History of the variations of Protestants*[39] we read:—

"*What was invented in order to render the Oblation in the Mass odious*. . . . In the Confession of Augsburg they even attribute to the Catholics this strange doctrine, 'That Jesus Christ had satisfied for original sin in his passion, and had instituted the Mass for mortal and venial sins which were committed every day'; as if Jesus Christ had not equally satisfied for all sins; and by way of necessary elucidation, they added, that Jesus Christ had offered Himself to bear the cross 'not for original sin only, but for others too,'—a truth which *no one ever doubted*. It is not matter of surprise that the Catholics, as Lutherans themselves relate, on hearing this reproach, all, as if with one common voice, cried out against it, saying, that 'never had such a thing been heard among them.' (*Chyt. Hist. Conf.*) But the people were to be made to believe that these wretched Catholics were even ignorant of the first elements of Christianity."

It is, however, a vulgar error to suppose that our Thirty-first Article was taken *directly* from the Augsburg Confession. The case stands thus. In 1530 the Protestants at Augsburg charged their opponents with

---

[37] *Pighii Controversias Ratisponenses.* Ed. 1549, p. 116.b.
[38] Op. tom. VII., col. 604. Ed. 1617.
[39] English Translation, Dublin, 1836. Vol. I., p. 126. Book III. §§ 53.

holding that Christ's passion sufficed for original sin, but that the Mass offering was instituted by Him for all daily sins after baptism. This error was, however, not described as being "commonly said"; and our English Article drawn up twenty-two years later did not repeat or adopt that statement. It had proved, in fact, to be untenable. Melancthon's *Apology* found an excuse for making the charge in what it described as "the error of Thomas," but which, in fact, was not his at all, and really belonged to the writings of Albertus Magnus.[39a] Mr. Dimock shews that even as to this writer the charge was due to a misunderstanding of language confessedly incautious: but that, in fact, neither Aquinas nor Albert did teach that the Mass had any atoning efficacy apart from and independent of the Cross.[40]

As a result, the charge was so warmly resented and hurled back that the Lutherans themselves abandoned it, and *it had disappeared from their subsequent Confessions long before our Articles were drawn up.* Our English Cranmer was keenly alive to the fortunes of the German Reformers and was little likely to repeat a blunder which had been so utterly exploded in the interval between 1530 and 1552.

The charge so far broke down that it was abandoned by Melancthon, when ten years later he drew up the amended "Confessio Variata" in 1540, and our Article has a closer verbal correspondence with this later

---

[39a] Prebendary Gibson in his book on the Thirty-nine Articles, II.-692, says, "it now appears that the sermons are not the work of Albertus Magnus"!

[40] The same thing is shewn from the Roman side in Vol. LIII. of the *Tablet*, 1895. pp. 766-804, as regards Catharinus, and p. 805 as to Pighius and Albert.

amended form.⁴¹ In the Saxon Confession of 1551 drawn up by Melancthon for presentation at the Council of Trent, the charge was left entirely unnoticed.¹² Mr. Dimock justly observes " we seem called upon here to give the Lutherans credit for desisting from a charge, the truth of which the papists had so strongly and indignantly denied. Is there not that which is full of instruction for us here ? Are we to suppose it likely that, *after this*, the English reformers would have framed an Article for the express purpose of striking down this repudiated opinion, and that in language which so entirely failed to describe it ? " He adds, "indeed all the evidence tends to shew that at the period of the Reformation, whatever hold the opinion attributed to Aquinas may still have had on popular ignorance, it had ceased to have (*if it ever had*) any appreciable support from theologians of repute, and that the imputation of any such notion was regarded as an insult to the educated mind of Christendom, as implying an inconceivable ignorance of the first principles of the Christian faith." " Is it credible that our English theologians, with Cranmer at their head, were concerning themselves to frame an Article on purpose to discredit a monstrous notion which had been denounced as nothing but a vulgar error of the grossest kind by leading divines of the Romish Church?" This alleged error was indeed so obscure and undefended that it was not even represented at Trent,¹³ though Catharinus was present.

Not one single Roman Catholic writer or speaker in England has yet been discovered who appears to have sympathised with the monstrous doctrine which Bishop

---

⁴¹ Dimock, p. 31.   ⁴² *Ibid.*, p. 32.   ⁴³ Dimock, p.61.

John Wordsworth has been at great pains to disinter. They all held and taught that the benefits of the Cross are APPLIED by means of the Mass-"sacrifice," and this was precisely the error which our English reformers denounced as being derogatory to the merits of Christ's Death as a "full, perfect, and sufficient" *oblation*, though but "once" offered. This was well expressed in the *Confessio Variata*—"quum sacramentis utimur, nostro opere ac nostrâ fide fit applicatio, non alieno opere. Etenim si non contingeret nobis remissio nisi applicatis missis, fieret incerta, et *fiducia transferenda esset a Christo in opus sacerdotis, idque, ut constat, accidit.*" [44]

King Henry VIII. (by the pen of Tonstal) acutely pointed out to the German ambassadors that their recital of "abuses" applied equally to the Mass itself in all its public celebrations every whit as much as to the "private Masses"—which alone they were attacking.[45] Cranmer, in his reply to Gardiner, does not even notice this heresy, though Bishop John Wordsworth gives a reference to pp. 361, 362 of his work *On the Lord's Supper*, as though it mentioned it. But what Cranmer denied in that "Fifth Book: *Of the oblation and sacrifice of Christ*" is precisely what Bishop John Wordsworth now holds for "Catholic" doctrine. Cranmer said, for instance (p. 345)—

"Thus, under pretence of holiness, the papistical priests have taken upon them to be Christ's successors, and to make such an oblation and sacrifice as never creature made but Christ alone, *neither He made the same any more times than once*, and that was by His Death upon the cross."

---

[44] Francke, App. 22.
[45] Burnet's *History of the Reformation*, I.-ii.-526. Ed. 1829.

"The very supper itself was by Christ instituted and given to the whole church, not to be *offered* and eaten of the priest *for* other men, but by him to be delivered *to* all that would duly ask it."[46]

"Christ made the bloody sacrifice, which took away sin: the priest with the church make a commemoration thereof with lauds and thanksgiving, offering also themselves obedient to God unto death." "And yet this our sacrifice taketh not away our sins, nor is accepted but by His sacrifice. The *bleeding* of Him took away our sins, not the eating of Him."[47]

"And as Christ only made this propitiatory sacrifice, so He made but one, *and but* ONCE. For the making of any other, or *of the same* AGAIN, should have been (as St. Paul reasoneth) a reproving of the first as unperfect and insufficient. And therefore, at His last supper, although Christ made unto His Father sacrifices of lauds and thanksgiving . . . yet made He *there* NO SACRIFICE PROPITIATORY; for then either the sacrifice upon the cross had been void, or the sacrifice at the supper unperfect and insufficient."[48]

Again, as if describing the modern "Anglo-Catholic" position, he said—

"You speak according to the papists, that the priests in their Masses make a sacrifice propitiatory. I call a sacrifice propitiatory, according to Scripture, such a sacrifice as pacifieth God's indignation against us, obtaineth mercy and forgiveness of all our sins, and is our ransom and redemption from everlasting damnation. And, on the other side, I call a sacrifice gratificatory, or the sacrifice of the church, such a sacrifice as *doth not reconcile us to God*, but is made of them that *be* RECONCILED to testify their duties, and to shew themselves thankful unto Him. And these sacrifices *in Scripture be not called propitiatory*, but sacrifices of justice, of laud, praise, and thanksgiving. But you confound the words, and call one by another's name, calling that 'propitiatory' which the Scripture calleth but of justice, laud and thanking."[49]

---

[46] Cranmer *On Lord's Supper*, p. 350.
[48] *Ibid.*, p. 359.
[47] *Ibid.*, p. 356.
[49] *Ibid.*, p. 361.

There is much more of the same sort, but these last words sufficiently shew where the shoe pinched. They prove moreover that the teaching of Article XXXI. was not primarily directed toward the obscure theory out of which, for obvious polemical reasons, Bishop John Wordsworth seeks to make such capital. He refers us[50] to Jewel, *Works*, II.-746-758. But that very reference is fatal to his theory. Jewel is there combating the theory now called "Anglo-catholic," viz. that the virtue of Christ's death is "applied" by the Mass to individuals. Thus Jewel says:—

"It is not the priest, but God only it is, that applieth unto each man the remission of his sins in the blood of Christ; *not by mean of the Mass*, but only by the mean of faith."[51] "Who ever bade you sacrifice Christ unto his Father? . . . or that Christ in your Mass should evermore appear before God and entreat for us?"[52]

The then Bishop of Salisbury might have had his degenerate successor in his eye when he wrote:—

"Where they say, and sometimes do persuade fools that they are able by their Masses to distribute and APPLY unto men's commodity all the *merits of Christ's* DEATH, yea, although many times the parties think nothing of the matter, and understand full little what is done, this is a mockery, a heathenish fancy. For it is our faith that *applieth* the death and cross of Christ to our benefit, and not the act of the massing priest."[53] "It is neither the work of the priest, nor the nature of the sacrament as of itself, that maketh us *partakers of Christ's Death*, but only the faith of the receiver."[54]

Archbishop Herman's *Consultation*, from which so

---

[50] *Responsio ad Batavos*, p. 8.
[51] Jewel, *Works* II.-748.
[52] *Ibid.*, p. 753.
[53] *Ibid.*, III.-556.
[54] *Ibid.*, p. 558.

much of the First Prayer Book of Edward VI. was copied by his friend Cranmer, and of which two[55] editions were published in an English translation in 1547 and 1548, exactly hits off the Roman heresy. He says:—

"Before all things the pastors must labour to take out of men's minds that false and wicked opinion whereby men *think commonly that the priest in Masses offereth up Christ our Lord to God the Father* after that sort, that with his intention and prayer he causeth Christ to become a new and acceptable sacrifice to the Father for the salvation of men, *applieth and communicateth the merit of the passion of Christ and of the saving sacrifice* whereby the Lord Himself offered Himself to the Father a sacrifice on the cross, to them that receive the same with their own faith ... the Holy Fathers by the name of sacrifice understood NOT APPLICATION, which was *devised a great while after* ... but a solemn remembrance of the sacrifice of Christ, as Augustine expoundeth it."

Bradford, who stood up almost alone in the Marian Convocation to defend the Thirty-nine Articles, and who suffered death at the stake for a testimony to their teaching, tells us that the "Romish doctrine" was this, that the "unbloody sacrifice" is "the principal mean whereby His bloody sacrifice is *applied* both to the quick and dead" ... "the supper of Christ is to them not only a sacrament but also a sacrifice, and that not only applicatory, but propitiatory, *because it applieth* the propitiatory sacrifice of Christ to whom the priest or minister will, be he dead or alive"[56] ... "whereas they call this sacrifice of the Mass, the principal mean to *apply* the benefits of Christ's *death* to the quick and dead," which he describes as "an

---

[55] See Dr. Jacob's *Lutheran Movement in England*, p. 353.
[56] Bradford's *Works*, II.-270.

abominable doctrine."[57] Geste in 1548 says the "English Catholiques" ("otherwise termed papistes") "avouch the full and entire fruit and virtue of the priest-Mass to consist in the *appliall* of Christ's merits unto us."[58]

This was what before the Reformation had been "commonly said" in England.

Bishop John Wordsworth would hardly venture to quote to his Old Catholic friends, the words of our Homily *Concerning the Sacrament*,—

"This is to stick fast to Christ's promise made in His institution, to make Christ thine own, and to *applicate His merits* unto thyself. Herein thou needest no other man's help, no other sacrifice *or oblation*, no *sacrificing*-priest. no Mass, no means established by man's invention."

because he would thereby lay bare what he is labouring to conceal, viz. that the error combatted in our Thirty-first Article was *not* that the Mass was independent of Calvary, but that it applied the benefits of Christ's Death to the "quick and the dead, to have remission of pain or guilt," BY A PRIESTLY OFFERING of the reproduced body and blood of Christ ON AN ALTAR. If such an offering by priests in the Mass be the sole means by which Christians may now obtain the benefits of Christ's Death, it follows that all practical hope and true piety must centre round that Mass-offering, and the mediation of the Mass-priests : just as men naturally betake themselves to the tap or the pump without wasting a thought on the hidden well or the far off reservoir from which, *in theory*, they may know well enough it "must" derive all its usefulness.

---

[57] Bradford's *Works*, II.-287, 289.
[58] Dugdale's *Life of Geste*, p. 97

All the "abuses" of money-making, multiplication of useless "celebrations," and scandals of whatever kind flowed from this notion that priestly presentation on an altar on earth is the Divine method for *communicating* the benefits of the Cross. That was the evil which the English Reformers set themselves to combat, and which the Council of Trent tried to bolster up.

And of it Cranmer says plainly—

"The Popish priests say that they offer Christ every day for remission of sin, and *distribute* by their masses the *merits of* CHRIST'S *passion*. But the prophets, apostles, and evangelists do say that Christ Himself in His own person made a sacrifice for our sins upon the cross, by whose wounds all our diseases were healed, and our sins pardoned; and so did never no priest, man, nor creature but He, NOR HE DID THE SAME *never more than once*. And the benefit hereof is in no man's power to give to any other, but every man must receive it *at Christ's hands himself*, by his own faith and belief, as the prophet saith."[59]

Bishop John Wordsworth, on the other hand, speaks of—

"The work of Christ, our high priest and advocate with the Father, which he is always doing in heaven, of the sprinkling of blood within the veil in the Holy of Holies, of the altar in heaven, and of the union of the earthly sacrifice with the heavenly work of our high priest "—

these notions he thinks would open a way of healthy conciliation which might bridge over the gulf between Trent and Lambeth. The answer is plain. The present work of Christ does *not* consist in ministration at an "altar," nor in presenting a sin-offering, nor in making sacrificial atonement for sin, nor even in sprinkling His blood upon the furniture of the

---

[59] *On the Lord's Supper*, p. 47.

heavenly courts. All these are mere human inventions. The typical symbolism of the Jewish Day of Atonement *broke down* when the blood had been sprinkled by a momentary act, and when the finished atonement *began to be applied* to the earthly temple and its worship. The anti-type of the GODWARD "sprinkling" was fulfilled BEFORE Christ "sat down." He "sat down" because His atonement was finished, and the *offering for sin* had *ceased*. Instead of the High priest "coming out," as in Jewry, the veil itself was rent so that the laity might press in "boldly," the very mercy seat being thenceforth accessible to the meanest laic. Nor was it ever the work of a priest to be always offering sacrifices for sin. On the contrary, spiritual worship only began on the foundation of the previous acceptance of the *finished* sin-offering. Till that had "ceased to be offered," no worship by sinners might even be thought of as possible. The *manward* functions of the High Priest after the order of Melchisedek, viz. "blessing," succeeded to His transient (Aaronic) ministration of sacrificing to God "for sin."

Christ is now presenting to the Father His people, and their gifts and graces, their praises and their petitions, but no longer any offering *for sin*. *That*, as a priestly *act*, is wholly a thing of the past both on earth and in Heaven.

"CHRISTUS SEMEL PRO PECCATIS NOSTRIS MORTUUS EST *ut nos* OFFERET DEO."
1 Pet. iii.-18. *Vulgate.*

INDEX

Adoration of Host, 32, 260, 268
" Advertisement " in Homilies an
" Erastian " notice, 236, 242 n
Advertisements of Elizabeth, 1566, on holy days, 7
Advertisements, wrong date of, explained, 77, 85
Advertisements of Elizabeth a " further order," 129
Advertisements contradict First Prayer Book, 88
" Agreeably," meaning of, 88
Altars removed by Cranmer in 1549, 282
Altars needed " other order " in 1559, 6, 46, 127
Altar lights, 26, 182
Andrewes, Bishop, on the Advertisements, 80
" Application " by " offering " denied by Bradford, Martyr, 304
" Application " by " offering " denied by Cranmer, 306
" Application " by " offering " denied by Geste, 305
" Application " by " offering " denied by Archbishop Herman, 304
" Application " by " offering " denied by Homily, 305
" Application " by " offering " denied by Bishop Jewel, 303
Article XXXVI. modified by Knox, 259, 279 n.
Article XXXI., 284
Articles, the eleven of 1561, 291
Aquinas acquitted by Hooker, 297
Augsburg Confession, error of, 299

Baring Gould on S. Catharine, 15
Baronius on S. Catharine, 15
Baxter did not know what " the Vestment " was, 145
" Be in use," meaning of, 102
Bishops, dress of, 121, 149, 164
" Bishops' Book, The," 230
Black-letter days, illegal observance of, 9

Black Rubric, The, 254
Bonner as " Minister," 23
" Bread " = loaf, 213
" Breaking bread " not "catholic " but primitive, 217
Bucer's description of Edwardian ritualists, 26
Bucer misrepresented, 180
Bullinger on the chasuble, 55

Calvin on Prayer Book, 182
Canon lxxxviii., 9
Canon xxiv., 89
Cecil's endorsement on Ordinal of 1552, 278
Cecil's endorsement on " Ordinances " of 1564, 61, 68
Chalices unlawful, 1559-1662, 74, 95
Chasuble, the sacrificial " Vestment," 117
" Commissioners under Great Seal," &c., 43-5
"Commonly said," meaning of, 299
Convocation on Calendar, 3
Convocation on Advertisements of Elizabeth, 75, 80
Convocation on Nowell's Catechism, 181
Copes tolerated by Sandys, 47
Copes used in sets of three, 89, 120
Copes destroyed by Royal Visitors, 109, 110, 115
Copes, non-sacrificial, 117, 119
Copes tolerated, though illegal, 42, 116, 120
Copes, why used in Cathedrals, 90
Copes, not used as in 1549, 117-122
Corporas, what, 94
Corpus Christ, illegal observance of, 4
Cosin, Richard, Dean of the Arches, 79
Cosin, Bishop, on black-letter days, 9
Cosin, Bishop, on the word " Mass," 28
Cosin, Bishop, on Prayers for Dead, 185

INDEX

Cosin, Bishop, on "sacrifice," 177, 179, 185
Cosin, Bishop, on "real" presence, 176
Cosin, Bishop, blunders of, 176-186
Cosin, Bishop, NOTES, First Series, 171
Cosin, Bishop, NOTES, Second Series, 178
Cosin, Bishop, NOTES, Third Series, 180
Cosin, Bishop, "Considerations," 185, 191
Cosin, Bishop, changed his views, 176, 211
Cosin, Bishop, on Kneeling at Sacrament, 267
Cranmer abolished "altars," 282
Cranmer denied Mass-offering, 301
Cranmer on "re-presentation," 302
Cranmer, author of "Black Rubric," 256, 265
Cranmer on "real" presence, 30, 31
Cromwell, State Paper by, 2
Cromwell preserves dedication festivals, 3
"Curiosity," what, 22
D'Ailly, Cardinal, 2
Debate in Parliament on First Prayer Book, 1548, 19
Deprivation of Romish Bishops, 44
Durel's Vindiciæ quoted, 164 ; its authority, 184
Durel's Vindiciæ on altar-lights, 183
"Durham Book," 187
"Durham Book," its date, 192, 203
"Durham Book," Photo-zincograph from, 146, 147, 222
Elevation, 32
Elizabeth's revision of "Church" documents, 125, 246, 253
Elizabeth's fraud rubric, 122
Elizabeth's fraud rubric compared with proviso, 123
Elizabeth's letter of June 25th, 1565, referred to, 57, 66, 77, 79
Elizabeth's printed Prayer Books, 125, 131, 277
"Et cætera" explained, 199, 164
Erasmus on Festivals of Church, 2
First Prayer Book of Edward VI., its compilers, 16

First Prayer Book of Edward VI., merely provisional, 19
First Prayer Book of Edward VI., copies rare, 138
First Prayer Book of Edward VI., failure of, 16
First Prayer Book of Edward VI., final rubrics in, 138-142
First Prayer Book of Edward VI., II. C. rubrics never revived, 142, 196
First Prayer Book of Edward VI., on saints' days, 3
First Prayer Book of Edward VI. not endorsed by Second Prayer Book, 19
First Prayer Book of Edward VI. not endorsed by Thirty-sixth Article, 275
First Prayer Book of Edward VI., changes forced by Gardiner's "mistakings," 28-33
"Form of Bread" rejected, 235, 245
"Further order," meaning of, 46, 129

Gardiner, Bishop, on the First Book of Edward, 17, 28
Gardiner, Bishop, his "mistakings," 29-33
Geste, Bishop, on surplice, 52
Geste, Bishop, on "distinctive dress" at Communion, 104

Homilies, dates of, 232, 242
Homilies, authors of, 233, 244
Homilies altered by Bonner, 234
Homilies in Rogation Week, 74
Homilies on Vestments, 112
Hook, Dean, on "pious" fables, 11
Hooker, 80, 111, 297

Injunctions of 1547, 4, 25
Injunctions of 1559 were under Great Seal, 36
Injunctions under 1 Elizabeth, cap. i., or cap. ii., 41
Injunctions required ornaments of 1553, 47
Injunctions, "other" or "further" order, 42, 126, 129
"Interpretations" suggested, 1561 (see Resolutions), 128
Islip, Archbishop, on multiplied holy days, 1

James I. revised a Homily, 252

310 INDEX

James I., his Prayer Book irregular, 136
James I., his Proclamation struck out, 152, 192
Jewel, Bishop, denied "application" by offerings, 303
Jewel, Bishop, knew only surplice in use, 112
Joyce, Wayland, misrepresents last revision, 153 n.

Kneeling at Holy Communion explained, 257, 266
Kneeling at Holy Communion, Knox on, 255
"King's Book," 234

Langdale, Alban, on Ridley's doctrine, 19
Langton, Archbishop, on saints' days, 1
"Latter year of King Edward," what, 39, 40, 105
L'Estrange on Advertisements and Orders, 81
Littledale on Purgatory, 14
Littledale on Advertisements, 61

MacColl, Canon, misquotes, 41
Mass abolished in 1549, 234, 236
"Maximum and Minimum" theory, 88, 165
Meopham, Archbishop, on Calendar, 1
"Ministers," what, 21-8
Missals, &c., defaced as illegal, 24
"Mistakers," what, 29-33

Newman on Mass-sacrifice, 285
Nicholls on black-letter saints, 10
Nicholls on Ornaments Rubric, 168
Nicholls published papers not intended for publication, 177, 209, 211

"Objective" presence repudiated, 218
Order, Royal, of 1561, 63, 78
Order for Tables "in every Church," 46
Ordinal of 1550, 274, 276
Ordinal of 1552, 278, 281
"Ornaments" defined, 91, 94
Ornaments of Church in 1549, 93
Ornaments of Minister in 1549, 95
Ornaments Rubric of 1549, 93, 95
Ornaments Rubric of 1552, 107

Ornaments Rubric of 1559, 123
Ornaments Rubric of 1604, 136
Ornaments Rubric of 1662, 137
"Other Order," 126-9
Overal wrongly cited, 170

Parker, Mr. James, misquotes Grindal, 71
Parker, Mr. James, misquotes Injunction, 37, 40
Parker, Mr. James, on the Order of 1561, 63
Parker, Mr. James, misconceives Bishop Cosin, 190, 209
Parker, Archbishop, enforces Surplice only, A.D. 1563-66, 48, 112
Parker, Archbishop, issues Advertisements as a Royal Commissioner, 62, 64, 77 n.
Parliamentary Debate in 1559, 19
Pastoral Staff, 135, 276
People's Hymnal on Purgatory, 15
Perry, Rev. T. W., mistakes of, 40, 79, 196
Pontius Pilate canonised, 13
Præmunire dreaded, 71
Prayer of humble access, 32
Prayer of Consecration, 30, 206, 220
Prayer for the Dead, 29, 185
Prayer for Parliament, 83, 205
Preces Privatæ of 1564, 7
"Public authority," what, 75

"Real" Presence, 19, 30, 31
Reception by wicked, 251
Relief bills did not touch "Vestments," 151
Resolutions of 1561, 7, 128
"Retained," varying meaning of, 101, 150
Ridley's "Zuinglianism," 19
Ridley on Altar Lights, 26
Ritual Commissioners on blackletter days, 10
Royal Visitation of 1559, 35-37, 108
Royal Visitors were "Commissioners under Great Seal," 43

Sacrifice of the Mass, Bonner on, 234
Sacrifices of Masses, 284-8, 293
Sancroft's Bodleian Book, 152-3, 162
Sancroft's MS. note, 163
Sancroft's Secretariat, 162, 198, 205, 209, 268
Sancroft's Visitation Articles, 163

INDEX

Scudamore on Saints' days, 13, 14
Second Prayer Book of Edward VI. asked for in 1662, 153
"Seventh year of Edward VI.," 39, 40
Shaxton's recantation, 295
Somerset's influence on Prayer Book, 24, 174, 181
Sparrow, Bishop, 81, 82, 84
Statutes :—
   4 Henry IV., cap. xiv., 2
   1 Edward VI., cap. xii., 25, 238
   2 and 3 Edward VI., cap. i., 16, 91
   3 and 4 Edward VI., cap. x., 24
   3 and 4 Edward VI., cap. xii., 270, 276
   5 and 6 Edward VI., cap. i., 18
   5 and 6 Edward VI., cap. iii., 4, 5, 6, 7, 9
   1 Mariæ, session 2, cap. ii., 4, 9, 277
   1 Elizabeth, cap. i., 35, 241
   1 Elizabeth, cap. ii., 5, 97, 106, 277
   1 Elizabeth, cap. ii., its synodical sanction, 105, 106, 153
   1 Elizabeth, cap. ii., its present supremacy, 125, 165
   5 Elizabeth, cap. v., 249
   8 Elizabeth, cap. i., 279
   13 Elizabeth, cap. xii., 290
   39 Elizabeth, cap. viii., 45
   1 James I., cap. xxv., 6, 9, 173
   14 Charles II., cap. iv., 279, 282
Strype's Errata, source of, 84
Supreme Governour, 34, 241
Supreme Head, 240
"Survey of the Common Prayer," 85, 88, 168
Surplice prescribed by Prayer Book, 1563 et seq., 48-53
Surplice with sleeves, 76, 87, 144
Surplice not consecrated nor Mass dress, 117, 119, 144

"Take Order," meaning of, 98, 126
Thirtieth Injunction, 1559, 38, 40, 54, 115, 184
Tillemont on Apocryphal Saints, 13
Tippet, 1562, 48
Tippet, 1564, 48, 49, 52
Trent v. Thirty-nine Articles, 255, 289, 290, 292

" Use "=employment, 103, 108

" Use of the Church," what, 102

Vestment, THE=chasuble, 117
Vestment, The, illegal, 109, 113
Vestment, The, rejected by Bishops, 135, 163
Visitation Articles :—
   Aylmer, 8
   Bancroft, 89
   Basire, 162
   Chaderton, 59
   Cosin, 156
   Croft, 158
   Dolben, 160
   Earle, 157
   Frewen, 154
   Gauden, 159
   Griffith, 159
   Grindal, 8, 103
   Gunning, 161
   Hacket, 156
   Henchman, 158
   Ironside, 157
   Juxon, 154, 158
   King, 158
   Laney, 158
   Lloyd, 158
   Lucy, 158
   Middleton, 8, 222
   Morley, 158
   Nicholson, 159
   Parker, 8, 47, 48, 49, 53, 56, 58, 74, 75, 112
   Parkhurst, 74
   Pearson, 161
   Piers, 158
   Pory, 83, 161
   Rainbow, 260
   Reynolds, 159
   Sancroft, 163
   Sanderson, 158
   Sheldon, 155
   Skinner, 158
   Sparrow, 161
   Ward, 158
   Whitgift, 59, 80
   Wren, 155
Visitors were " Commissioners under the Great Seal," 35, 43
Wheatley on " Romish " saints, 10
Wordsworth, John, Bishop, his notions, 296, 306
Wren's influence on present Prayer Book, 198-201
Wren, author of changes in Ornaments Rubric, 1662, 155, 194

www.ingramcontent.com/pod-product-compliance
Lightning Source LLC
Chambersburg PA
CBHW022024240426

43667CB00042B/1088